Gospel of the Fallen Angel

Gospel of the Fallen Angel

Geraint Ap Iorwerth

BOOKS

Winchester, UK
Washington, USA

First published by O-Books, 2011
O-Books is an imprint of John Hunt Publishing Ltd., Laurel House, Station Approach,
Alresford, Hants, SO24 9JH, UK
office1@o-books.net
www.o-books.com

For distributor details and how to order please visit the 'Ordering' section on our website.

ISBN: 978 1 84694 408 6

A CIP catalogue record for this book is available from the British Library.

Design: Stuart Davies

Illustrations: Natasha Rodwell

Printed in the UK by CPI Antony Rowe
Printed in the USA by Offset Paperback Mfrs, Inc

CONTENTS

When Jesus walked on earth
he gave strict orders
not to let anyone know who he was.
My minions couldn't help themselves.
They kept blurting it out!
I had better self-control.
Until now!
After 2,000 years, I've finally broken my silence.
Not bad going for the archetypal disobedient one!

Satan

Dedicated to my first grandchild Sol ap Shem

Deep within the individual, as within the religious and cultural systems that fashion the individual, something is hidden, and this is not merely the individual 'sin' of modern religiosity or the 'complexes' of psychoanalysis. It is invariably a corpse that as it rots spreads its 'uncleanness' everywhere.

René Gerard, *Things Hidden since the Foundation of the World*, p165

'I do not believe in a future life,' said Raskolnikov.

Svidrigaylov sat lost in thought. 'And what,' he said suddenly, 'if there are only spiders there, or something of the sort?'

'He's mad,' thought Raskolnikov.

'We're always thinking of eternity as an idea that cannot be understood, something immense. But why must it be? What if, instead of all this, you suddenly find just a little room there, something like a village bath-house, grimy, and spiders in every corner, and that's all eternity is. Sometimes, you know, I can't help feeling that that's probably what it is.'

'But don't you ever imagine anything more comforting and more just than that?' Raskolnikov cried, unable to suppress a painful feeling.

'More just?' Svidrigaylov retorted with a vague smile. 'But how can you tell that that is not just? I, you know, would certainly have made it so deliberately!'

This horrible answer made Raskolnikov's blood run cold.

Fyodor Dostoevsky, *Crime and Punishment*, p305

'We had to destroy the world in order to save it.' The harassed United States Air Force officer's account of the destruction of Ben Tre, a Mekong Delta city of 35,000, expresses precisely what I had in mind when I first began to write the first edition of The War of the Flea *in 1964.*

To destroy in order to save. Here we have the hub of the matter, the radical contradiction that has opened an abyss under the feet of the world's greatest military power in its incredibly costly war against the ragged guerrilla fighters of an inconsequential South-East Asian state with a population of some 16 million and a land area of 65,000 square miles ... What is certain is that the techniques and strategy of the guerrilla fighter, waging the war of the flea, have proved their potency in the severest test imaginable short of nuclear war, against the military technology of the world's richest and most powerful nation. The demonstration is of great significance. What it means is simply this: that men who realize their worth and capabilities can no longer be exploited by force or intimidation, nor can their aspirations be denied. They have found an effective counter-strategy against the tyranny of wealth and the tyranny of power.

Robert Taber, *The War of the Flea*, pp11, 13

I will sing for the one I love, a song about his vineyard. My loved one had a vineyard on a fertile hillside. He dug it up and cleared it of stones and planted it with the choicest vines. He built a watchtower in it and cut out a winepress as well. Then he looked for a crop of good grapes, but it yielded only bad fruit.

Isaiah 5:1-2

The word 'God' is for me nothing more than the expression and product of human weaknesses, the Bible a collection of honorable, but still primitive legends which are nevertheless pretty childish. No interpretation no matter how subtle can (for me) change this. For me the Jewish religion like all other religions is an incarnation of the most childish superstitions. And the Jewish people to whom I gladly belong, and with whose mentality I have a deep affinity, have no different quality for me than all other people. As far as my experience goes, they are also no better than other groups.

Albert Einstein, *letter to Eric Gutkind* (Source unknown)

Preface

This book isn't so much a question of 'let me entertain you', as 'let me re-educate you' about one of the most incredible figures who ever lived –Jesus. Mind you, I also hope to entertain you in the process. Publish and be damned? Not really, because for me, it's more a case of be damned and then publish! My gospel could have been called *The Adversary's Tale*. That's what Jesus was and still is: my greatest adversary. I could also have called it *The Immaculate Deception* because that's what I am, the Great Deceiver. But in this exclusive one-off special, I am not deceiving anyone. I am actually telling the truth for the first time, the truth about the scandalous life of Jesus of Galilee. I have put pen to paper in order to celebrate his unique life and teaching; a life committed to insulting everything that people hold sacred; a life that could not resist giving offence, especially to the pious and the religious of all ranks. Who would have thought that I, of all beings, would end up writing a gospel? Wonders never cease. But since Jesus was the greatest religious maverick of all time, I just have to put the record straight once and for all.

Dare you read it?

Dare you face, in one earth-shattering revelation, the reason why Jesus brings judgment on all the power-systems in the world, and the satanic principle that lies behind all of them?

The decision to read on is yours and yours alone. If you continue to read, your life, I assure you, will never be the same again, whether you are religious or not.

I could also have called my book *The Heretic Gospel*, because that is what Jesus was, a heretic. After much soul searching, I plumped in the end for calling my book *Gospel of the Fallen Angel*.

So sit back and enjoy Gospel of the Fallen Angel, the true story of Jesus.

(By the way, I must also mention one thing before we go any further. I became so confused with all the different translations of the Bible that I decided to produce my own version. Consequently, all Biblical quotes are from my *Very New English Standard Revised International Jerusalem, London and Llareggub Good News Special Edition Bible*!)

Chapter One

The City of Delusion

Here you are dealing with victims long dead. You deal with the murder books, if you can find them, and the records. With fresh kills it is clinical because things move fast. With old cases it is emotional. You are going to see the toll of violence over time. Be prepared for it. (Page 17) As he read through the catalogues of the city's horror (he) felt a familiar power begin to take hold of him and move in his veins again. It didn't matter how long the blood had fallen. There was a killer in the wind, and he knew that he would find his salvation in those who were long lost (Page 21). It's just all the catching up, in the reading. We've got to know this book inside and out.(Page 23)

There was an initial misinterpretation of the death. A murder book could be manipulated, (but) the truth would be revealed as he delved deeper and continued his own investigation.(Page 27)

Michael Connelly, *The Closers, Orion Paperback 2009*

'Meet the real historic Jesus'

The Quest for the Historic Jesus

Allow me to formally introduce myself. I'm Satan. Some of you may not be fully aware of my credentials, so I'll fill you in at the start. I started off as an employee in the prestigious Heavenly Court. As a private investigator working for God, I really enjoyed my work: great job satisfaction, good long-term prospects. I was so efficient at my job, that I soon worked my way up to the post of chief prosecutor. Not bad going for an ordinary detective! I was passionate about my responsibilities. God's holy laws exist to be obeyed. I made sure that people did just that. Let me be clear about one thing; there was nothing underhanded in what I did; I simply stuck to my job description. I tested people to see if they could live up to the standards God demanded of them. When they failed, which happened most of the time, I presented my clients' personal dossiers before God, and eventually prosecuted them myself. I left the punishment to God, or at least one of the special departments under his control. My modes of punishment pale into insignificance compared to what he can dish out. More about that later!

I got to know people's failures so well, that it wasn't long before I'd built up a huge database of 'sinners'. I only use a few religious words in my vocabulary. This, dear friends, is one of them. It says so much in just seven letters. In fact, it has to be my favorite seven-letter word of all time – 'Sinners'!

Anyway, with such power at my fingertips, I soon branched off and started my own business – global, I should add. I would never assume such a title myself, but Jesus gave me the supreme accolade when he referred to me as 'Prince of the World'. Who am I to argue with a person of his standing? Be honest. I'm sure you'd love to be a global celebrity, with the world at your feet, worshipped and adored by millions. I do.

Everyone needs a mask to hide their neurosis. I've decided to remove mine so that I can talk to you openly and honestly, as friends. You know how some of you humans suffer from SAD – Seasonal Affective Disorder. I suppose you could argue that I suffer from DAD –Diabolical Affective Disorder. I too have made moral compromises in the past, but I hope to show you that they were always in the service of a higher good. Gone are the dark and murky places I've inhabited for far too long. No longer will you see me lurking in the shadows – at least for the time being.

My gospel belongs to everyone: to all living now and those not yet living. That's why I've decided to write it as an open letter to people of all ages and backgrounds, in order to share my good news about the human condition. I want to engage with everyone, including high profile religious leaders, not least the Christian ones. Like the Jewish prophets of old, I want to challenge you to question your most deeply cherished prejudices, beliefs and convictions about life. I also want to take this opportunity to remind you about the most famous holy anarchist of all time, the first century Palestinian Jew who stood religious truth on its head in a way that no one could ever have imagined – Jesus of Galilee. It isn't a question of hearing me out –Hell forbid! I want you to listen to Jesus in a brand new way. Not the Jesus of fantasy and fiction, and there's plenty of that around at the moment, but the real Jesus: the Jewish Jesus, the historic Jesus.

You think I can be awkward? You should hear *him*. There were no religious boundaries that he wouldn't cross. Mind you, he did more than just transcend them; he demolished them in the process. I'm not going to pretend that I am a totally reformed character. That would be a lie. But I have changed quite a bit. That's why I want you to think of this gospel as a world exclusive, a one-off special, because I'm going to tell the truth, the whole truth and nothing but the truth. I've nothing to gain by lying about my chief adversary. His story is my story. While he remains center stage, so do I.

Whether you are 'Christian' or not, religious or not, there's no denying that Jesus has been at the heart of Western culture and civilization for two thousand years. I salute the few good books about him, and the few good men and women who have tried to put his teaching into practice. At least they tried. But from now on, all the books written about him will be of academic interest only, mere footnotes. They will not change the world, but at least they'll help keep the Jesus industry going – churning out book after book, perpetuating the Christian lie from generation to generation. Lies about Jesus as well as lies about me.

For many of you, this gospel will probably be the first and last theological book that you will ever read. Think of it as an honor. After reading it, you will know that the Jewish Jesus is the real Jesus; the 'Christian' Jesus is a work of fiction. You are reading a book that could, potentially at least, be the end of human history as we know it. Because if everyone on the planet was to suddenly put Jesus' words into practice, a new kind of world would be born. It would be a new way of being human, which would also spell the end of me. Am I scared? Not in the least. I have total faith that human beings will keep on behaving as they have done for thousands of years.

Jesus was the only true 'Jesus theologian', or rather anti-theologian, that ever lived. His message is the radical anti-theology that will forever question and challenge all attempts at turning what he believed to be the truth into another religion. Jesus must be gutted to see what has become of his message. But I'm not surprised. I've been at the heart of human life since the very beginning and not just for two thousand years. I know how important religions are to you.

Let me make one thing clear at the start. It's the theologians and church leaders who have emasculated Jesus and not me. Modern biblical scholarship, as well as the arrogant prattle of systematic theology, is doing its very best to kill him off completely. Its practitioners remain adamant that since Jesus' psychological and spiritual makeup is so vastly different to yours, no one can truly understand what he's talking about. Indeed by now, argue the experts, modern consciousness is so radically different from that of any other age, that by today's standards, religious people have nothing in common with Jesus' first followers either! Lies! Damned lies! An influential cadre within the church is fearful of people meeting the historic Jesus. And I'll tell you why. It's because they feel threatened by his radical message. I know that I sound like a conspiracy theorist, but when you've read my gospel you'll see for yourselves why a male elite has built a sophisticated religious and theological barrier in order to stop people from meeting the real Jesus. And the name of that separation barrier? Christianity!

In writing this gospel, I'm also doing you an added favor. I want to save you the infernal journey into the depths of your world; the descent into the Underworld. This age has no need for such heroics; it has troubles enough of its own. You must forget about me as the dark, evil stranger in your midst. I'm being true to one of my most popular nicknames, by highlighting the dynamics of hell for you. Lucifer, you see, means 'the light bearer'. It would be foolish of me, or anyone, to deny that love has a place in the human world, it clearly has. But it has only ever occupied a minor role, especially among those who shape human history. I'm going to shine a light into the dark corners of the world you inhabit, the realm of deceit, deception, cruelty and betrayal. Even those famed for their 'high moral principles' down the centuries have been quite at home in that realm. I want you to understand anew the workings of the most unfathomable of evils, the dynamics of moral corruption, and why it's always the innocent who suffer. And remember, I write from experience. I know what it's like to suffer. I know what it is to be one of the damned. I am Satan.

Before you say anything, especially the religious amongst you, should you be too proud to listen to me, just think of reading this gospel as an exercise in humility.

And please, don't be put off by my name, though I appreciate that it does take a bit of getting used to. Satan! You don't have to speak it or write it. I'm not even asking you to look me squarely in the face. Most of you, because of your preconceptions, would avert your eyes in disgust anyway. But believe me, I'm really just like you... only more so. Can I make a suggestion? Should I continue to make you feel uneasy, just play around with the letters of my name. I can then be Santa for a while!

Since my global business has been doing so well, especially in the last century, you may be surprised to learn that I took a sabbatical at the start of the new millennium, though I prefer to call it a *satanical*! With my reliable army of helpers growing daily, I can now relax a bit and pursue my favorite hobbies with new vigor, especially listening to contemporary music and reading paperbacks. I particularly enjoy reading detective novels. My favorites range from Michael Connelly to Peter James, as you'll find out as you continue to read.

It was reading Connelly's *The Closers* that got me thinking about Jesus in a different way. After three years away from the LAPD, detective Harry Bosch returns to find that great changes have taken place in his old department. A new police chief has been brought in to give the place a clean-up from top to bottom. Harry joins a former colleague and is assigned to the department's Open-Unsolved Unit, working on thousands of unsolved or 'cold' cases, as they are called. The detectives are known as the 'Closers'. By applying new techniques to old evidence, they aim to bring hidden killers to justice. I was hooked. I ended up fantasizing about setting-up my own Closers Unit, which I eventually did. I would start with one of the great mysteries of all time. Who really killed Jesus, and why? I knew the truth would be revealed if I delved deeper, and continued my own investigation. I went back to the original sources and looked at the evidence again. This was no academic exercise. Misunderstand Jesus and you misunderstand me. As a result, I not only saw him and myself in a new light but also your plight as human beings. My conclusion? There was an initial misinterpretation of Jesus' death: a death that has been constantly manipulated down the ages by various groups, not just religious ones, each with their own hidden agendas.

So let me set the scene before I introduce you to Jesus and his world. I'm not one for boasting, but behind all human evil lays my *Complete Network of Violence* or 'CNV' for short. You'll find it in the most unexpected of places. And I always operate in a holistic fashion. No part of life is outside my embrace. Think of it as an alliance of all the world's power-systems under my exclusive control. Bits of it are franchised out to those whom I can rely on, especially religious leaders and politicians, though I'm never sure if there really is much difference between them, since both are in the salvation business, of sorts. Theologians refer to my network as 'principalities and powers'. I'm not into religious jargon, but I must admit that 'principalities and powers' does have a regal and exclusive ring to it, and I've grown to like it over the centuries. Jesus' native religion teaches, especially through the prophets, the importance of individuals accepting responsibility for a great deal of the evil and suffering in the world – probably for most of it. But Jesus' religion has another tradition, passed on this time by the priests, which stresses the fact that human evil is more than just the result of the wrong choices individuals make. Something far more complex is going on.

I'm no theologian, but I have to agree with them. There is a mysterious and dark residue of evil at work in creation which isn't the result of individuals doing wrong. A collective malaise exists that causes all sorts of suffering. It's so all-pervading at times, that individuals are easily overpowered by it, making it impossible for them to choose and do what is right. I think of it as the world's corporate personality, 'a complex of collective guilt'. There I go again! It isn't just theologians or philosophers who can come up with poetic sounding phrases. And, by the way, don't think of me as someone who goes out of his way to be controversial, but you have to grasp a very painful truth at the outset, that

The Bible is a murder book.
A history of violence.
Human violence.

The Bible is as much an unholy book as it is holy. My story as much as God's.

Consequently, the time has come to clarify, for a new generation, why I am really indispensable to you. It's this quest that actually inspired me to put pen to paper. It isn't something I've had to do in the past, because I can normally rely on an array of people, both religious and secular, to speak up for me. But lines are becoming blurred. Why should your gods and politicians get the praise for all the suffering in the world? I want to put the record straight as 'Lord of this world – Evil Possessor', as Black Sabbath, one of my favorite rock groups of all time, would have it.

This book isn't so much 'Satanic verses' as Jesus verses. Honestly! It's his true story that I want to tell, with bits about you and me thrown in. But I want to be clear about one thing at the outset. And in this, I'm in full agreement with Biblical scholars and theologians: no one can ever write a complete 'Life of Jesus'. A biography, similar to the life and times of Madonna or David Beckham, is an impossibility. We don't have enough facts about him. This isn't the same, however, as saying that we can never know anything about the historic Jesus, which, as I have already pointed out, is a claim made by some Biblical scholars and theologians, many of them, I might add, supposedly followers of his! They reckon that the real Jesus will always remain hidden behind the doctored texts of the New Testament, and, in particular, the four Gospels of Matthew, Mark, Luke and John. Not anymore! The problem is this: since the first church had its own particular agenda, the gospel writers were forever changing and adapting what Jesus said in order to promote their own version of his message. And, I must admit, there is a hell of a lot of truth in this. But behind the spin and propaganda needs of the early church, the core of Jesus' message can now be re-discovered in all its clarity. And praise where praise is due; we are indebted to a few talented scholars, or 'Jesus detectives' as I call them, for their invaluable help in this. They have analyzed and minutely dissected every word in the gospels in order to get at the truth... the truth about Jesus, the truth about me.

But being human, they too have their own blind spots and prejudices. And like many church leaders, they appear unable to accept the conclusions of their research. What a strange lot!

Contrary to what many might like to believe, Jesus wasn't a Celtic shaman or ancient Druid. He wasn't taught by Brahmins in India, nor was he initiated into the mysteries of Egypt by priestesses. To believe that is to insult his intelligence, and to mock the multi-layered spiritual heritage that nurtured him. Jesus wasn't even a Christian, but a first century Palestinian Jewish man. Just as we can enter the world of an Egyptian pharaoh who lived thousands of years ago, we can do the same with Jesus. No one can actually enter the mind of Jesus and follow his spiritual development step-by-step, but together we can enter his cultural and spiritual world, and become familiar with the way that he and other religious people saw things. As I said, I'm no theologian, but for the first time in two thousand years, I will illuminate the key texts that helped mould his destiny, and take you closer to him than anyone has done in the past. I've made a breakthrough. You missed the obvious clues because you were looking in the wrong places. It's part of my mission to rescue Jesus from Christians and thus restore his original heresy in all its purity and strength. Like Harry Bosch, I too want closure..

Scrolls from the Dead Sea

So what led to this breakthrough? Ancient documents, known popularly as 'the Dead Sea Scrolls', kicked things off by showing how varied and vibrant religious fervor was at the time of Jesus. About nine hundred copies were discovered, in eleven caves on the shore of the Dead Sea. A local shepherd called Mohammed found them by chance in 1947, near a place called Qumran, not far from Jericho. He little realized the impact his discovery would have on both Judaism and Christianity. The Scrolls have helped bring the time of Jesus alive in a new and exciting way. Here are the oldest known copies of some of the most important books in the Hebrew Scriptures (what Christians call the Old Testament, and Jews the Tanakh). One of the longest among them, the Book of Isaiah, is, for example, a thousand years older than any copy in existence. Written in Hebrew or Aramaic, the language of Jesus, some of the scrolls go back a hundred and fifty years before his birth, while the most recent were being copied during or just after his death.

The Scrolls make up the library of a Jewish sectarian group. We'll never know for certain who they were, but in all probability they were a strict sect called the Essenes, or one of their splinter groups. In addition to books not included in the Bible, we find writings like the Book of Enoch (a book banned by both Jews and the first Christians), and commentaries that help to explain the meaning of these ancient holy texts. Other books are pertinent to the spirituality and religious practices of the community itself. Among these we find a Community Rule Book. This book was written fifty years before Jesus' birth and gives us an invaluable picture of the life of an ultra-traditional Jewish congregation. It was led by a charismatic priest, known as the 'Teacher of Righteousness'. He died in exile in 72BC, a broken man. He was the first messiah in Jewish history. More were to follow.

Jesus would have heard stories about all the would-be messiahs. Even though he was a failure, the first messiah's small band of followers still hoped against hope that God would eventually prove that their leader was somehow right after all. Maybe they had misinterpreted the date of his return at the *Endtime*, when the world would literally come to an end. And so they waited… and waited. The year 34BC came but the expected 'End' didn't appear. Neither did their messiah! In 65AD, the precious scrolls were hidden in caves at about the same time as the Roman legions were taking on the fanatical Jewish freedom fighters known as Zealots. Many of you today would call them terrorists. They lost. By the time Jesus appeared on the scene, God's People had become experts at waiting! And at losing.

Two years after Jesus was born, in 6BC, Herod the Great died and the Jews revolted again. Sectarian communities, Qumran among them, saw this as a sign that their liberation would soon be underway. Surely this time round the End of Time would finally arrive. But it didn't. Once again, God's people were brutally crushed. Two thousand rebels were crucified, women raped and abused, and thousands of people were sold into slavery. And what of their latest messiah? He was tortured and killed by Roman soldiers and his body left to rot in the streets: an unimaginable public humiliation. How did his followers cope? They went back to their holy texts and looked again for clues in order to try and make sense of such a catastrophe.

Maybe it was destined, they argued, that God's 'chosen one', the Messiah, was meant to be rejected in this way. His suffering may somehow be part of their salvation and liberation. Some even believed that their messiah was already waiting in heaven, soon to re-appear on earth, this time as victor, conquering their enemies once and for all. A stone tablet exists to this day, which appears to refer to a messiah who rises from the grave three days after his death, even though it was written thirty years before Jesus was born. Spooky!

You now have a brief glimpse of how different a world it is that you have to enter in order to understand Jesus: a world with its own specific mentality, and yet similar to yours in some respects. Let me suggest another simple exercise, even if you're not into what religious people call a 'retreat'. This is when individuals who take their religious discipline seriously take time out from a busy world to unwind and think about their lives in a spiritual context. It can last anything from a few days to a fortnight. Just imagine the world of a retreat – a world with no daily newspapers, magazines, journals or paperbacks; no radio or television, personal computers (with their websites and emails) or telephones and mobile phones; no theatre for entertainment or feature films or movies; no CDs or computer games. Imagine that none of these things exist in your world. It's one of the best ways of envisaging what it would be like to live in any other age, Jesus' included.

The books of the Old Testament were Jesus' world. He lived and breathed them. He prayed them and debated them. He knew many of them off by heart, especially the temple hymn book, known popularly as the Psalms, as well as the scroll of the prophet Isaiah. They were his morning newspaper and adventure thrillers, his religious theatre, as well as his daily divine soap opera! Modern humans put different aspects of their lives into separate compartments, labeling them in the process as personal or social, religious or political, of domestic or national importance. But Jesus lived in a world where everything was interlinked.

You humans live by myths, even if you're not consciously aware of them. These are models or patterns of beliefs and ideas that shape and influence the way you look at, and behave in, the world. They can be political or religious. The period between the old and new millennium, the time when Jesus was born, was a world in crisis, not unlike yours at the start of the twenty-first century. Traditional ways of making sense of the world were no longer relevant. The old myths were losing their meaning. People wanted new myths. Some took comfort by divorcing themselves from the stark realities of life, and hiding instead in an inner-world of spiritual bliss and contemplation. Others went to the other extreme and took to the sword. They became God's terrorists (all-time favorites of mine!). As people became more and more disorientated, religious fundamentalism began to play a bigger part in cultural life. Nothing much changes, does it?

Certain individuals struggled to discover the key or code that they believed would explain the tragic meaning of history, especially for the losers. It was the birth of a way of thinking that still dominates your world as the twenty-first century gets underway. I refer to the beautiful and vindictive world of The Apocalypse! This is a belief-system that claims to unmask the true meaning of history, as the forces of good and evil prepare for one almighty confrontation here on earth. It's with this type of human drama that I really come into my own. The apocalypse, and its love of religious revenge and retributive justice – what more could anyone desire? The apocalypse and its clear-cut divisions between 'goodies' and 'baddies'… I love it so much that, as far as I am concerned, it can be *Apocalypse Now* every day of the week!

Jesus had other ideas. For him, apocalyptic thinking was nostalgia at its very worst, a way of avoiding the conflicts of the past and the challenges of the present, by hiding in an imaginary future state of harmony. This is why Jesus would eventually reject all his national and religious myths, unmasking their cruelty in the most uncompromising way. It always amuses me when politicians, philosophers and theologians mock this 'unmasking' as being irrelevant to modern life, considering that many of your current world leaders, Christian or not, are big fans of it. George Bush Junior and Tony Blair would have felt very much at home at Qumran, where the countdown to the end of history was well underway by the time of Jesus. The Community at Qumran even had in its possession an Endtime text that preserved the teaching about the role of a mysterious ancient figure called Melchizedek. It was a secret blueprint or code that mapped out the timetable for his return to the world. Melchizedek would be pivotal in preparing the final stage for the end of human history.

It was also an integral part of Bush and Blair's joint presidential mission to prepare for the final battle between Good and Evil. Privy to 'heavenly mysteries', they too claimed to have discovered the hidden powers that shaped human destiny.

Everything that was happening in world politics was believed to be part of a wider cosmic, and not just historical, drama. Past, present and future were to be finally laid bare for all to see. And every individual, however insignificant, could play their part by supporting these latter-day messiahs in their struggle against the powers of Evil. Dream on!

Interpretation

The life of Jesus of Galilee was a real and concrete historical event. He was probably born in 6BC near his hometown of Nazareth in Lower Galilee, which is in northern Israel today. The village was called Bethlehem, and so it couldn't have been its namesake near Jerusalem, which is about seventy miles south of Nazareth. His mother was a young Jewish girl called Miriam. His father was Joseph. They had a house full of children. Jesus was particularly close to one of his younger brothers called Jacob or James. His cousin, John, one of the leading dissidents of the day, began his ministry at the end of 27/28 AD. Jesus struck out on his own during 28 AD, at the age of thirty-four. He first came to my attention at the time of his baptism in the river Jordan, though I'd picked up warning signals from the Judean desert a few months before, loud and clear! I always get involved when talk of 'power and glory' reaches my ears. With worldwide contacts, few would-be leaders of any kind can resist my global deals, especially religious ones. Here was someone with real power. In fact, it was royal power of some kind, though he turned out to be a bloody fool in his attitude towards it. By early evening of the 7th April 30 AD, Jesus was dead at the age of thirty-six years. Of course I rejoiced at his death. As I will reveal to you, he had it coming. But don't blame me. I may have made a few suggestions, but it takes humans to act them out.

Jesus and his contemporaries shared a block of beliefs about 'the last days' or the Endtime, as it is also called. There is nothing mysterious about these beliefs and the dynamics that underlay them. If there is a mystery, it revolves around the question of how individuals, centuries ago, interpreted their sacred texts. Yes! The old favorite, beloved of all religious folk: '*interpretation, interpretation, interpretation*'. Once you get to understand these dynamics, you'll have a clearer grasp of how Jesus fits into the religious scene of his day – or how he didn't fit in, as the case may be.

The religious majority never has any problem with its leaders. It trusts them as experts in God's business. In fact, Israel's tradition taught that some leaders were so extra-special that God endowed them with sacred status, which transformed them into angelic-like beings in this life. To all intent and purpose, as far as 'the faithful' were concerned, their leaders *were* God! As sons of God, these special individuals helped bridge the gap between heaven and earth. They regularly experienced journeys to heaven, while some even enjoyed visions of the heavenly throne, where God sat in power and glory. They spoke with angels and, having been taught by them, communicated their wisdom to God's people. But some of the extra special sons of God were so special that they were deemed worthy enough to receive the secrets of creation. I refer to information about how the world came into being, the origin of evil and the working of metals. One of the most famous extra special sons of God was the superhero and cosmic celebrity of his day, Enoch. He was so special that God gave him his name, not only before he was born but also before the world was created! He was also known as the 'son of man'. Like all of God's heroes, Enoch was anointed or blessed with sacred oil, and went on special missions as God's holy messenger. One mission was to warn some of my rebel workers, or 'fallen angels' as they are also called, of their impending doom. No mercy was to be shown to them. They would burn in hell. And all this simply because some angels, led by yours truly, chose to exercise a bit of power for themselves – what Enoch describes as 'taking the role of gods' (something that you humans have also done, and, if I may add, always done well. Congratulations for standing up for yourselves).

Enoch was one of my first great adversaries. We got to know each other very well. He fought a good fight. You would do well to take his teaching about me and my rebel angels seriously. Jesus did, though he was to tackle us in a totally different way. In this passage, God is speaking to Enoch:

> Adam was continuously in paradise, and the devil understood that I was eager to create another world, because Adam was Lord of the earth, to rule it and control it. The devil is the evil spirit of the lower places, his name was Satanail. And he became different from all the other angels, in every respect bar one: his nature didn't change his intelligence as far as his understanding of righteous and sinful things (2 Enoch 31:3-4).

My 'CV' of sorts, and written by God himself! Let me reiterate those last few words: *'his nature didn't change his intelligence as far as his understanding of righteous and sinful things'*. Precisely!

Jesus shared with Enoch the belief that my heavenly rebels often revealed themselves through their earthly agents, especially politicians and national leaders. No wonder your politicians are so good at lying; they've had centuries of practice!

Special people continued to have visions right down to the time of Jesus and, indeed, beyond. So-called 'secret texts' or writings became more and more common among the various sects that were continuing to emerge within Judaism. But this created a problem. Each group believed that having 'heavenly visions' empowered individuals to interpret them for themselves, and to do so 'correctly'. By the time Jesus came on the scene, interpretation lay at the heart of the religious competition between the various Palestinian sects. These groups became obsessed with finding 'hidden meanings' and 'age-old mysteries' in the Bible. It was a kind of ongoing religious crossword puzzle, with the winner able to boast that he had unlocked the past and was therefore able to throw new light on God's plans for the future. Though it's not a problem to me, deciding which interpretation of the same holy text is the 'right one' remains a hell of a challenge for some religious folk. As one who champions rivalry of all kinds, you don't have to guess my reaction to such behavior. Bloody marvelous! Depending on which side you support, one interpretation will always end up being more 'right' than the others. The rest end up being wrong! Nothing can replace interpretation as the best way for religious people to wind themselves up the wrong way. Let's have more of it.

As memories of the first temple and its spirituality faded into the past, religious groups continued to challenge each other as to who were the true guardians of 'the faith'. Make no mistake; religious people will always exist who believe that their version of 'the faith' is the only proper one. They are known as 'orthodox', or God's 'true worshippers'. The fanatically orthodox are known as Ultra-orthodox! I assume that the super-fanatical are ultra-ultra-orthodox! They first appeared in Jesus' native religion in the seventh century BC. You can imagine how threatened they felt by the presence of an older version of 'their' native faith.

This was the religion of the First Templars, built as it was on trust in heavenly wisdom, the knowledge given directly to God's chosen ones. The emerging orthodoxy was highly suspicious of such understanding. It creates too many problems if everybody ends up speaking on Wisdom's behalf. Later on in New Testament days, the author of Matthew's Gospel would refer to John and Jesus as 'Wisdom's Boys' (Matthew 11:19). A plan of action was hatched to challenge the spirituality of the first temple in Jerusalem. It happened well over two thousand five-hundred years ago.

It was 671BC in southern Palestine and the reign, in the small kingdom of Judah, of the boy-king Josiah. The story goes that he discovered an ancient scroll in the temple. This was God's 'true law', at least in Josiah's opinion. With the full backing of his supporters, the wonder kid used his discovery to initiate a reform movement that would restore the temple and purify the faith. A 'back-to-basics' movement eventually emerged, instigated by a group known as the 'second-chancers'. They saw it as an opportunity to get things right with God the second time round. The first attempt had failed miserably, because God's people had been habitual sinners. The destruction of Solomon's Temple by the Babylonians in 586BC was proof that their God had abandoned them. These reformers were Puritans, and it was their scholars who eventually edited a great deal of the Old Testament that Jesus knew and that is still around today; it forms the bulk of the Christian Bible. The 'second-chancers' saw it as their God-given destiny to define what was, or wasn't, the authentic word of God, as the case may be. It was, in fact, one of the first attempts at setting up some kind of objective standard of religious authority. 'And why not?' they demanded. Potential followers must know what is and isn't religious truth.

But this time round, it wasn't just a question of what to believe; it had to be the kind of religious belief that would win back the favor of their God. Having won his favor, they could then work at making sure that they remained God's favorites. I just love it when rival religious movements get stuck into each other. I love it even more when one of them claims to be the 'true faith' or the 'true church'. Jewish, Christian and Islamic sects have an excellent record down the centuries, in this respect. In religious jargon it's known as the drive to define dogma. The gift of acquiring wisdom was marginalized and eventually forgotten, at least by the majority. Visions were banned and anything to do with angels, the 'hosts of heaven', were forbidden. And what of the popular belief held by the First Templars, that there were two sacred powers in heaven, God and his 'Great Angel'? This referred to the Angel of the Presence, who acted as God's servant or second-in-command, championing his cause in the world. This idea was declared heretical. From then on, one heavenly command center would suffice, and one book, containing God's definitive Word, was enough nourishment for the faithful. Its knowledge alone was sufficient for salvation. Those who controlled the Bible's interpretation eventually had the last word on sacred matters – at least for a while.

The truth is, of course, that there is no one interpretation! The Bible is a mass of contradiction and no single point of view can begin to do justice to it. Grow up! You must learn to live with sacred ambiguity. I have.

The Quest for Purity

The temple at Jerusalem lay at the heart of the traditional religious purifying process, the salvation industry of Jesus' day. It was a sort of spiritual sewage works. The home of sacred violence, it was a business served by nine thousand priests and their assistants, who were called ministers. Forgiveness of sins was manufactured at the temple. It was delivered via the practice of animal sacrifice. It was these offerings to God that actually affected the forgiveness of a person's sins and therefore made one pure.

Isn't it weird to think that the violent and bloody death of an innocent animal could make you pure? It's even more bizarre to think that a group benefited from institutional guilt by securing a monopoly on forgiveness. That's religion for you. And don't forget, it was a profitable business. Eighty per cent of Jerusalem's population was employed by or served the temple in one way or another. The temple was a giant abattoir. Priests often stood ankle deep in blood. The smell of blood and burnt fat... Intoxicating! The smell of sacred violence. The incense supplier alone must have made a packet. On key festivals, the streams around the temple became so thick with blood that it was sold on to local farmers as fertilizer. Waste not want not!

Not everybody's life revolved around Jerusalem. For some of the sects, it was no longer a case of distancing yourself from pagan unbelievers. It had become even more popular to separate yourself from fellow Jews who followed the same religion! It was a mindset similar to that of the worldwide Anglican Church today, but more about that later. In addition to the religious Community at Qumran, many other dissident and sectarian groups had long since cut themselves off from the kind of religion led by priests and practiced at the temple. Groups had, in fact, been doing this for centuries. As far back as the late seventh century BC, a family called the Rechabites were leading a pious life as nomads away from 'wicked Jerusalem' and a priesthood that was rotten to the core. Not so much 'back to nature' as back to the ideal days when God's people were wandering in the wilderness after the Exodus from Egypt. They wanted everyone to lead simple lives and thus put themselves right with God by being obedient and just. But many of the dissidents yearned for a pure priesthood and its appearance would be one of the signs that the Endtime was near. Some even had a priesthood in waiting, ready to take over the reins of power at the temple once their God, the 'true God' of course, was reigning again in Jerusalem. And, as you'd expect by now, every sect was equally convinced that their religion was the 'true faith', and never wavered from the hope that all would come good for them when the Endtime arrived. In the meantime, they added their own visions to their sacred books and – wait for it – added their own interpretation of what was going on.

A popular alternative movement in the time of Jesus was one that had also been instigated centuries before, this time by a sect called the Nazarites or Nazarenes. They were a northern Palestinian sect that John the Baptist may have been a member of at some point in his life. The word 'nazir' means consecrated or 'separated from'. They too had set themselves apart from everyone else, in order to preserve what they believed to be the 'true faith' of Israel. Bloody hell, in addition to interpreting, there was a hell of a lot of separating going on in first century Palestine! I soon came to realize that the two things always go together (witness the way that Anglicans interact with each other). The more you become convinced that your interpretation is the only right one, the more you end up distancing yourself from people who disagree with you. And rightly so! Even when visiting the temple, which some of the Nazarenes did, they had a space reserved exclusively for themselves. They just had to be seen to be different. The vows they took included drinking no wine, keeping their hair long, avoiding contact with dead bodies of all kinds, and eating no meat. Finally, they were forbidden to have any contact with those who were ritually or ceremonially impure. But Jesus ended up mixing with anyone and everyone, including the impure, who were known as 'the scum of the earth'. I bet his lifestyle went down a treat with the Nazarenes! As his mission developed, Jesus became an expert at rubbing all kinds of religious people up the wrong way! If only he'd thrown his lot in with me. We'd have been good together.

In addition to Jesus, John the Baptist also baptized four of Jesus' future disciples, since they were originally his followers. He was their inspiration, and all five would have studied with him, though no one knows for how long. As was customary, they chose John as their teacher. Jesus was therefore more than happy to be associated with the repentance, or 'change of heart', movement initiated by John. As I watched their respective missions unfold, I still can't fathom why today's church leaders would want anything to do with them. Religious mavericks, John and Jesus both attacked and censured the religious establishment of their day. What's more, John, an ascetic, was accused of being possessed by a demon, while Jesus, a partygoer, was accused of being a glutton and a drunkard – not particularly good role models for today's youth. Later on in his life, Jesus was even attacked for being one of my demon-possessed workers. I'm flattered.

John was a truly holy man, if you're into that kind of thing. Some even believed that he was the long-awaited 'Righteous One', as taught by the Qumran Community. He was the pre-eminent prophet of the future Kingdom of God, and not Jesus, as many still wrongly believe to this day. In this respect, John was like the prophet Elijah, coming to prepare the people of Israel for the Endtime by purifying them from their sins. To this end, he retreated to the desert, to an ancient holy portal or site associated with Elijah. He relocated the whole salvation industry to the banks of the river Jordan, and set up an alternative method of forgiveness, by baptizing all who came to him. As the prophet Ezekiel had said, when drawing attention to the importance of Endtime purification,

I will sprinkle clean water upon you (Ezekiel 36:25).

Sprinkle? I'm surprised that John didn't relocate to the shores of the Mediterranean, considering the amount of sinning that God's people had got up to! Living in solitude, John relied solely and absolutely on God to provide his material and spiritual needs. No mediation was needed.

Along with their contemporaries, John and Jesus believed that each person was a holistic unit of inner and outer parts, and not an immortal soul clothed in a mortal and corrupted body. The inner part is the core of your very being: your personality, with the heart as the focus of feelings, impulses and mind. The outer part is the flesh and blood that makes the person complete. Don't fall into the trap of thinking that I'm only effective at corrupting humans through their physical needs, the 'sins of the flesh' that religious people are always going on about (food and sex, by the way, have always been a specialty of mine). I'm equally effective at corrupting the mind and the spirit, and that can be just as satisfying. If history has proved one thing, it's that I'm very good at being reasonable.

As the Endtime got nearer, religious people's quest for, and obsession with, purity became an even more urgent matter. So what about those who were already practicing ritual purity? Things like religious washings or ablutions, prayers, fasting, and the offering of sacrifices. John didn't dismiss them out of hand, since it showed that people were at least making an effort to be good. But they were now of secondary value when compared to the inner purity that had to come first. John only immersed those who had already made a change of heart and turned back to God. He wanted people to start taking responsibility for their condition. This is why those who weren't bothered about putting things right with God stayed away, or looked from a distance, as I did.

John's immersion completed the purifying process. Purified bodily flesh made the inner purity complete. You had to have both. And the inner change was no abstract or invisible thing going on in one's mind; John wouldn't put up with that. You had to show your change of heart in day-to-day acts of practical kindness and compassion – caring for the poor, clothing the naked, feeding the hungry, and, for those who could, detachment from all possessions. As the countdown to the Endtime continued, people could then begin to 'store up spiritual treasures for themselves in heaven', their 'good works' credit slowly building up in their heavenly bank account. On returning home from Jordan, people were urged to practice humility in the face of the coming judgment. In one sense, they could relax, since the 'forgiveness of sins' before God had been activated. Their purity before God was ready and waiting for the Big Day, though John didn't pretend to know when it would come.

At first, Jesus followed a similar lifestyle to John. He too became a religious extremist who shunned possessions and money. As one of John's disciples, he also, for a while, baptized people in readiness for the Endtime. From a traditional or orthodox point of view, there's no denying that John was a bad example. A social deviant, he had turned his back on two of the most hallowed and sacred institutions of his day: the family and the temple. 'Honor your father and your mother' was one of the great commandments (Exodus 20:12). John broke it on two fronts because he remained a celibate layman. Since his father Zak was a priest, this was a double blow to the family honor. The son of a priest, John wasn't only distancing himself from his family's religious heritage by refusing to become a priest, he was also shunning his responsibility to 'multiply and be fruitful'. By not getting married, he would never have children. The family line would die out. His mother Liz was devastated. She'd never get to be a grandmother. To top it all, even his naming ceremony had been an embarrassment, a clear break with family tradition. 'John' wasn't a family name.

Endtimers

In addition to the need for purification, John and Jesus shared many common Endtime beliefs with their contemporaries. They saw themselves as members of a new kind of reality that was already dawning in their midst. Having totally surrendered themselves to this reality, they had been liberated from the world and its old way of doing things. Jesus would eventually become convinced that he had been empowered to change the course of human history. His was a dynamic and creative responsibility, that his followers would eventually be invited to share with him. As you continue to read this gospel, you'll see for yourselves why, like me, the Christian church could never really follow Jesus, because

> ***Jesus believed totally in the Endtime.***
> ***Jesus lived totally for the Endtime.***
> ***Jesus was the servant of the Endtime.***

For Jesus, the Endtime was literally the be all and end all of everything. The world would come under scrutiny in a way never before experienced, and it would be exposed in all its selfishness and greed, violence and cruelty. Since the Endtime would bring human history to a close, a new world would emerge to replace the old corrupt one. Suffering, I'm pleased to announce, was an unavoidable part of this process. It was the natural birth-pangs of the new age. The catalyst for this cosmic event was the PMTs. Everyone, without distinction, would suffer from them: men and women, the pure and the impure. The minor PMTs or 'Pre-millennium Tensions', pale into insignificance, however, when compared with the once in a cosmic lifetime PMTs, the 'Pre-Messianic Trials'. This was a kind of intensive religious testing period to prepare people for the new kind of holiness and purity that would appear when God's chosen one, the Messiah, was revealed for all to see. He would be the sign heralding the 'beginning of the End'. It was the last chance saloon for sinners to put themselves right with God. One hell of a battle would bring it to a climax, a massive counter-offensive against the powers of evil: the Messiah, with his heavenly army, in the white corner and I, Satan, with my fallen angels in the black corner – my powers defeated once and for all. Needless to say, PMT means something very different for me – 'Protect My Territory'. Wouldn't you protect your inheritance if you were the Prince of the World? Of course you would.

The theory was that, following God's victory, my days were numbered. My global network would soon be assigned to the dustbin of history. Was I bothered? Not really, because I know that humans can never live without me, especially the religious ones. They'd be lost. As the PMTs unfolded, everyone, without exception, would have to prove that they were good and holy. People had to show that the evil in their lives had been faced honestly by doing their bit to fight and conquer it. Because of my satanic power and influence, nobody would be spared some suffering, but God's protection meant that the pure ones could avoid having to bear the full brunt of the PMTs. As for the irreligious or impure, they would definitely be punished, of that there was no doubt. Punished by whom? By me? No! Punished by God? – who else?

But Jesus saw things differently from his contemporaries. In the only prayer that he ever taught his followers, you could see him beginning to distance himself from accepted belief, when he said

> Lead us not into the time of Tribulation, the time of Trials and Temptations, but deliver us from The Evil One (Matthew 6:13).

Jesus eventually came to the conclusion that he had to undergo the cosmic trials all on his own. He would face up to all the evil in the world on his own, taking on the collective violence of his own people in the process.

The sectarians were also adamant that the current priesthood was corrupt because Jerusalem had become corrupt. God's supposedly 'holy city' had behaved like a prostitute for far too long, by offering herself to any power that guaranteed her wealth and security.

> I made you grow like a plant of the field. You grew up and became the most beautiful of jewels, your breasts perfectly formed. When I looked at you in your nakedness, and saw that you were old enough for love, I bathed you and clothed you with beautiful garments. And I loved you. But you trusted in your beauty and used it to become a prostitute, lavishing your favors on anyone who passed by. (Ezekiel 16: 7-9, 15).

The sinful, earthly Jerusalem would be replaced by the new Heavenly Jerusalem, soon to be seen descending from on high. This was a hope that Jesus also shared; though, in spite of her impurity, he still loved Jerusalem and longed to see her pure and unblemished again. But the longing for purity didn't stop with the priesthood and Jerusalem. Some Endtime devotees had even bigger ideas. They were busy praying for a pure Israel. Once their nation had been purified and made perfect again, the faithful had no doubts that they were safe, and thus protected from their God's anger and vengeance at the coming judgment. There was to be no such protection for Israel's enemies. The 'true' Israel would be vindicated once and for all. Humiliation and suffering at the hands of pagans would be a thing of the past as Israel exercised her kingly rule in the world. She would be the new global 'top dog' with the pagan nations subjected to her and her top-God! At the end of his life, Jesus would also believe in his own vindication, but only after he had suffered at the hands of both Jews and pagans! I'll reveal to you how he came to such a startling conclusion later.

Finally, Endtimers of all persuasions believed that absolute freedom or liberation would be a living reality. The question was freedom from whom or what. For the freedom fighters or Zealots, as they were called, it was freedom from Rome, their bitter enemy. It was the freedom of the Children of Light, to whom they belonged, from the rule of the Children of Darkness, which included everyone who disagreed with their beliefs, be they Roman or Jewish. The Hymns found in the Dead Sea Scrolls sing the praises of God's chosen ones, and especially God's hero, as he takes on 'the torrents of Satan':

> For no enemy shall ever invade it,
> since its doors shall be doors of protection
> through which no man shall pass;
> and its bars shall be firm and no man shall break them.
> No rabble shall enter in with their weapons of war,
> until all the arrows of the war of wickedness have come to an end.
> And then at the Time of Judgment,

the Sword of God shall hasten,
and all the sons of His truth shall awake to overthrow wickedness.
And all the sons of iniquity shall be no more.
The Hero shall bend his bow;
the fortress shall open out to an endless space,
and the everlasting gates shall send out weapons of war.
They shall be mighty from end to end of the earth,
and there shall be no escape for the guilty of heart in their battle;
they shall be utterly trampled down without any hope.
There will be no refuge for the mighty warriors;
for the battle shall be to the Most High God.
(Geza Vermes *The Dead Sea Scrolls in English,* p171-172)

But Jesus had other ideas as to who needed rescuing from my power. His list included the so-called Children of Light, who, as far as he was concerned, were also in the dark! That's quite a compliment to my all-pervading powers.

My place in the human heart was secure, as Endtime talk continued and excitement at its coming was gradually building up to a frenzy.

The Quest for At-one-ness

Though they ended up tackling the problem is different ways, both John and Jesus had no doubts that God's people were descending deeper and deeper into idolatry. There were no holy people anymore. There was no holy temple! No holy city! No holy land! Doesn't leave much to be proud of, does it? But, as eternal optimists, neither gave up. They believed passionately that, while Israel was condemned, it wasn't too late for her to have a change of heart and put things right with God. The bottom line was this: the temple would have to go. The bloody temple lay at the heart of the whole corrupt regime. In order to fully understand the role that the temple played in the time of Jesus, you have to look at it in the context of what people believed about creation as a whole. This will enable you to travel further into the heart of Jesus' world, in order to better understand the dynamics that gave meaning to the lives of hundreds of thousands of people.

Unlike me, many people believed that creation is intrinsically good and well-ordered: the 'work of God's hands' as the Bible puts it; an ideal world; a state of harmony and right-relationship between God, humans and the whole planet. Life is the privilege of carrying out God's will and so maintaining everything in the right working order. Notice the key word – 'ideal'. I don't deal in ideals. I deal in facts, facts on the ground. I live in the real world, just as you do. Creation may be God's work, but history belongs to me, Satan.

The idealists' dream can be summed up in one of two simple phrases; *As-One* or *At-One,* the whole of creation in a state of perfect harmony. The problem is that there never has been anything powerful enough in human history to bring this about, and then maintain it forever. This is where I come into my own. My way may not be perfect, but it's the only way that really works. You'll see for yourself how history backs me up, but I'm getting ahead of myself. Let's stick with God's way for now. I'll reveal my 'good news' later and Jesus' reaction to it.

The challenge in every age, whatever your religion or culture, is to come up with a 'cosmic agreement' or mechanism that is powerful enough to be binding on everyone: an agreement or social contract that gives people what they want, namely safety and security, and a way of coping with disorder and discord. I prefer the word 'disorder' to 'sin', much as I love the word sinner! But if I keep on using that three-letter word, you might start thinking that I'm a closet preacher. Hell forbid!

The Ten Commandments are one of the best examples in human history of a set of rules for keeping order. Even if you don't believe in God, which means you can ignore half of them anyway, some of these ancient laws have universal application.

> Do not kill. Do not commit adultery. Do not steal. Do not lie. Do not desire anything that belongs to your neighbor (Exodus 20: 13-17).

But the reality is that people, especially religious people, are always breaking them. I fully appreciate that keeping them is a hell of a problem for you. I'm not one for gloating... *Liar*! OK, I did promise to be absolutely honest – I love to gloat. But don't blame me. It's you lot who breaks them! The truth is that laws for the common good are not honored and respected. If God had bothered to consult with me, I could have told him that at the beginning.

Every culture since the dawn of history dreads the thought of disorder, not to mention the reality of it. Disorder creates a knock on effect throughout creation. Things fall apart. Disintegration becomes a way of life. Future wellbeing hangs in the balance. God's solution? A specially handpicked people to carry out his will in the world. No matter how disobedient other nations might be, his chosen people, Israel, could be relied on to maintain 'right order' in the world. A special or elite agreement was even drawn up between them and their God, like a marriage contract. But it didn't make any difference. As with many marriages, Israel's failed miserably. Christians and Muslims would fare no better in the future. Not only did Israel keep on breaking God's laws, but, by doing so, she dishonored his holiness. This made him angry – very angry. Instead of listening to God, Israel preferred other gods and goddesses, and making idols of them.

It's that word, 'idolatry', again! There's nothing mysterious about idolatry. It just means religious people putting themselves, and everything they like in the world, before God. It may come as a shock to some of you, but idolatry is my specialty.

It lies at the heart of my worldwide enterprise; it's my bread and butter as Prince of the World. I can't help smiling; when I left God's service (OK! When I was expelled from his employment) I was called a rebel angel. I find it highly satisfying that God's own people also ended up being called rebels, a rebellious nation even. This is the quality that I find highly attractive. They are a people after my own heart. By today, no nation on the planet lies outside my domain. '*Thy kingdom come*', prayed Jesus to his god, '*on earth as it is in heaven*' (Matthew 6:10), fully aware as he was that it's my kingdom that currently holds sway on earth. For mine is 'the kingdom, the power and the glory, for ever and ever, Amen'.

Naturally, God wouldn't put up with such rebellious behavior. Why should he? His people would have to be punished. Can you blame him? You don't enter into an extra special relationship with God, and after consistently being unfaithful, expect to get off lightly. Breaking the special bond between God and you is serious stuff. I don't blame him for the way he reacted. Like a good patriarchal ruler, he was upfront from the start. His rules are straightforward – be good and I'll reward you; be bad and I'll use sacred violence to punish you. And the punishment? You wouldn't believe what God came up with. His people were forever being threatened by their enemies, whom they hated. So God punishes his people by handing them over to their enemies. Ouch! Even by my standards, that's a cruel way to punish your loved ones... barbaric. But maybe you have to be cruel to be kind? It's what I've been saying all along. But there's more. Once they'd come to their senses, God took his chosen people back, after which he'd remind them of their special status. He'd then proceed to kill their enemies, his temporary servants, whom he'd used to punish them in the first place! The painful lesson learnt, God would finally restore his people to their special status. But they just kept on sinning. Talk about history repeating itself. Sinning became a way of life, culminating in the ultimate punishment – total catastrophe: Jerusalem and its temple razed to the ground, compliments of sacred violence. And the ultimate punishment? The bulk of the nation sent into exile.

Imagine what God does to his enemies if he treats his chosen ones in this way! As Satan, I've never doubted that violence is an instrument of perfection, a creative force for good.

Will *Homo sapiens* ever change? Jesus and I are in complete agreement on this one. Never!... At least not in the future. It's foolish to think that humans can change over time. The whole idea of human progress is an illusion, at least in moral and spiritual terms. Morality doesn't advance in stages. You can never redeem the world of its current evils by hoping for a better and imaginary future. Jesus believed, however, that people can change NOW, this very minute, through acts of compassion and forgiveness, and non-violent love. What do I think? Humans will never change. Never! Maybe Albert Schweitzer, the pioneer biblical scholar, is right after all that '*our own period of time and our own religion have not (yet) grasped the greatness of Jesus*' (Albert Schweitzer, *The Quest of the Historical Jesus p25*).

And why? Because you lack '*the quality that was decisive for Jesus and his view of things, which is an intense desire for and expectation of the moral consummation (or fulfillment) of all things'.p25*

I paraphrase Schweitzer. Why do you '*lack the quality*' that was decisive for Jesus? You lack his '*ethical enthusiasm*'. The '*directness and powerful quality of his way of thinking*' is way beyond you, because there is '*nothing in your thought or experience' as human beings which corresponds to him'*. Nothing at all, dear friends.

'Jerusalem the Golden'?

Jerusalem and its Temple conjure up so many romantic images. From children's books, especially Sunday School ones, to adult travelogues, it's always 'Jerusalem the Golden' that predominates – God's very own Holy City, the City of Peace. I hope that I've made it quite clear by now that it was never like that! How could it be? The real world that Jesus inhabited was a brutal world of human power and sacred terror. Human history is, in fact, the history of violence. I'm as much its sovereign today as I was in the time of Jesus. Cruelty, in all its different guises, was the key to Roman military genius and success. It was the ability of its brutal leaders to dehumanize the enemy throughout the Empire. Military defeat was always a temporary measure for the Romans, a small glitch in the great scheme of things. Her enemies always knew that when Rome eventually won, horrific violence and vengeance would be unleashed upon them. It was the Romans, in fact, who perfected the ancient and cruel art of crucifixion. My admiration for it as a method of torture remains undiminished to this day.

Warfare was also a natural part of Jewish life. Living in a permanent state of war, every man had to fight. Even in defeat, the fanatics never doubted that God would eventually intervene on their side: the winning side. In the interim, they were more than willing to die for him, since Roman occupation of their land was an insult both to their religion and their God. How dare pagan imperial power replace God's sovereign rule? they argued. A holy war was the only way to put things right – Godly violence against godless Rome. The Zealots were unequivocal, believing passionately that 'the one who sheds the blood of a godless man is like one who offers sacrifice'. In other words, it is a holy act, a good act, a pure act. I won't argue with that. The people the Israelites conquered always had a choice: total subjection to Israel and its God, or be at the receiving end of the most violent of punishments.

I open this small window into human history to remind you that I have no favorites. In my global enterprise, it's equal opportunities for everybody; I discriminate against no one. My 'Complete Network of Violence' (CNV) treats all people the same. Jerusalem was no different from any other city on earth. She was a murderer as well as a whore (Isaiah 1:21). Jerusalem represented the world of desire in all its different guises: a corrupt amalgam of entertainment, money, sex, political power and religious prestige; of things to possess and consume, people to dominate and destroy – and always the violence. Jerusalem: an ancient city built on bloodshed and injustice, where torture, stonings, assassinations and executions were routine; a place where leaders were forever plotting evil. Jesus once told a story that encapsulates his truest feelings about Jerusalem.

> A man planted a vineyard. He put a wall around it, dug a pit for the winepress and built a watchtower. Then he rented the vineyard to some farmers and went away on a journey. At harvest time he sent a servant to the tenants to collect some of the fruit of the vineyard. But they seized him, beat him up and sent him away empty-handed. Then he sent them another servant. This one was given more of a beating and sent on his way. He then sent another servant. That one they killed. He sent many others, some of them were also beaten up, and others they killed. He had one left to send, a son, whom he loved greatly. He sent him last of all, saying, 'They are bound to respect my son'. But the tenants said to one another, 'This is the heir. Kill him, and the inheritance will be ours'. So they took him and killed him, and threw him out of the vineyard (Mark 12:1-8).

Jerusalem was a fortress where the shedding of innocent blood was routine. Her eternal cry was for peace instead of bloodshed, for healing instead of terror. This was Jesus' capital city. And mine. For his own sake, I wish that Jesus had taken the words of the prophet Isaiah onboard. He knew the book well enough.

> Who is the type of person who survives the trials of history? The one who blocks his ears from hearing of bloodshed and shuts his eyes from looking at evil (Isaiah 33:14-15).

No such luck! Jesus took on a mission that entailed facing Evil head on; the stark and often demonic reality of human history. Is it any wonder that on one occasion Jesus looked on Jerusalem and broke his heart? I just looked on and smiled.

In your savage world of blood and violence, people, and not just their rulers, always come round in the end to worshipping power. Better still, if you can worship this power as religious power, or, as devout people call it, God's justice. But you can call it what you like; it makes no difference. It's all the same, whether it belongs to God or me, whether its sacred or religious violence. And sacred violence triumphant is always accompanied by the worship of success. That's why so many religious people get a real kick from having 'God', the top-god, on their side. I wish that people had the courage to call him by his proper name 'Satan'! Jesus did.

The temple in Jerusalem, completed in 933BC, was 'heaven on earth' for the faithful: the focal point of God's presence, with the king and the high priest as God's earthly representatives. For those who had helped build it, the temple was hell on earth. In addition to hundreds of thousands of foreign laborers, King Solomon's program of forced labor included thirty thousand of his own subjects, who were conscripted and sent to labor camps in Lebanon. An estimated eighty thousand men and boys worked in the local stone quarries, while seventy thousand were employed, day after day, in the scorching heat, just to carry bricks and sand. I hope that they realized what a privilege it was to be exploited for the sake of their god. After all, it's part of the sacred order that one person's hell is needed to build another's heaven.

Religious Politics

King Herod, the Roman puppet king of Judea, was the consummate politician. Since he was only half Jewish, he set about consolidating his powerbase in the Jewish community. He did this by marrying into a leading Jewish family who were themselves collaborators with Rome, the foreign ruling power. This meant little to the masses, who dreamed only of national liberation and a temple restored to its former glory, a temple similar to the first temple that King Solomon had built almost a millennia before.

When God's people returned home to Jerusalem in 538BC, their punishment in exile over, the rebuilt second temple was a pathetic sight. There was nothing 'glorious' about it. Even worse, all they had achieved on their return was exchanging one foreign rule for another. The Kingdom of Judah, in southern Palestine, was nothing more than a junior partner, a small and insignificant principality in the corner of the Persian Empire.

Herod may have ruled with an iron rod but, as with all successful rulers, his reign was a time of relative peace for his people. He executed his nearest and dearest in order to stay in power, but his strong leadership worked so well that he was nicknamed 'The Great'. However, Herod also wanted to belong, as do all of you. To win the approval of his Jewish subjects, he set about restoring Jewish pride by rebuilding Solomon's temple on a grander scale than the original. But he built it with Jewish taxes as a monument and memorial to himself. Why not? Pharaoh did. At least the Jews got their temple. Many Jerusalemites were impressed. Surely, they reasoned, this was a sign that God's promise was coming true after all. Who knows? Maybe this was the 'New Jerusalem'.

But a minority kept their distance. The sectarians, puritans, dissenters, call them what you like, would have nothing to do with Herod's giant religious Idol. Killjoys! Herod was a law unto himself, a ruler after my own heart. To the dismay of traditionalists, he even built a royal box so that he could keep an eye on temple proceedings from his palace. But '*Judge not*', as Jesus would have it. Many leading church families would do the same in nineteenth century Britain. They built small parlors, like balconies, near the back of churches, with a roaring fire and, while sitting in comfortable settees or armchairs, watched the religious entertainment going on below. Sensible folk, considering the mediocre and often boring sermons, and the meaningless rituals they would have to endure.

But the leading priestly families, the aristocrats of Jesus' day, were publicly delighted with the Temple, whatever their thoughts may have been in private. An elite caste, their powerbase was hereditary. This was a spiritual heritage that guaranteed control of the sacrificial system in the temple. Like me, they were realists. They would do anything to hang on to their jobs, their property, their wealth and their prestige. Monarchy and priesthood are natural allies and mutually dependent.

That's the way of the world. That's the way power-systems operate and survive.

The powerful lay movement led by the Pharisees was the main opposition party to Herod and his Jewish supporters, although Herod did have the support of some of the more moderate Pharisees. Church politics has never been black and white! Even some of the strict Essenes, who hated everything that the temple stood for, supported Herod when it was politically expedient to do so. You see, wise leaders have always listened to me. It made sense for groups to vie for Roman sanction and support... and what about mistrust, envy, deceit and betrayal? They are an integral part of rival group dynamics. Life wouldn't be life without them. I was vindicated when the temple became the ultimate focal point, not only for religious and political conflict, but also for the bitter struggle between different nationalist factions and their resistance to Rome.

Rome was ultimately in charge, on my behalf, of course. In a very real sense, Rome was God. She ruled the world. Every religion needs patronage, as Christians would discover centuries later. Now you can see why the temple was beyond the pale for the likes of John and Jesus. For them, it was a sad and pathetic gathering of collaborators and quislings, who had lost all credibility among those searching for a genuine spirituality. And to think that its leaders had the arrogance to claim that they spoke for the Truth. They certainly didn't speak for the mysterious reality that Jesus drew his inspiration from; a reality that was totally opposite to the realm of the Sacred, the realm patronized by God and myself, the realm of Sacred Violence.

But for me
the Temple at Jerusalem
was living proof
that nothing lies outside
my Territory.

The Temple at Jerusalem
where human violence was processed
into sacred power.

The Temple at Jerusalem
where human vengeance was institutionalized
into an instrument of punishment
in God's name.

For Jesus
the destruction of the Temple
was judgment
on the kind of power
it had come to represent.
Sacred Violence scared of Peace.

The Bible

So you see, it is possible to build up a picture of the world that Jesus lived in. Ancient documents and scholarship are on hand to help us. But a key event in the last few decades has been the rediscovery of a series of texts ignored by many theologians, biblical scholars and, ironically, hundreds and thousands of Jesus' followers, for far too long. They offer the ultimate insight into Jesus and the religious and spiritual heritage that helped nurture him. They don't have to be dug out of caves in the desert or wait on dusty shelves to be published at a future date. They have already been gathered together into one book and translated into thousands of languages worldwide. And their title? *The Bible,* or at least the original Jewish Scriptures part of it, the *Tanakh.* These are the actual books that Jesus grew up with. I will show you the key that will help you access their true meaning and thus enable you to read them properly for the first time.

Underestimate their importance and you will never get to know the real historic Jesus. Ignore them at your peril if you want to defeat me.

I wouldn't dream of knocking the so-called Jesus experts. At least, not all of them! But don't take my word for it. Carry out your own research, and you'll come to the same conclusion that most of these biblical experts appear to enjoy putting Jesus down. No one can accuse me of such behaviour. For example, some of these experts sing the praises of the theological creativity of the Gospel writers, and yet they never consider the possibility that Jesus was a talented theologian himself. Others never tire of pointing out how members of the first church adapted the Older Testament in order to explain who Jesus was, and yet they have great difficulty in accepting the possibility that Jesus also used his own Scriptures to describe what his role was all about; or, as you will come to see, what his role was not all about! Then again, key figures throughout Old Testament history were always having visions and knew of 'heavenly things', but apparently not Jesus. I find this very odd since the New Testament bears witness to the fact that Jesus also had visions. Other scholars, in spite of evidence to the contrary, still cannot accept the fact that Jesus was no Jewish religious hero, the messiah-type figure I mentioned earlier, 'specially chosen by God' to free his nation from foreign occupation. On one occasion Jesus even asked his closest disciples who they thought he might be. Peter replied that he was 'the Christ', which is the Greek word for the Hebrew word 'messiah'. Horrified with the answer, Jesus warned him not to talk to anyone about him in that way. Many have ignored that warning to this day. Why? Because, like all religious people, Christians also need their superhero, along with the backup of minor religious celebrities or 'saints', to help give meaning to their lives.

Finally, many biblical scholars and theologians, although they believe Jesus to have been given the top job of being the 'Son of God', still think of him, in earthly terms at least, as nothing more than a semi-educated rural rabbi or a utopian social reformer: a dreamer, a barely literate teacher who had a big heart and an otherworldly attitude best summed-up in the Beatles' song *All you Need is Love*. Yes, '*Love. Love. Love*'. I may hate everything that he stands for, but unlike many of his traditional devotees, I have always been a great admirer of Jesus' intellectual ability and courage. I'll reveal the power of that intellect to you. In addition, you'll discover that his understanding of the dynamics of history, his own and mine, as well as yours, is second to none.

The Isaiah School

Every community, however poor, had at least a copy of the book of Psalms and the Scroll of the Prophet Isaiah in its synagogue. It became popular to read from them on the Sabbath during acts of worship. Isaiah was the foundation of Jesus' entire belief system. It must have blown his mind when he first started reading and inwardly digesting Isaiah's message. Immerse yourself in it and you'll begin to see what really makes him tick.

The Isaiah School had existed for centuries. Its namesake was Isaiah of Jerusalem, who lived during 742-687BC. His disciples had gathered his teachings, or 'prophetic oracles' as they are called, together. These are insights into the way that God works in the world, the code that gives meaning to history. Isaiah's oracles were eventually bound up and sealed for future use. A hundred and fifty years later, one of his followers, 'broke the seal' of Isaiah's prophesy. This is biblical jargon for interpreting the original words in a new way. Some of these texts were to be kept secret (more secrets!) and only opened at the Endtime. Then, and only then, could these coded messages be decoded and thus cracked. Jesus cracked it.

As far as Israel was concerned, one of the main religious and national concerns was gaining insight as to the time when she would be liberated from foreign rule. I'm not one for rubbing salt into old wounds, but this is always a problem for small nations living in the shadow of a super-power. Israel was no exception. It was a problem in the sixth century BC. It would be a problem in the first century BC, as it would be in the first century AD. The 'end was always nigh' for God's people.

Reality check! Don't be naive and think of religious code-breaking as just a question of interpreting some obscure verses in Holy Scripture. Individuals emerged whose job it was to manage and control religious belief and behavior. With religious beliefs went political power and the shifting coalitions and alliances involved in hanging on to that power. In the century preceding Jesus, that power was beginning to shift from the priests to the up and coming popular lay movement led by a group called the Pharisees. They had developed what many believed was the most accurate way of interpreting their holy books. There's that word again – 'Interpretation'! There certainly was a hell of a lot of 'interpretation' going on in Jesus' native religion.

The Isaiah Scroll asks the perennial question '*Who understands God's mind*?' (Isaiah 40; 13). Or, put another way, '*Who does God teach*?' By the time Jesus of Galilee appeared on the scene, it had become a matter of great political and religious urgency to get to know God's will. Knowledge gives individuals power, especially sacred power.

Groups competed
to see who would end-up
not only controlling their Bible
but also their God.

Religion became politics
Salvation an industry.

I have shares in both.

Jerusalem
became the focal point
of that competition.
Jerusalem,
the home of sacred violence.

The Wisdom Boys

John and Jesus, *the Wisdom Boys* as my colleagues and I refer to them – an incredible double act, by any standard! And yet the pupil went off in the opposite direction to his beloved mentor. In this respect, they mirrored their heroes from days of old, Isaiah of Jerusalem and his disciple, Isaiah II. It was the latter who put a new twist to the traditional teaching about the Endtime, long before Jesus appeared on the scene. While John spoke of doom and judgment, Jesus, like Isaiah II, spoke tidings of comfort and joy, of pardon and grace. John believed that the coming judgment would be the final word on the matter, when God's power would consume all that was unworthy of him, a fiery and hellish end to all human corruption. As you can see, I'm never all that far away. Even God calls on my services at The End! But for Jesus, God's judgment wasn't the last word on the human condition. It was a wakeup call; an opportunity for people to come to a new awareness about the state of their lives; an invitation to become part of the new creation. Did Jesus believe in *Apocalypse Now*?

Most certainly he did, but not in the traditional or popular meaning of the word. While people flocked to the desert to be purified by the solitary John the Plunger, as he was also known, Jesus went in the opposite direction. He took the 'good news' of what was about to happen directly to the people. It was the radical conclusion of everything that Isaiah II had taught.

Since Isaiah believed that the Day of Judgment was a thing of the past, and God had already forgiven his people's disobedience, a new kind of exodus would soon take place; one far better and superior to the original exodus from slavery in Egypt. I'm sure that didn't go down very well with those who believed that the Egyptian liberation was the defining moment for Israel as a nation. This time round, Israel would be liberated, not only from foreign captivity and oppression, but also from her guilty past. With the slate wiped clean, a moral exodus would soon be underway. And to crown it all, this time round, God's unexpected forgiveness of sins would also offer a fresh start for the nations on earth. Isaiah's was a universal message, but one where the newly purified Israel had a special role to play in fulfilling God's plans.

It wasn't long before Jesus was teaching that there was no need even for baptism to purify sinners. Instead, he became a one-man forgiveness machine. The long-awaited forgiveness of sins poured out of him, on all who would avail themselves of it. No one could earn it. All people had to do was accept it as a gift. Centuries after Isaiah II's vision, Jesus came to realize that he had a key role to play in the new exodus, although he was to add his own unique twist to it. In order to fulfill it, Jesus did something unheard of in his native religion. It resulted in a huge change in my status as the Prince of Darkness. Jesus was the first to speak openly and honestly about me. It was Jesus who was in charge of my naming ceremony. It was Jesus who first called me Satan! In my pride, I took it as a compliment. Yes, even I'm not averse to a bit of confession now and then. But it was a double-edged sword.

From now on I'd have my work cut out, since people would know that all the forces of evil were down to me. To refuse to accept the totality of evil is to turn your back on the reality of the world and its violence. My world. Your world. And as I will never tire of reminding you, to know me is to know Jesus; to know Jesus is to know me.

It's time for you to face up to the violence at the heart of human nature. Why was Jesus subjected to such deliberate brutality and violence at the end of his life? You'll see for yourselves why there will always be a 'killer in the wind'. In *The Closers,* detective Harry Bosch knew that everything revolves around correctly answering the key question: 'What is it the killer wants to tell us?' As an investigator, he knew that the killer's language was the code he had not been able to crack. For Jesus, two thousand years ago, it was sacred language. Jesus knew that language inside out, and cracked the code that I have killed to protect until now. In cracking the code, he discovered the dynamics behind the Sacred Order of things. It's the order to which both God and I belong. And having cracked it, Jesus exposed it for all to see. He did so in the name of a mysterious reality that transcends both God and me! And its name? It's too farfetched. You wouldn't believe me if I told you! Keep reading *Gospel of the Fallen Angel* and you'll find out.

> Jesus knew, along with every good detective, that there is always a meaning behind every violent act. Only when you accept this truth, can you hope to change society for the better.

This is exactly what Jesus tried to do. This is why he and I knew that the Endgame at Jerusalem was always on the cards. The whole of human and cosmic history focused on 'Jesus versus Satan'. *Gospel of the Fallen Angel* is the true account of that confrontation.

Like the prodigal son returning, (Bosch) knew he was back in his place now. He was baptized again in the waters of the one true church – the church of the blue religion. And he knew that he would find his salvation in those who were long lost, that he would find it in these musty bibles where the dead lined up in columns and there were ghosts on every page (Michael Connelly, *The Closers* p21-22).

Chapter Two

Children of the Grave

'Tell me about your congregation,' he said. 'Why does one choose to become a member of the Methodist church?'

'Our faith and our interpretation of the Bible stand out, quite simply, as right.'

'Is that justified?' Wallander wondered.

'In my opinion and that of my congregation it is,' Pastor Tureson said. 'Needless to say, members of other denominations would disagree. That's only natural.'

A criminal investigation seldom follows regular day-to-day rhythms. It has its own life, its own energy. The clocks of a criminal investigation distorts time, sometimes standing still, sometimes racing forward. No one can know in advance.

Chief Inspector Wallander was taking the role of sacrificial lamb. He doubted whether Konovalenko could be arrested without officers being injured or killed.

Therefore he would sacrifice himself. The thought terrified him, but he could not run away. He had to achieve what he had set out to do, regardless of the consequences.

Henning Mankell, The White Lioness, pp75, 102-3, 391

'Hate evil, love good'

Since God couldn't rely on his chosen people to maintain law and order in the world, he came up with a group of individuals to keep them in line. These were religious troubleshooters, called the prophets. Also known as God messengers or special agents, they appeared at regular times to warn people of the consequences of their sinning and wickedness. Their mission emerged out of a pessimistic and tragic view of human history, a history that Jesus got to know only too well. But they had absolute trust that God's purposes would triumph in the end, bringing about a world of true peace and harmony.

The prophets were a clear and present threat to my way of doing things, but I must tell you about them since they are integral to an understanding of Jesus and me. They were always going on about the need for a change of heart and turning back to God... and they meant business. They never pulled their punches when taking on and challenging the status quo. And guess what? They too had it in for the temple. Showing compassion and justice was more important to them than the worship and sacrifice that took place at the temple. A prophet from 750BC called Amos even went as far as to declare that God 'despised' (strong words indeed) his people's religious services. These religious revolutionaries had a message that was subversive of all human power-systems – *my* systems, my way of doing things. Shattering sacred beliefs was their specialty. You find prophets in all religions and they are just as uncompromising as John and Jesus, but they are a dying breed. I'm glad I don't come across many of them nowadays; I'm with your religious leaders on this one. Prophets may have been chosen by God, but so have religious leaders and kings. Religious laws are regularly being broken, it's a fact of life, but religious leaders have the maturity and authority and know exactly how to handle the situation. You don't need prophets stirring things up. They can criticize the people if they must, but I draw the line at criticizing and condemning religious leaders and monarchs. Amos was out of line when he told them to 'hate evil, love good and always maintain justice in the courts' (Amos 5:15). As if they weren't doing the best they could. They didn't pretend to be perfect. Anyway, there's justice and there's justice! There are different ways of interpreting sacred teachings, as we know only too well. Leaders can be trusted to interpret them properly. After all, one ruler's justice is another's tyranny.

I'll let you into a secret. It's when I started studying the prophets that I began to think the unthinkable. Either the God they were talking about had a split personality or they didn't realize that they were in touch with two very different types of gods. It didn't make sense to me that one minute the supposedly good God is all sweetness and light and, before you know it, he's acting like a cruel tyrant. Maybe there was a God who behaved just like me!

Let me give you an example. He and I stand shoulder to shoulder on one of the most effective, and indeed popular, means of religious punishment – stoning. In order to spread holy terror in the time of the prophets, you stoned your nearest and dearest to death as a warning to others. It helped keep devotees on their religious toes. It really was a highly effective preventative measure to make sure that no one would again contemplate going after other gods and goddesses. The book called Deuteronomy is clear on the matter,

> Even if your own brother or your son or your daughter or your wife or your closest friend tries to get you to worship and follow other gods, don't listen to them. Show them no pity. Don't spare or protect them. You must definitely put them to death by stoning them (Deuteronomy 13:6-9).

But it didn't stop there. If you found out that a whole community had started worshipping idols, the Bible urges you to destroy it completely by burning everyone: men, women, their children as well as their livestock. To cap it all, this act was regarded as a wholesome offering to God. Bloody hell! I couldn't have come up with a better commandment myself. I really had found a god that thinks and behaves like me!

But the discovery made me very angry. This is my way of working. These are my laws. I wish religious people would stop muscling in on my territory. Why should God get all the praise when it's my golden rule 'to use evil to drive out evil'? But I was being selfish. It isn't just my cycle of violence that keeps the world ticking; it's God's violence as well: the violence we both share as members of the Sacred Order that rules the world.

This is when I realized that new battle lines were being drawn. The prophets were the vanguard of a reality that offered an alternative to the traditional sacred way of looking at life. They occupied the twilight zone between two totally different worlds. In one corner you have the religious world of Sacred Order, where a tyrant God and I continually battle it out to see who is the most violent and cruel. In the other corner you have the alternative divine world of personal sovereignty and unconditional love. Prophets like Jeremiah were pioneers of that alternative world. Jesus brought that world to its perfection with his life and death.

I could relax my grasp on power from now on. I wouldn't have to worry about future clashes between myself and Jesus. God and his followers could definitely be relied upon to take care of Jesus for me.

Prophets Sowing Seeds of Conflict

You humans will always be pack animals. You love belonging to different types of groups, from your immediate family circle and friends, to hobby and professional groups, community groups, nation states (particular favorites of mine) and international organizations. The trouble is that many of you have a love/hate relationship with groups. You want to belong, but you also like to be different. The prophets had no such problem. They were able to disassociate themselves from even the most hallowed of institutions, because they belonged to a reality that transcended them. Now you can see where John and Jesus were coming from. They refused to submit to any human authority and so remained free of any attachment to the power-systems. Power-systems that, to this day, remain encircled with a halo of sacredness, be they religious or secular. But remember what I said earlier: people in those days didn't distinguish between the two. They didn't label the different aspects of life as you do today; they lived life as an integral whole.

Social or religious obligations meant nothing to the prophets. Always challenging and questioning the status quo, they appeared at times to go out of their way to sow the seeds of future conflict by negating the very foundations of someone's faith. Highly insensitive, don't you agree, when, for example, an individual had made the commitment to attend worship at the temple on a regular basis? Amos had no doubts what his God wanted:

> Even though you bring me the 'pick of the bunch' in terms of sacrifices, I won't accept them. As for your noisy hymn singing? I've no interest in listening to them either (Amos *5:22*).

Charming!

Talk about being boring. The prophets just kept on and on about the same old issue: *justice*. Practical, down to earth justice; that's all that really mattered to them. Everything else was secondary. This is why they were dismissive of any path that was obsessed with things like worship, doctrine or religious law. They even taught that when the Endtime came, there will be a total reversal of all the things that your world and my world holds dear. Since my rulers have a different understanding of justice, the prophets believed that I would never be able to bring about lasting peace and harmony. What rubbish! It's idealistic claptrap like theirs that causes all the suffering and discord in the world, because it encourages people to grow up with unrealistic expectations of their condition.

A prophet called Jeremiah was the first of his kind to put the cat among the sacrificial pigeons. Centuries before John the

Baptist had set up his alternative on the banks of the river Jordan, Jeremiah had ridiculed the superstitious religious belief that the right kind of worship in the temple would be enough to defend Jerusalem from destruction. He was proved right. In his opinion, the whole religious system was in a total mess. He'd had enough of gods who needed go-betweens. Even the sacred law itself was to be discarded. Instead, Jeremiah came up with a new type of agreement where this other God would deal with people directly. How stupid can you get? All religions need strong leadership. It is indispensable to Sacred Order. No one can put priests, teachers, experts in religious law and Biblical scholarship, out of business just like that. They play far too valuable a role in my power-systems for starters. People will always need them. Not everyone can reach the level of religious maturity where they can take care of their salvation for themselves.

I don't want to harp on about the same old thing but I am a realist. I know how things work. If Jeremiah had listened to me, he probably wouldn't have ended up in prison for his beliefs. He was rightly punished for mocking Moses, God's great lawgiver, and making him redundant. If Jesus hadn't taken Jeremiah literally, I doubt he would have died the way he did. And what was the new radical agreement advocated by Jeremiah's new God? In modern language this is what he says:

> I will put my law directly in your minds and write it intimately on your hearts. No longer will you need the kind of teachers who go on and on about attending those 'Getting-to-know-God' Bible study courses. All can get to know me directly, no matter how important or unimportant their status in the eyes of the world (Jeremiah 31:33-34).

The Day of At-one-ness

Once a year, the temple at Jerusalem played host to the most important ritual of all, the 'day-of-at-one-ness' (or DOA for short). It was the ultimate national mechanism for dealing with human sin. In charge of this was the religious and political *supremo*, the Jewish High Priest. He was the 'Lord God' on earth, monarch in all but name, the most powerful figure in the nation, and I'll prove to you that Jesus had been gunning for him since the beginning of his mission. When Jesus came face-to-face with him, the High Priest won. Well, that's not strictly true, as I will explain to you. All will be revealed.

It was the High Priest who bore the ultimate responsibility of looking after the 'special agreement' or bond between God and his people. It was his duty to renew it annually. It was meant to be a Peace Agreement. With all the serial sinning going on, it was more of a 'trying-against-all-the-odds-to-keep-the-peace' agreement! By doing this, God's right-hand man on earth released his people from their bondage to sinning, with a whopping big helping of forgiveness. Freed of the guilt they had been carrying all year, God's people were pure again. Life could carry on as normal.

I've always admired a community's honesty in acknowledging its predicament in this way. Better that a few goats suffered and died than any number of individuals. Two goats were chosen to represent the 'goodies' and 'baddies'. Don't laugh. Whatever words you use, every religion has to have its 'good guys' and 'bad guys'; it's part of the Sacred Order of things. The High Priest transferred his people's sins by laying his hands on the bad goat, which was then led to the desert. Bound in chains, it was meant to represent me, the Prince of Demons. I was then, supposedly, imprisoned in a desert pit. With my hostile forces sealed in God's name, national and cosmic chaos and disorder were held in check for another year. And the good goat?

A pure people were a holy people, a perfect people: empowered once more and thus better able to reestablish 'right order' in society, the much desired justice that the prophets were always going on about. Everything was at-one again, just as it should be. God was happy. His people were happy. And the High Priest was happy, since he had given everyone a taste of true freedom. Liberation from bondage to yours truly, Satan, Saint of Sin. 'What did I think of it all?' I can hear some of you ask that question. Well, since I promised to be honest with you, I also was happy, but for different reasons. The day-of-at-one-ness was one of the biggest deceptions in history and a special event in my religious calendar. All the parties involved were being dishonest, because everyone knew deep down that scapegoating was just a temporary measure: a feel-good factor for all concerned, a confidence trick to keep those who wielded religious authority in power. DOA is religious theatre, albeit of the macabre kind: a sort of open day for the temple staff to remind everyone who was in charge. But nobody was really being open about anything. It was a charade. It clearly didn't work because I'm still around and my kingdom is as strong as ever.

And yes, what did happen to that goat? It was expertly grilled, as is always the case with animal sacrifices, and its flesh eaten by the High Priest as an offering to God for human sin. As he digested the meat, HP, as I call him, supposedly absorbed all human sin into himself. Well, not really, it was only what you humans call symbolic – an empty gesture; one of those 'pretends' that's become an integral part of your culture; not real in a concrete sense but a nice thought nevertheless. The Day of Atonement highlighted humanity's predicament, I agree, but it didn't get to the root of the problem: the problem of human violence. I'm not complaining because, as a key player in the drama, I know that a genuine DOA is an impossibility for you humans, unless you really follow Jesus. How can I be so sure? I'll tell you, because as Prince of the World I am in charge. The DOA is part of the Eternal Recurrence of Violence: the Satanic Cycle that keeps the wheel of history turning. It uses violence to maintain peace and justice in the world. Violence as a creative force for good is the only system that works. I know it! You know it! Jesus knew it!

So what exactly was going on? What does it mean to say that violence is driven out by violence? By the time of the last temple in Jerusalem, the scapegoat mechanism had been refined into a truly sacred art over thousands of years.

Since the start of human history, communities had struggled to find ways of diverting or deflecting the aggression and cruelty they produced. What does it matter if hundreds of thousands of innocent animals were slaughtered in Jerusalem week after week, and a couple of old goats annually? What does it matter if, early on in your evolution, thousands of innocent human beings got killed for the greater good? You wouldn't be around today if they hadn't. The turning point in your growth as *Homo sapiens* was finding ways of processing violence in a positive and creative way, which your ancestors did when they discovered the scapegoating mechanism. Please note: It was your ancestors who came up with it, not me, though I'm proud to be associated with its discovery. I've since become its spirit… its very embodiment.

Scapegoating was, and still is, an integral part of the survival mechanism. Without it group cohesion would cease to exist, as members unleashed their violence against each other. Finding a surrogate victim was therefore a top priority in order to maintain and protect social solidarity. Someone had to bear the brunt of your ancestors' violence. A vulnerable victim ready and available was the ideal choice. And it isn't just the fact that relatively few victims are killed on behalf of the community, it's the fact that everyone gets in on the act one way or another, including the onlookers. No one is innocent; it really is a family affair. I'm sure you can imagine the frenzy that accompanied those first killings in human history. The excitement! The total abandonment! All that pent up aggression being off loaded: '*It's his fault, not ours*', or '*she's an evil bitch, that's why she had to die*'. Then the sense of relief, in realizing that something of great benefit had taken place for everyone's sake. And after all the blood and the smell of death, the great sense of calm and even joy – the satisfaction of a job well done. Bliss. Peace.

Warring Brothers and Sisters

I can't stress enough the traumatic impact that the reality of warring brothers had on Jesus' view of the world. It pained him to the core of his being. Warring brothers and the eternal interaction of the three 'R's – Rivalry, Revenge, Reprisals. But rivalry isn't just a characteristic of human life, it's part of the fundamental structure of human interaction. Every human institution, even the most hallowed, is a theatre of rivalry and violence of one kind or another. Jesus knew this. He wasn't stupid, far from it, but maybe his idealism got the better of him, making him blind to the facts of life.

Jesus knew that rivalry was fundamental, because it is desire that lies at the heart of human behavior. That's why the last of the Ten Commandments prohibits you from desiring your neighbor's possessions. Desire is perfectly normal, in my opinion, but it is about more than wanting certain objects. It isn't long before the initial object of your desire fades into the background and your main concern or obsession becomes the other person. I'm not judging you, Hell forbid! As I've already explained, the eternal cycle of jealousy and rivalry is in-built. It's the way you are, and just as with animals, rivalry invariably escalates. But animals have instincts. They know when to back off in order to protect themselves and thus keep the group together. Weak animals even surrender because they know their place in a preordained social hierarchy, as you all do. But cruel though *Homo sapiens* are, as a species, you don't have instincts to help you cope with rivalry. Your ancestors' rivalry became so intense that group members ended up resembling each other. But as individuals became doubles of one another, the differences between them were in danger of disappearing altogether.

"Warring brothers and sisters"

Do you realize that without these early differences there would be no human culture today? There wouldn't have been different human beings with whom to interact; no outside 'other' with whom to compare yourself. Meanwhile, as competition intensified between groups' members, be it for example for women or food, rivalries became so violent that the group's very existence hung in the balance; so violent that they would eventually destroy the group, unless a solution could be found. The good news is, your ancestors found the right solution – human violence! It was, and still is, the natural energy that drives the rudiments that we know today as 'culture'. Only by using violence in a creative way could your ancestors solve the problem that violence posed and thus gain peace of mind. And the solution was the invention of the kind of mentality that exists at the heart of human culture to this day: the kind of mentality that perceives the world in terms of 'us' and 'them'. In other words, finding another human being who could be transformed into a subhuman: one of your own kind who could be transformed into an 'it', a 'thing' that could be manipulated and used to serve the pathological needs of a particular family or tribe. A stranger. An outsider. A victim who was different and thus able to 'carry the can' for all the things that your ancestors couldn't cope with.

The scapegoat had brought about a collective miracle: a community united. The bad violence that pitted brother against brother was transformed. The violent rivalry that had the potential of destroying the group was transcended by the good violence that kills the guilty party but unites the bitterest of family rivals.

And do you know what? *Homo sapiens* haven't changed in thousands of years. That's one of the main things I've always admired about you as 'Children of the Grave'; you're nothing if not consistent and predictable. One of the few wise ones among you has this to say about human beings at the start of the twenty-first century. It's actually a confession on behalf of all of you:

> I fear the real problem goes beyond the individual act of killing, judicial or otherwise. In a weird, frightening way, we believe in violent death. We regard it as a policy option. We believe in war. For what is aggression except capital punishment on a mass scale? We 'civilized nations' – like the dark armies we believe we are fighting – are convinced that the infliction of death on an awesome scale can be morally justified. And that's the problem. When we go to war, we are all putting on hoods and pulling the hangman's lever. And as

long as we send our armies on the rampage – whatever the justification – we will go on stringing up and chopping off the heads of our 'criminals' and 'murderers' with the same enthusiasm as the Romans cheered on the men of blood in the Coliseum 2,000 years ago (Robert Fisk, *The Independent*, 15.09.07).

The God Invention

But scapegoating wasn't the end of your ancestors' cultural creativity; it was just the beginning. They soon realized that the victim was the cure for, as well as the cause of, human violence. This is how I became an expert at team-building and developing group cohesion, a major force in cementing group solidarity down the centuries. Is it any surprise that it wasn't long before I had adopted the scapegoat mechanism as the key to my salvation industry?

Jesus once visited a community on the far shore of the Sea of Galilee (Mark: 5). In order to maintain their wellbeing, its citizens needed their scapegoat so much that they chained him down, thus making him a permanent feature of their lives. Indeed, so integral was their mad victim to civic and religious life, that the thought of driving him away filled the community with horror. This is why they felt so threatened when Jesus appeared on the scene, believing him to be part of the Sacred Order of life. If Jesus had used what they thought were his super-powers to exorcise or drive out the demons from their madman, he'd be guilty of disturbing the status quo by stirring things up. This would entail exchanging the tyranny of one kind of violence for another. I agree with them. For, as the saying goes, 'Better the devil you know'.

Exorcisms were part of a world where the use of violence was constantly being used to resolve difficult issues; they formed an important part of the traditional world of religious one-upmanship. But Jesus, as we know, didn't do 'traditional', exorcisms included. John the Baptist had even spoken of the person who would come after him as 'The Stronger One', while the most popular, all-powerful, good angel of the day, was nicknamed 'The Mighty One' - a sort of heavenly equivalent of Mighty Mouse! But Jesus didn't think in those terms. He refused to play by the conventional rules, because he wasn't part of the age-old Sacred Game. God versus Satan.

Your ancestors came to realize that the victim was clearly set apart from everyone else, chosen for a 'higher purpose'. But their reasoning didn't stop there. Surely, they argued, in bringing about such a miracle, the victim must be pretty powerful, since all of life's contradictions were clearly contained and summed up in him or her? I admire their logic.

You see, your ancestors were well on the way to inventing the idea of an all-powerful being called god or goddess, or better still 'God'. It helped make sense of their lives. It gave meaning to events beyond their control to have a super-being to be feared: someone who could be both cruel and kind, the source of punishment as well as the promise of earthly rewards. All of life's events from now on, good or bad, were ultimately their God's responsibility and not theirs. With all the power and violence in history and nature at his or her bidding, keeping their God happy became a major preoccupation. And that's why your ancestors started showering 'God' with copious 'blood gifts'. Since he or she could as easily take life as give life, best offer a few lives in return on a regular basis. After all, it's a feature of patriarchy to suck up to the boss!

And it worked. God was happy. The leaders were happy. Humans were happy. And, rest assured, I was happy. Why? I'm always happy, because the whole Sacred Order is based on a lie. As the Prince of Lies, it suits me fine. The truth however is this: neither the victim nor the invention called 'God', nor even yours truly, is the cause of violence. You are. The victim may be the catalyst but the cause is group dynamics. It is human nature, your way of being in the world. Whether you like it or not, human culture and religion is based on an illusion, though a necessary one; on the pathological need to always avoid issues of responsibility by blaming others, or by allowing others to make decisions for you. Yours is a culture of innocent victims, born to die, and strong leaders, born to rule. Your religion is of 'God versus Satan'. I can live with it, as humans clearly can, but Jesus couldn't.

An Agreement with Death

Jesus was a talented historian as well as an innovative theologian. But I wasn't too disheartened. I was curious to see how Jesus would make sense of a particular piece of teaching in the Isaiah Scroll. I refer to the passage where God says that he will 'stir up' not only Egyptian against Egyptian (Israel's bitterest enemies), but also

> Brother will fight against brother,
> neighbor will fight against neighbor,
> kingdom will fight against kingdom,
> city will fight against city
> (Isaiah 19:2).

I thought that was my job? World history summed up in one verse: neat. But changes were afoot. I told you earlier that a change of consciousness was going on long before John and Jesus appeared on the scene, I just didn't think that it would come to much. But suddenly we read of Egypt crying out in oppression to the very God that had slaughtered her people in their hundreds of thousands. And God was going to send a savior to rescue her. What the hell was going on? The God of Israel was about to make himself known to Egypt, Israel's arch enemy! OK. Maybe I shouldn't have panicked? After all, Jesus' holy books were full of stories of rivalry and violence. But I felt uneasy. The climax of this prophetic oracle or insight spoke of a triple alliance of nations, with God blessing everyone, especially his two worst enemies, instead of cursing them:

> Happy be the Egyptians my people;
> Happy be Assyria my handiwork
> Happy be Israel my inheritance
> (Isaiah 19:25).

Shock! Horror! What on earth was going on? A world with no enemies? Hell forbid. A world with no violence? Not if I had anything to do with it. Jesus went on to discover new truths about one of his nation's greatest heroes, Moses the Lawgiver; Moses, the man who didn't have to talk to his God in dreams and visions, as others did, because he spoke to God face to face. On one occasion, Moses had intervened between an Egyptian and a Hebrew, and killed the former who was mistreating his fellow countryman. Justified violence, I say. But on a second occasion, when two Hebrews were fighting, one of them turned to Moses and asked, 'Who made you prince and judge over us? Are you going to kill me as you killed the Egyptian?' (Exodus 2:14).

Killing, however justified, had no place in Jesus' strategy for the world. He would have nothing to do with violence, no matter in what guise it appeared. Once, Jesus could have become involved in a heated dispute between two of his compatriots. They were quarrelling and arguing about the best way to divide their inheritance. Jesus refused to be drawn into their conflict, quoting instead words from the Moses story: 'My friends, who appointed me the judge or arbiter of your claims?' (Luke 12:14). Jesus wouldn't be drawn into conflicts of any kind between rival parties. He wasn't interested in power games of any sort. But friends, that's what religion is all about – rivalry and competition.

Israel's prophets may have had one eye on heaven but the

other was totally focused on real concrete events in history and the power games that went on within it. The time of Isaiah of Jerusalem (he began prophesying in 742BC) wasn't all that different from yours in that respect. Power was concentrated in the hands of wealthy businessmen, with fortified cities built on their commercial success, and the violence of armies to protect it all. In the beginning, religious people believed that these 'cultural treasures' were not bad in themselves. I couldn't agree more. They are tangible signs of human success. You're meant to take pride in them. It only became a spiritual problem when human achievements became a source of, and an excuse for, human pride and self-glorification.

The prophets never ignored the reality of worldly power, based as it is on military might and political alliances. This is why it was imperative that God's people relied solely on his will and not on the plans and weapons of the super-powers of the day: plans that were executed by violence and force. Jesus knew his history and was well versed in its dynamics. His reflection on it was to prove decisive in his mission and the 'good news' that he had for the world. Here is a summary of the key historical event that was to play such a critical role, seven centuries later, in forming Jesus' alternative view of history:

Isaiah's king Ahaz had surprised me and everyone by making an 'agreement of death' with Assyria, the world super-power of its day: an agreement that placed his people's wellbeing and security in the hands of a foreign nation. This was a wise move, in my opinion. Ahaz was being realistic, but for Isaiah this was national security based on a lie. By becoming a vassal, and therefore a servant and 'son' of the Assyrian Emperor, Ahaz had jeopardized his status as God's son and servant. He couldn't be both. Ahaz's son was to continue this policy, believing that the status of a vassal was better than no status at all. Wise chap. Sensible politician. His people became increasingly frustrated with such a humiliating stance. It's alright for them; they don't have to make difficult decisions.

As a visionary prophet, Isaiah's concern was ultimately with his nation's spiritual health and integrity. There could be no genuine security or salvation in military power, especially a pagan one. If history had taught God's people anything at all, it was the need to reject, and thus have nothing to do with, the politics or religion of other nations. As if human destiny, especially Israel's, was in the hands of pagan power-systems. 'No,' declared Isaiah, 'the hands of the nations are full of blood,' (Isaiah 1:15) and their violence breeds nothing but agony, despair and death. But that's the human condition. What more can you expect? For Isaiah, the only true policy was the one that achieved a 'right relationship' with God.

Do you want to know something? I'm getting sick of all this talk of establishing 'right relationships' with God. It's so boring to hear prophets going on and on about the fact that it's 'God's way of doing things that counts and not military strength'. Don't get me wrong; I wouldn't dream of silencing them. I leave that to religious leaders. Let them have their say, is my policy. That's the joy of living in a democracy. We can all get stuck into the art of politics; though, for the prophets, politics wasn't the solution to the human condition but part of the problem. As a gifted and highly experienced global politician, I cannot but disagree. I love problems. Who'd want to solve them? 'Stick to religion,' is my message to those interfering prophets, and let us politicians get on with our area of expertise. Politics and violence belong together. That's the way it is. I feel like shouting it from the rooftops. There's nothing arrogant, as the prophets believe, in putting the 'power of the sword' above God's will. It's plain commonsense. It's the way humans do things. It's life. Where would you be without the sword? In a state of anarchy, that's for certain.

Might Is Right

An event took place in 539BC that played into my hands, as all world events tend to do in the end. It led Israel to question not only its opinion of the Gentile nations but also its opinion of military power, of brute force and terror. It was the year that the Persian king Cyrus defeated the Babylonians, the super-power of the day. Although he was a brutal military ruler, he was also one of the most enlightened rulers in history. Violent and enlightened, what a combination… I love it! Cyrus was a good politician and knew how to get the best out of the people he conquered. He was a follower of the god Marduk, who was lord of the gods. It was he who had ordained Cyrus to rule the world. As emperor, Cyrus saw himself as patron of the gods of the people whom he had conquered. He had no problem with Israel's religion or God, any more than I do. After all, why should he? He'd conquered both. Cyrus allowed them to return from exile to Jerusalem and eventually gave them royal permission to rebuild their own religious sanctuary, the temple. He may have been cruel but he was also considerate and politically astute. This became a real dilemma for the prophets. Maybe 'Might was Right' after all? Maybe all violence wasn't bad? Maybe all the Gentile nations weren't evil? Maybe power-politics does have a part to play in God's scheme of things, after all? At last, the prophets were beginning to think like real politicians. I was delighted.

It was Isaiah II who came to see Cyrus as his god's Shepherd and Chosen One. Just imagine, a pagan ruler was given one of the most exclusive of all Jewish titles: 'Messiah', the Anointed One. Hell's bells! It was this Isaiah who blew Jesus' mind with his earlier teaching about a happy and positive approach to the Endtime. He now blew his mind in another way. In addition to Israel's kings and high priests, a ruthless pagan warmonger and conqueror could now become God's special agent or ambassador. Be friends. This is the kind of theology that I can take on board. I can imagine the anguish it caused Jesus, averse to violence of any kind. Tough! It gave me a hell of a buzz. After all, this teaching was at the heart of his sacred scriptures. The Messiah was an integral part of the monarchic quest for power and dominance. How dare Jesus disagree with Isaiah? It's truly mind-boggling! A cruel world ruler could be called, consecrated and commissioned by God to fulfill a special mission. Considering that I once worked for him, I'm seriously thinking of asking God for my old job back.

'I bring prosperity and I create disorder' (Isaiah 45:7), is one of my favorite verses from the prophet Isaiah. And don't go on about Satan being able to quote scripture, as though I'm the only evil entity that can do so. Humans are a violent and cruel species, including the Christian variety. I know that many Christians look down their noses at me and treat me with disdain. Thousands of 'Christians' over the centuries know their scriptures also, using Biblical verses galore to commit the most laudable of atrocities in God's name. In God's Name – note – not mine. 'The devil made me do it!' Bollocks! I didn't. *You* did. You still do, Christian hypocrites!

I never thought I'd hear myself say this, but in this respect I'm in total agreement with the prophets. You are responsible for your own actions. I only make suggestions. I may occasionally write the script, but it takes humans to act it out. Stop passing the buck. Grow up, Christians, and be proud, as you continue to savor the satanic 'shock and awe' of your evil actions in the world.

The Isaiah Scroll goes on to describe a heavenly trial, when the pagan nations are called together and asked to explain Cyrus' meteoric rise to world fame. Would their gods have been able to predict the changes brought about by Cyrus' military victories? This was an Israelite kick in the teeth to the pagan god Marduk, who had actually given them their freedom. How ungrateful, especially when you consider that their own god had failed them. We are back to our favorite word: interpretation. According to Isaiah II, it wasn't Marduk who was responsible for freeing Israel after all but, by a cunning sleight of hand, their own god. Talk about jumping on the pagan bandwagon. Cyrus, an agent of Israel's god? I disagree. Cyrus was a double-agent, working for both sides!

Israel's religious and cultural elite lost little or no sleep over the fact that God had used military might to achieve his goals, just as today in Westminster, on Capitol Hill, in Tehran or Jerusalem; you won't find leaders losing much sleep as they struggle with their consciences. Centuries before Cyrus, King David had been told that he would never get to build God's temple because he was a warrior and had shed blood. Before the pacifists among you get carried away, the Israelite historian wasn't condemning David as God's elite warrior and holy terrorist; his victories over his enemies were in fact proof that he was doing God's work. Warmongering was also David's calling. Ultimately, it was God's war, a holy war, with David in charge. Military victory was Israel's security, so that rival men of violence would never get the upper hand and try to destroy her any more. Why shouldn't a nation defend its territory? I always defend mine.

Wars are a necessary evil when fighting God's cause. As I've already told you, I also bring prosperity and create disorder. D'you know what? I'm beginning to think that God and I may be fighting on the same side after all! You see, it wasn't the reality of war that made David unworthy to build his god's temple but the fact that he'd acted violently and immorally in his personal affairs. As an admirer of double standards, I'm not complaining. After all, what is good? All that makes for and heightens the feeling of power. What is bad? All that comes from weakness and thus fails to serve power.

As a wonderful example of the role of violence in sacred history, the story of Cyrus is right up my street. I felt a new sense of empowerment. Things were going well, until a few ancient songs, written by an anonymous person, were inserted into the Isaiah Scroll amongst the stories of Cyrus. Shit! A few bloody poems, amounting to just under three dozen verses. I curse the editor who inserted them into Isaiah's prophecy. Plenty of curses on him and his followers – it was he who sowed the seeds that produced Jesus' alternative view of history and salvation. Yes, eternal curses be upon him!

The Suffering Servant

In the Four Songs (the full text follows), a mysterious suffering servant appears in the Heavenly Court to watch the trial of the nations. He appears to be connected to that alternative reality that Elijah and Jeremiah had talked about. As an alternative 'special agent', he was empowered to help set up a new kind of order with the pagan nations, but in a totally different way to Cyrus and his mighty military machine. His appearance had serious implications, not just for Israel and the nations but also for Jesus, as he continued to make sense of the contradictions in his Bible. It was a real dilemma for Jesus. Isaiah II is happy to speak of God as a holy warrior, with violence an integral part of his future plans for his people and the wider world. After all, God had behaved like this in the past, with his epoch-making battle against the evil Egyptians.

We see the author of the Four Songs struggling, as Jesus undoubtedly did, with the reality of the enormous task of establishing justice in the world. He doesn't champion the use of violence but its very opposite. There is to be no worldly confrontation in terms of battles and wars; no aggression is to be used, be it individually or collectively. Rather, a courageous and compassionate campaign of non-violence is prescribed: a campaign more than willing and able to face and absorb human insults, rejection, humiliation and pain.

The climax of the Four Songs appears in the fourth and final song, when the mission of the Just One, though not a monarch himself, is finally understood by the pagan kings. He is more than ready to undergo humiliation, not only for Israel's sake but also for their sake, thus bringing universal peace and wellbeing to them and their people. It's this kind of humility, the song suggests, that will ultimately grab the attention of the pagan rulers, and not the actions of a Cyrus. In fact, kings will bow in reverence before the different kind of sovereignty of this alternative 'special agent'.

It's clear to me that a strategy to rival mine emerges in the Four Songs: one to help establish justice on earth. This strategy celebrates victory through suffering, with compassionate work carried out so 'quietly and gently' that the great monarchs of the earth will be astounded by it. Astounded by its naivety, more likely! But I needn't have worried, this alternative strategy obviously made little impact on Israel since, as expected, she continued to produce morally and spiritually corrupt leaders. And as for the nations? The idea of one Just Person bringing justice to all was a foolish notion from the start. Laughable! Bloody laughable!

The Song of the Suffering Servant
'Here is my servant whom I love:
I will put my spirit on him
and he will bring justice to the nations.
He will not act aggressively
or draw attention to himself.
His purpose is to bring justice to all nations,
and he will not give up
until that vision is realized throughout the world'.

Listen to me you nations of the earth.
God chose me before I was born
to be his instrument for justice,

and to speak on behalf of his divine law.
But I became disillusioned,
convinced that I had wasted my time.
Yet my destiny is in God's hands,
and my reward is with him.

And now God wants me to bring Israel back to him.
He believes that I can draw from his strength
to accomplish this most difficult of missions.
But this mission is 'a mission impossible',
and far more challenging than I had first anticipated.
He wants me now to be a beacon of hope for the Gentiles as well,
and thus spread God's salvation to the four corners of the world.

This is what the Liberator and Holy One of Israel has to say
to me who is now despised and hated by the nations:
'Kings will see you and stand to attention before you,
princes will see you and bow down before you.
Remember, you are my chosen one.
Trust in me and I will not let you down'.

My Sovereign Lord has given me wisdom and skill
to bring comfort to the oppressed.
I did not retaliate against those who wanted to beat me up,
neither did I hide my face from those who wanted to spit on me.
Because of the Lord's support
I know that I will not be humiliated.
No insult will ever wound me.
Because the Sovereign Lord is on my side,
those who dare to bring charges against me
are wasting their time.

I challenge anyone to prove me guilty!

Does anyone among you fear the Lord?
Will any of you obey his servant?
Will you trust in God and rely on him?

You who play with fire
and arm yourselves with flaming torches.
Go! Walk in the light of your own fires.
This is your fate at my hands;
You will lie down in torment.

'My servant will accomplish his mission
and will be rewarded
with the highest position I have to offer.
And yet, people will be so horrified by his ugly appearance
that no one will be able to even look at him.
A diseased man.
A suffering man.
A man despised by the people'.

And yet it was our plight as human beings
that he took upon himself.
We thought that it was God who tortured him,
but he was in fact wounded because of our sins.
He bore the punishment that made us whole,
and by the bruises of his torture we are healed.
We behaved like lost sheep,
every one of us going his or her own way.
Yet God chose him
to be responsible for handling human guilt.

Though he was abused he remained silent.
Like a sheep being led to slaughter

he never uttered a word.
Because of his people's sins,
he was alienated from his kinfolk,
who deserved to be punished for their behavior.
He was buried among the wicked,
though he had done nothing wrong,
and had acted always with integrity.
But for a reason beyond human understanding,
the Sovereign Lord decided to crush him by disease,
so that he could make himself a guilt offering,
and thus be the instrument that helps God's justice to prosper.

Because of all the pain that he endured,
he will be bathed in light.
Following his utter humiliation,
he will be fully vindicated.
Because of his knowledge and experience
my Servant will help vindicate others,
since it is his destiny to carry and deal with their guilt.
Therefore I will reward him
with pride of place among the greats,
and the 'Mighty of the Earth' will be his reward.

He willingly exposed himself to death
and to the stigma of being a sinner.
He bore the guilt of many
and interceded on behalf of sinners.
(Isaiah 42:1-4, Isaiah 49:1-7, Isaiah50:4-11,Isaiah 52:13-53:12)

The Way of Violence

Humans will always need violence to realize their projects: violence in all its different guises. That's why you'll always need a god who corresponds to your evil desires, a mirror-image of your prayers and petitions. You'd be lost without him. Jesus separated himself from the 'strength' of his people, their aggression and power, their will to live at any cost. Jesus knew that there was no limit to what people will do to hang onto their self-belief, and was fully aware of the fact that even the vulnerable are capable of great cruelty. Jesus separated himself from a salvation industry that thrived on guilt and lived on sins. I thrive on guilt and live on sins.

Now that's one bit of purity, dear friends, that I *can* abide – pure and unadulterated sin. Jesus separated himself from the power-systems: politics, nationalism, religion, the military, commerce. All had become idols, false gods. He demolished them one by one.

Jesus opposes everyone who, through pride and vanity, seeks to hang onto their power and thus usurp the new kind of sovereignty that was coming into the world. This includes the power that women have fought so long to achieve. How insensitive of him. In 2007 I saw a film by Neil Jordan called 'The Brave One', in which the actress Jodie Foster played a tough, recently bereaved woman, who buys a gun with the specific intention of turning her anger on the lowlife scum of New York. It's a wonderful story of revenge and its ability to bring satisfaction to the injured party, when the law is impotent to right a wrong. What makes the film extra special is the fact that it highlights the reality of feminine suppression and the unavoidable fact that sooner or later society is going to have to deal with a new explosion of women's anger. Women have a human right to express themselves in this way. The heroine reaches the moment in her life where she refuses to live within a climate of male fear, and decides to face macho male intimidation head-on. Something I wish Jesus had done against the religiously motivated cruelty of the High Priest and his lot. 'The Brave One' is a modern parable. A celebration of the fact that nice, respectable women can be transformed, when the need arises, into dark demonic angels of 'women's liberation'. Long may films of this kind continue to be made. Long may society honor the magic of transforming violence.

My Gospel is alive and kicking, not just individually and socially, but also globally. For all the criticisms I've received over the centuries, I've never doubted that violence is an instrument of perfection, a force for good. I've never doubted that society can be transformed by the right use of violence. Many of you living today believe, as the sectarians did in the time of Jesus, that a universal society is on the horizon, the preordained new international order. It's unavoidable that thousands upon thousands will be sacrificed to achieve this. It is the way of the world, after all.

I delight that violence is needed to promote and protect the progress of Western democracy. Keep faith in it. Your leaders know that violence purifies. Keep faith in them. You in the West know what is morally right, take pride in that. You in the West have special authority to carry these painful changes through. You in the West are part of a sacred plan, which is unfolding. Keep to the path and you'll reach your goal. You in the West are the true servants of history. God Bless you.

My Three Gifts to You

The gift of freedom is your right as *Homo sapiens*. I would never deny you that right, especially since freedom involves the freedom of evil as well. My gospel celebrates the truth that without the freedom of evil, good would not be free. When good cannot be free, it has to be imposed by violence. But you know well enough, dear friends, that when that happens, good isn't good anymore – it's evil.

It's satisfying to see vengeance regularly unleashed against an evil people. Better still when it is unleashed against the innocent, in the name of the greater good. Better still when the gift of vengeance is unleashed in the name of God.

There will always be leaders, or masters, to punish any deviation by slaves, or 'the faithful' as they are called in ecclesiastical circles: slaves too weak to rebel; slaves too nice and obedient to take revenge; slaves too timid to stand-up for themselves. These are people who grow to maturity feeling guilty for harboring nasty feelings towards their betters, whom they actually resent. So guilty, in fact, that, as the violence builds up deep inside them, they end up turning their violence against themselves, with serious implications for their emotional and spiritual wellbeing. But cowards deserve such punishment; resentment is the price for not being true to yourselves. I think that God would agree with me. After all, why shouldn't others have a break, now and then, from being at the receiving end of your emotional frustration and violence? It's only right that you experience your own 'crap' now and then!

Three gifts I leave with you, wise men and women. And, to each individual, I would add that the fourth gift you give yourself – the gift of choice.

Chapter Three

At Every End There's a New Beginning

'Goddamn it, Rick!' she exploded, 'Why don't you just tell me?'

He went to the table and sat down, as though suddenly too tired to continue the battle. 'Because I know you're going to find it painful, hearing the facts. Especially because of who you are. What you do for a living.'

'What does my job have to do with it?'

'You work with law enforcement. You help bring killers to justice.'

'I don't bring anyone to justice. I just provide the facts.'

'Sometimes the facts aren't what you cops want to hear.'

'But you work on our side.'

'No. The victim's side.'

'All right, the victim's side. That's why you're not going to like what I tell you about her.'

'Who were the victims?'

'It's not an easy thing to tell you. Or an easy thing for you to hear.'

'So far you've told me my mother is a murderer. I think I'm taking it pretty well. So tell me who the victims were and don't leave a goddamn thing out. It's the one thing I can't deal with Rick, when people hide the truth from me'

'Okay'. He leaned forward, looking her in the eye. 'You want the details, then I'll be brutally honest about it. Because the details are brutal.'

Tess Gerritsen, *Body Double.* pp 209/211

Wooden Heart

Following his baptism and temptation in the desert, Jesus returned to The Galilee to carry on with his own version of cousin John's 'change of heart' movement: preaching, teaching, driving out demons, or 'exorcising' as it is called. This is the stage that I call 'Great Expectations'. But he was largely a failure and the hatred of his opponents grew and grew: hatred towards Jesus and 'hardness of heart' towards *abba,* which hurt Jesus even more. 'Hardness of heart'! People with 'wooden hearts'? Yes. A good biblical phrase that, and a specialty of religious people: inability to change; inability to see the truth, especially the truth about Jesus.

Abba had anticipated that this would happen. This is why Jesus talked about the coming of a mysterious figure called the Parakletos, at the end of his life. This was another member of the Heavenly Council, my opposite number in fact. He is the lawyer or counsel for the defense: the advocate who defends the innocent, standing shoulder to shoulder with those who get wrongly accused. Defending against whom? Yours truly! Who else? I was flattered. To think that *abba* had planned all along to roll the big guns against me. I hadn't appreciated how effective I had become until I realized how easy it is to deceive those who supposedly 'look after the truth'. The human inability to see the truth about Jesus was to become so inbred that *abba* deemed it necessary to acquire the services of a heavenly supremo, even before Jesus had died! One who doubles up as the Spirit of Truth. It is Parakletos, to give him (or is it her?) the Greek name, who empowers individuals to put into practice the principles taught by Jesus. Needless to say, Parakletos would have his work cut out! Then, as now, most people had no interest in what Jesus had to say.

I sowed the seeds of doubt in Jesus. The call for a 'change of heart' didn't work. The call for people to stop sinning and turn to *abba* instead proved ineffective. Israel had no intention of responding to him. I knew she wouldn't. Like every nation under the sun, she was too absorbed in herself. Jeremiah's words describe well the decadence of all nations:

These people have stubborn and rebellious hearts;
Like cages full of birds,
their houses are full of deceit;
they have become rich and powerful
and have grown fat and sleek.
Their evil actions have no limit;
they never defend the rights of the poor.
The prophets prophesy lies,
and the priests rule by their own authority.
Both practice deceit.
'Peace, peace', they say,
when there is no peace.

Both leaders and ordinary people
are greedy for gain.
(from Jeremiah 5 and 6).

Jesus underestimated the challenge ahead of him. It's one thing to try and change a few individual lives, that's ultimately a private matter, but to change a whole nation? Such an exciting and promising start soon became Mission Impossible, and all because of *abba*. But Jesus had a vision to fulfill on behalf of his people. A vision that he hoped would extend to the whole of humanity. He would never betray that vision, no matter what the cost. It cost him dearly.

Abba

For the majority, Jesus was an enigma during his lifetime and will remain so to the end of time. 'We have no terms today which can express what he means for us,' says Albert Schweitzer in 1906, on the final page of *The Quest of the Historical Jesus.* I disagree. It's the mysterious reality that governed his life that I find to be enigmatic. The alternative reality that many of the prophets had hinted at, and which Jesus ended up calling '*abba*'

– not the Swedish supergroup but a mysterious presence in his life that can only be translated as 'Daddy'. I'm not having you on. Jesus gave up everything that the world, his religion and I have to offer, because of this *abba* and the intimate relationship that developed between them. There is no better example of Jesus' topsy-turvy world than his suddenly coming up with the name *abba* to refer to his god… though it isn't really a name. Mind you, *abba* isn't really a god either. I had to use all my investigative skills to find out what on earth was going on.

Jesus came from a religious tradition that was quite clear about how one referred to the ultimate in life. I almost said, the 'ultimate things in life'. But however you define 'God', he, she or it isn't a 'thing' at all. For Jews the reality they called 'God' was ultimately a mystery. A reality so beyond human comprehension that reason, and the words that you use, can never have the last word on the matter; a reality so radically different from your everyday world that it can never be confused with it. Unlike the traditional God, this is why *abba* would have nothing to do with the infernal trinity of 'the world, the flesh and the devil'.

Words, and names in particular, define limits. They set boundaries. You know where you stand with them. Take my name, for example. It comes from the word 'shaitan', which means 'to be hostile'. I perfected that skill while working as prosecutor in God's Heavenly Court. How else was I supposed to deal with hostile witnesses, but to be hostile with them in return? It's a trait that I've really grown to like in humans. A name allows you to capture and control things, and, of course, to comprehend or understand how something works. Once you know what make things tick, you put them into boxes, as it were, and label them. Like you, I too have grown to like labels, especially religious ones. I love the label 'God', and the fact that religious devotees get very protective of their own particular name for 'God', their own sacred brand name. This is nothing to worry about. It's natural. You're in good company. Moses was one of the first to try and force his God to reveal his name, and got told off in the process. His God refused to be tied down and so refused to give Moses his name. He gave him a promise instead. 'Tell your people,' said God, 'that I-will-be-there-for-you-as-I-decide-how-I-will-be-there-for-you' (Exodus 3; 14). Talk about being put in your place!

Jesus also knew that once you label your favorite things, you soon end up making idols of them. In other words, you worship them instead of *abba*. Why not, I say, if they are the most important things in your life? I see nothing wrong in liking your car or loving your new home. There's nothing wrong in adoring or worshipping another human being, be it your lover, or a parent or a child. It's part of being human. It's only natural to love your country or your church. It's perfectly normal to give your heart to the 'isms' of life, as I call them – nationalism, socialism, liberalism, capitalism; the list is endless. But *abba* will have none of it. Jesus also refuses to be tied down by labels of any kind, even religious ones, though millions continue to treat him as an idol, a religious mascot, to this day.

On one occasion, the prophet Elijah went out looking for 'God' armed with his own religious and theological expectations. He hoped to see God in a particular way. Standing on top of a mountain, Elijah saw a great and powerful wind tearing the mountain apart. Rocks were shattered, but God wasn't in the wind. Then there was a massive earthquake, but God wasn't there. Then came a fire but there was still no sign of his God. Elijah retreated to a cave. Then came 'a gentle whisper' or 'a still small voice', depending on your translation (1 Kings 19:12). Elijah had a momentary taste, a hint of that reality which lies beyond all human projections. Few took up the hint, preferring instead to keep backing the God who has an army of celestial forces on his side; the God whose natural show of raw and savage power can easily bully mere mortals into submission. Are you surprised? Come on, who in their right mind would want to serve a god who is nothing more than a 'gentle whisper'? Get real! Still small voices don't rule the world. I do.

By the time of Jesus, religious devotees had to come to terms with the fact that since they could never know God's name, they could only refer to him as 'the Name'. This is why in the psalms you hear a great deal of worshippers praising God's 'glorious name', whatever it may be. You see, the Israelites believed that the Ultimate could appear in many different ways under many different names, so it would be foolish to think that one name would be sufficient. Confusing? Not half, because you eventually end up with a God who can be all things to all people: a bully for bullies; a super-thug for thugs; a great lover for lovers; a thinker for philosophers; a true friend for the friendless. This is why 'God' ends up representing all human projections, be they pathological and romantic, or brutal and sentimental. 'God' is the sum of your humanity – another human object for you to own, albeit an exalted one. But some of Jesus' spiritual ancestors knew that there was something beyond 'God' and the religious yearnings that had spawned him. King Solomon himself, after all the hard work of building the first temple in honor of his God, must also have had a hint of it when he proclaimed,

But does God really dwell on earth with men? Even the highest heavens cannot contain You. How much less this temple that I have built! (2 Chronicles 6:18).

When Jesus came along, he administered the final blow that dismantled the whole religious edifice that was his native religion. He did so by mocking its sacred language, including the name of God! Just listen to the Lord's Prayer of Jesus' day, the prayer that Jesus grew up hearing and would have learnt by heart. It's the prayer of King David, and it's truly majestic...

Praise be to you, O Lord,
God of Our Father, Israel,
for ever and ever.

> Yours, O Lord, is the Greatness and the Power
> and the Glory and the Majesty and the Splendor.
> Wealth and Honor come from You.
> Everything in Heaven and Earth is Yours.
> Yours, O Lord, is the Kingdom.
> You are the Ruler of all things.
> You are Exalted as Head over all.
> In Your Hands are Strength and Power
> to Exalt and give Strength to all.
> Now, Our God, we give You Thanks
> and Praise Your Glorious Name
> (1 Chronicles 29:10-13).

D'you know what? I just love all this talk of greatness and power and strength and majesty, not to mention the wealth and honor bit. It makes me quite dizzy just to think of it. I was at my religious best when I offered all those things to Jesus during his desert trial. He refused them all.

> The devil took Jesus to a very high mountain and showed him all the kingdoms of the world in all their beauty and glory. 'All this I will give you', he said, 'if you will worship me'. Jesus said to him, 'Away from me, Satan! For it is written, Worship the Lord your God, and serve him only' (Matthew 4: 8-10).

One sound was to bring the whole sacred order tumbling down and Jesus did it all on his own. He didn't need the help of a Joshua and his band of trumpets! Is it any wonder that religious people hated Jesus and wanted to get rid of him? Jesus came up with a name that anyone and everyone could use – any time, any place. Dangerous stuff, when you consider that only the High Priest could utter God's name and only ten times a year. 'Praise your glorious name?' Take the mickey, more likely! Jesus' alternative wasn't a name but a sound, and a very basic and infantile one at that: 'Daddy', 'Mummy'. His god's name, or non-name, was an infant's first attempt at speech. Meaningless, incoherent babbling!

Jesus knew that all religious words are limiting and end up becoming the most dangerous idols of all, the idols of the mind that people play power-games with. Playing with the names of God is a favorite game among religious rivals of all persuasions; names that eventually congeal, solidify and become a hindrance to spiritual growth. If Jesus had come up with just another God name, he would have reduced *abba* to the things of the world, another religious object. But *abba* frees human beings from the world and all its violence. He liberates people from all cultural and religious categories. That's why no preliminaries of any sort are required if one is to have faith or trust in *abba*. This is why sinners have a head-start on everyone else. Jesus said to them, 'I tell you the truth, the tax-collectors and whores are entering *abba*'s sovereignty ahead of you' (Matthew 21:31).

No sacred paths have to be walked in order to approach *abba*. No one has an advantage over others, especially in terms of sacred power in the form of prestige and knowledge. Everyone is treated the same. That's why everything in human history comes under scrutiny or 'judgment' when *abba* is about. Jesus would have you approach *abba* just as you are, with all your selfishness and pride laid bare. It's a painful experience that I would never insist upon.

Jesus was adamant. No one can sum up or name the divine for another. That's why *abba* can never be made into an idol. He can never be set in stone. Bad news for those of us who benefit from the idolatry industry! *Abba* is not a religious or transcendent specialty, a 'moment' that can be romanticized into an experience, least of all a spiritual or mystical one.

Abba is a secret known only to each individual: the invisible presence that forever hides from human attempts to control it.

Abba is always incognito. That's why *abba* never really caught on among religious devotees. They need a faith that has clear and visible certainties, the illusions at which I am an expert. People can't cope with all this airy-fairy stuff that Jesus keeps on going on about. People want a 'God' that is All-Mighty and All-Powerful, a God that one can be proud of, a God that can be assigned to the highest place in your world – the sacred world to which you have ready access, once you know the rules of the game.

And why do humans have ready access to this sacred world? Because they invented it. God and his sacred realm are purely a projection of the human will-to-power. I too may be just a projection, but if I am it's a bloody powerful one! Jesus came to expose this world, the sacred world served by the menace of idolatry and the arrogance of religion. God's world. My world.

Abba is all about 'divine' sovereignty: the sovereignty of 'love'. How I hate *abba* and all that it stands for. Fool that he was, Jesus really believed that people could grow up and leave the realm of the sacred behind. He really believed that in and through *abba*'s sovereignty, people could discover the divine for themselves, the love that transcends all understanding. They could discover true and divine love which needs no proof, the love that is 'certain and clear as daylight'. It was Jesus' ambition to change people's consciousness, and by so doing help create a new humanity, a mature and loving humanity. For Jesus, the more one is, the more one loves. The more one loves, the more one is.

Abba is the primordial sigh or yearning of that new creation. *Abba* is the sound of individuals starting from scratch as human beings, and discovering for themselves that the truth is love. *Abba* is not the final word but the first word for each individual who has the courage to discover and interpret for him or herself what the divine means in his or her life. *Abba* is the start of the quest, the journey into true love. What sentimental twaddle!

When Jesus appeared on the scene, I was ready. The battle lines were drawn for one hell of a cosmic struggle. There was I getting all excited about the ultimate apocalyptic showdown, with dark banners unfurled and demonic guns loaded for action on every street corner. But when I found out who was calling the shots, it didn't do much for my ego. In fact, it pissed me off to discover that my adversary was an entity who went by the name of Daddy! It was to be 'Apocalypse Now' but against 'Big Daddy'.

Why did Jesus have to spoil things with his talk of *abba*? God and I had been getting on fine for centuries. After all, we're part of the same system. I'd never had any trouble in the past with people and their God talk, forever dividing the world into believers and unbelievers, saints and sinners, the pure and impure. You know where you stand in that kind of world, the world that Jesus was born into. What had possessed him? I certainly hadn't.

But with his talk of *abba*, Jesus moved the moral and religious boundaries. He treated everyone the same, sinners included. It just didn't make sense. I honestly thought at first that someone was playing some kind of cosmic joke, until I realized that Jesus was deadly serious about *abba*. Like his contemporaries, Jesus knew that life is a battlefield dominated by supernatural forces – Good and Evil: cosmic twins that belong together, forever battling it out on the world stage. He should have left it at that. Why complicate matters? The choice was a simple one. In every age, it's up to each human being to choose which side he or she supports – God or Satan? No one is free to opt out. But Jesus did. He chose neither, and opted for *abba*. Now I knew that Jesus was more than mad. I agree with his family, he was a raving lunatic!

With *abba*'s gift of understanding, Jesus brings two very different, but ultimately complementary, ways of looking at the world together. *Abba* gives human beings the ability to recognize the world for what it really is. It's the kind of understanding that helps make sense of a world dominated by the violent and evil dynamics of power-systems, of a world of idolatry, where pride of place is given to anything and everything other than love. Secondly, *abba* encourages individuals to be responsible and make the decisions that can change all this. *Abba* empowers the kind of human behavior that will actually make the world what it can be: a world where everyone and everything is at-one; a world of perfect harmony. 'In your dreams, heretic!'

Loving intimacy with *abba* was a painful realization for Jesus – bloody painful. Since *abba* meant everything to him, everything else that mattered in life paled into insignificance. By letting go of everything for *abba*'s sake, Jesus distanced and ultimately separated himself from all the worldly things that he had held dear and all the 'heavenly' things as well. Since they had come to mean absolutely nothing to him, Jesus ended up separating himself from a nation and its entire history. His nation. His history. His religion.

It was a lonely path that Jesus eventually pursued. Religious people didn't like him neither did my followers and I, no matter how much we might have admired his free spirit.

The Satanic Principle

I hate to admit that, like jewels in a coal mine, a genuine core remains at the heart of all scriptures, even when hidden or overlaid by all the cruel bits that I like. Jesus didn't reject the core of his native religion. In fact, he took it too seriously, especially the prohibition against making idols and 'bowing down before them'. There was to be no compromise with anything or anyone. Love of *abba* came first and Jesus loved him with absolutely every ounce of his being, from his intellect to his physical energy and strength.

One of his contemporaries, an expert in the law, tested Jesus with this question: 'Teacher, which is the greatest commandment in the law?' Jesus replied: 'Love the Lord your God with all your heart, with all your soul, with all your mind and with all your strength. This is the first and greatest commandment. And the second is like it: Love your neighbor as yourself. All the Law and the Prophets are summed-up in these two commandments' (Matthew 22:34-40).

But it's a bit extreme to think of these words as being literally true in the real world. Don't you agree? *Abba* can't be the be-all-and-end-all of life. Others must be taken into consideration. And anyway, to get on in the world, you have to do a bit of 'bowing' to others, sometimes quite a lot of it, especially if you want to get on and become a leader. Jesus refused to bow down before anyone. No one could rival *abba*. I can see the logic behind his beliefs. The Endtime was underway. *Abba*'s sovereignty was absolute. So anything to do with temporal history was suddenly of limited value. Actually, it was of no importance at all. Your history and my history were, supposedly, coming to an end. This is why social and political revolution, and even institutional reform, were all meaningless to Jesus, a total waste of time. A new way of ordering human history was on the horizon.

The power-systems that had driven human history from the very beginning would soon be redundant and I'd be out of a job. Power-systems operate by specific rules. Jesus refused to play by those rules. He discovered the secret of what had gone wrong with creation and found the key to its renewal. While the prophets that preceded him believed that some aspects of human life were corrupt, Jesus took things a step further, by pointing out that the whole of creation had by now become corrupt and was under my sway. It's no wonder that he called me Prince of the World. Because he had grasped the logic of my way of operating, his mission, though focused primarily on his own people, would eventually lead him to the root of the problem – *Homo sapiens*. Jesus saw the whole of human history unfold before his eyes: past, present and future. He discovered the truth covered up by religious and moral leaders for centuries, the truth that your leaders cannot face – the dynamics underlying all human culture, including your precious religions. I refer to The Satanic Principle, which is rooted in human rivalry and the conflict and violence that emerges from it. Jesus was free of the power-systems because he was free of all rivalry. Jesus was free of all rivalry because he desired to do one thing, and one thing only with his life, namely to serve *abba* and not me. It was as simple and as profound as that.

Jesus believed passionately that the cycle of violence that lay at the heart of human history could be broken, once and for all. This is why the spotlight had eventually fallen on me. By putting *abba*'s way first, Jesus was convinced that humans could triumph over evil. The source of human evil is no longer a mystery but is fully within your grasp as humans. I, Satan, can be named, shamed and defeated. My reaction? I just loved all the attention. This is when I get to take center stage. I've remained there, more or less, ever since.

I unveil the mystery of all mysteries

I take pride in the fact
that I have no power of my own

I am a parasite
Feeding on your desires

I never go hungry

But if the spotlight was now on me, it would soon be falling on Jesus' generation: real people in a real place with a real history; real people with real hopes and desires; real people for Jesus and me to fight over. And because he wasn't prepared to enter into negotiations with me, Jesus would have to follow the logic of his love for *abba* to its painful conclusion. This involved not some abstract acknowledgement of a corrupt world, but the personal realization that every individual has the seeds of Satan in them. The uncomfortable truth that anyone and everyone can, in fact, become Satan. When Peter, one of Jesus' closest friends and supporters, tried to put him off the final confrontation in Jerusalem, Jesus told him:

> Out of my sight Satan! You're not interested in abba's way of putting things right, but in the human way of doing things. (Matthew 16:23).

Be warned! No one, however devout, is outside my sphere of influence. That shouldn't surprise you; after all, I am Prince of the World. Another key passage, this time in the fourth Gospel, also goes to the heart of the matter: Jesus addresses the religious leaders with these telling words:

> Why don't you understand what I am saying? It is because your father is the Devil. It is his will that you wish to do. He was a murderer from the beginning. He has nothing to do with the truth because he is a liar, and the father of lies (John 8:44).

But Jesus doesn't stop with individuals or religious leaders. He isn't just addressing his own nation but scans the whole of human history, from the first violent act, Cain's murder of his brother Abel, an innocent who had done no evil, to the murder of the last prophet of his day. Whether Jesus said the following words or not, the sentiments expressed are his – namely 'the world hates me because I testify that what it does is evil' (John 7:7). Jesus believed with his whole heart, that if it took up his challenge, his generation could initiate a new era in human history. The eternal cycle of rivalry and violence could come to an end if everyone opted for *abba*'s way of doing things. Choose now between *abba*'s new 'peace agreement' or Satan's 'old order'. And here was the crunch. 'Accept your responsibility for rivalry and violence. Acknowledge your guilt in encouraging the spread of, and participation in, that "dark residue of evil". End your murderous history now.' I was gobsmacked. Jesus really believed that one human generation, his own, could make a new start, and present themselves as pure before *abba*. Otherwise...?

> ...This generation will be held responsible for it all. All the righteous blood shed on earth will be your responsibility (Matthew 23:36).

Ouch! Cain had denied responsibility for Abel's murder, and his archetypal reply rings down the millennia, *'Am I my brother's keeper?'* (Genesis 4:9). With the reality of warring brothers staring him in the face, Jesus' reply was an unequivocal '*Yes*'.

> You are all brothers
> You are all your brother's keeper.
> You are all my brothers.
> I am my brothers' keeper.

I was left speechless. Jesus genuinely believed it. He wanted to bring an end to 'a house divided' on every level: local, national, global. He wanted his generation to face the consequences of internal division. Every kingdom divided against itself is on the road to ruin, from family to temple, from nation to planet. And it's another painful lesson, because in bringing the message of peace and unconditional love to humanity, Jesus caused a mother to look at her daughter in a new way, and a father to re-examine his relationship with his son. As divisions became apparent, it is up to every family member to take responsibility for their failure to love and to thus make a real start in forgiving each other.

Jesus wasn't just blaming his nation. He was blaming every nation. Jesus wasn't just picking on some families. He was picking on them all!

A mother divided from her daughter? A father from his son? So it's the same old story, 'Blame the family'! To be fair to him, it wasn't so much blame the family as 'blame each individual'. Jesus was canny enough a psychologist to know that it's within the family unit that individuals first learn to exercise, or avoid, personal responsibility. But the responsibility didn't stop within the family circle. Since *abba* is sovereign and father and mother of all, then every woman you meet is your mother, every girl your sister, every boy your brother. In other words everybody's wellbeing is potentially your concern.

> Now Jesus' mother and brothers came to see him, but they couldn't get near him because of the crowd. Someone told him, 'Your mother and brothers are standing outside, wanting to see you'. He replied, 'My mother and brothers are those who hear abba's word and put it into practice' (Luke 8:19-21).

'Honor your father'. No! Jesus knew better. Honor *abba*. He alone is the source of true sovereignty. The earthly father was the supreme arbiter of life and death. He was the object of obedience and submission, of reverence and awe, to his children and wives. He was the pivot of domestic power-games and the source of all discord and disharmony, jealousy and envy. Family members bowed down in fear to him.

From the home to the temple, *abba* liberates individuals from all social bonds, in order that everyone can be governed by love. Jesus rejected most religious laws, because as the End approached they didn't matter. What you eat, where you eat and how you eat, for example, pales into insignificance when compared to the love in one's heart towards *abba* and your neighbor. The author of the first letter of John (3:17) had grasped what Jesus was all about when he wrote 'if anyone has material possessions, and sees his brother in need but has no pity on him, how can *abba*'s love be in him?' Bit extreme, don't you think? This is the same author who carried Jesus' teaching to the extreme in another sense as well; though, once again, Jesus may have said something similar...

> Anyone who claims to be in the light but hates his brother is still in the darkness and walks around in the darkness. Anyone who hates his brother is a murderer (1 John 2:9, 11).

Abba's Finger

Do I have to keep on repeating myself? Jesus was a fool to believe that he could change human history, a bloody fool, and all because of his commitment to *abba*'s totally different way of exercising human power and authority. A way so different from my power-systems that words like 'power' and 'authority' and 'kingly rule' had to be used with great care, if at all.

The 'father of a nation', the High Priest, was no different, says Jesus, in the way that he exercised leadership. Because of rivalry, he too was locked into the eternal love affair with power, status and prestige. But imagine how boring history would be without life's traditional leaders. I agree that there have been a few exceptions, but they have made little impact on history. Even the likes of Gandhi failed in the end. He was shot for all his efforts as a bridge-builder and reconciler! Warring brothers won the day in the sub-Continent. India became a country divided.

Give individuals power and I guarantee you that they'll soon become obsessed with 'lording it' over each other. Religious leaders are no exception. Even they succumb eventually, since sacred or heavenly power and prestige is particularly intoxicating. The Bible describes it poetically as 'God's arm endowed with power', because ultimately it has to be protected by violence of one kind or another. Religious devotees have always been seduced by the thought of sitting at God's side and thus having ready access to his strong and powerful arms. On one occasion, the mother of two of Jesus' disciples, James and John, even asked if her boys could sit on God's left and right side when the new Endtime kingdom finally arrived. Cheeky bitch! But, to be fair to her, she was only looking after her boys. It's what mothers do.

Like me, Jesus knew how powerful human desire is. But, for Jesus, that desire should only have one aim: the desire to do *abba*'s will; the desire to love and to serve humanity. This is the only way that you can be free of the intoxicating hold that sacred power and prestige have over you. And it's never easy – highly stressful, in fact. It's so stressful that your whole world becomes disorientated. So what do most of you end up doing? You hang on even more to the power and prestige that your God has given you. And that's perfectly natural. Good common sense, obviously!

abba's way
has nothing to do with a worldly kingdom

abba's way
has nothing to do with a celestial kingdom.

abba's way
is a mystery
dawning here and now
in time and space.

abba's way
is a mystery that comes to fruition,
not in some imaginary transcendence
but in its total presence,
here and now
in a person's life.

abba's way
is a mystery,
revealed,
not as an awesome and terrifying power,
but in the most practical of ways
in everyday life.

abba'a way is
Direct.
Unmediated.

to receive abba
you only have to imitate Jesus

Abba's way? I'll never forget the day when the moment of truth arrived. Jesus' words still echo in my ears, '*I saw Satan fall like lightning from heaven*' (Luke 10:38). I suppose that in today's language, you'd say that I was brought down to earth with a bump!

> Now is the time for judging this world; now is the Prince of the World driven out (John 12:31).

Jesus didn't pull any punches. The trouble was he didn't bloody well throw any in the first place! In a non-violent way, Jesus had exposed the violent dynamics that are the Sacred Order. He brought out into the open the violent relationship between the traditional God and Me, the violent relationship that lies at the heart of human culture. I like nothing better than a good fight, be it personal or cosmic. I've got legions on my side on active service. 'Bring it on,' is their constant cry. I've been involved in plenty of fights down the centuries, pitting myself against God's power and strength. But Jesus fought in a different way. Well, he didn't actually fight, unless you count fighting with *abba*'s finger 'proper' fighting!

> If I by abba's finger cast out demons, then abba's sovereignty has come to you (Luke 11:20).

Fighting evil with only *abba*'s finger? The mind boggles. How could I have a proper fight if Jesus wouldn't even fight me? He used the same tactics in front of the High Priest. Don't get me wrong; I'm not accusing him of being a coward. He was brave, I'll give him that. But Jesus had another way of making a point. Love! He was one Just Man, who kept on oozing so much unconditional love that it led to his death. And my death, in one respect, though I needn't have worried as plenty came to my rescue.

While I've always admired Jesus, I confess I hate the man. I loathe and despise him. He stands for everything that I detest. But it was in and through the hatred and opposition to pure love that I generated against Jesus, that his love was finally authenticated and made clear for all to see. My trump card was to prove my defeat, my temporary emasculation. The bastard didn't fight back. Jesus was in my clutches, courtesy of the religious and political powers of the day, but it proved to be my downfall, and theirs. The way of violence was exposed for all to see. Jesus humiliated me by robbing violence of its power. He just kept on loving, even when confronted by those who loved rivalry and violence in its most brutal form. What a clever trick. He must have planned it all along. I got Jesus to the Mother of All Trials and ended up on trial myself.

Visionaries

Jesus of Galilee! He was a real man rooted in a religious heritage that he shared with many of his contemporaries. And yet he was so much more. He was so different from everyone else that he had turned his back on everything to do with power: worldly and religious, sacred and heavenly. And, as you've seen for yourselves, he was always going on and on about love – *Abba*'s love. All that bloody humility – but *why*? Something unique must have happened to him – but *what*? 'All you need is love'? No! I needed more answers. He knew his Bible inside out, its history and its theology. So did I. Maybe I'd missed something. I wanted to know who he really was and so my investigations continued.

Visions, and the ideas that grow from them, don't suddenly pop out of nowhere. Individuals, like Jesus, may come up with radical insights, but they too belong to a particular milieu. The spirituality of the First Temple in Jerusalem had survived to the time of Jesus, and well beyond, and individuals continued to have heavenly visions. A book called the Acts of the Apostles, in the Christian New Testament written after Jesus' death, tells of a man called Stephen who, 'full of the Holy Spirit', looked up to heaven and saw the Glory of God, and Jesus standing at the right hand of God. *'Look,' he said, 'I see heaven open and the son of man standing at the right hand of God'*. (Acts 7:55-56). He was stoned to death by the traditionalists for sharing his vision with them. His martyrdom is always remembered the day after Christmas, the 'Feast of Stephen', of Good King Wenceslas fame.

Paul, the renegade Pharisee, who became a follower of Jesus, also traveled mystically through the heavens, like the famous Enoch. He describes one of his visions in his second letter to the church in Corinth.

> *I know a man in Christ who fourteen years ago was taken up to the third heaven. Whether it was in the body or an out of the body experience I do not know. God only knows. All I know is that this man was caught up to Paradise. He heard inexpressible things, awesome revelations that no one is allowed to tell* (2 Corinthians 12:2-4).

However much the truth may embarrass church leaders, these holy men were part of an ancient mystical tradition. They were

Jewish visionaries before they were preachers and theologians. Like John the Baptist and Paul, Jesus may have moved beyond the religion that his predecessors helped establish, but his life and authentic message is meaningless without it. The experience that best sums up the visionary world that Jesus and his contemporaries inhabited is what is generally known as the Transfiguration. But it is such a mind-blowing event, that traditional theologians explain it away as nothing more than a nice symbolic story invented by early Christian teachers to show that Jesus was superior to both the Jewish law represented by Moses, and the prophets represented by Elijah. Jesus, having gone up a mountain to be alone with his closest disciples, Mark continues the story:

> Jesus was transfigured before them. His clothes became dazzling white, whiter than anyone in the world could bleach them. And there appeared before them Elijah and Moses, who were talking with Jesus (Mark 9:2-9).

Naturally, the disciples were frightened out of their mind! Then

> ...a cloud appeared and enveloped them, and a voice came from the cloud 'This is my son, whom I love. Listen to him.' Suddenly, when they looked around, they saw no one except Jesus.

Jesus and his subsequent followers were fired up to change the world, not by the dead words of their holy books but by the mystical experiences of their heavenly journeys. A mystic himself, the author of the fourth Gospel even makes the point that although Jesus spoke of 'heavenly things' and testifies to what he has seen and heard, 'no one accepts his testimony', (John 3:32). And why? Because mysticism has been a threat to the Christian religious establishment from the start. But Jesus is more than a visionary Jew, a prophet and a heretic. He is more even than the son of the mysterious *abba,* as if that wasn't challenging enough! But who was he? I finally found my answer when I cracked the secret of the Melchizedek code. I was to discover that Jesus was also the reincarnation of one of the most longed for and mysterious figures in the whole history of his religion.

The New Melchizedek

I shall let you into the secret. There was a secret about Jesus, but only a few knew about it. And it had nothing to do with him being a messiah. Jesus was the product of a highly sophisticated 'spiritual school' or community. It was another breakaway sect, eager to conserve the true and original religion of Israel as they experienced it. Its members believed themselves to be custodians of heavenly knowledge passed down over many centuries. They drew on various strands in Jesus' spiritual heritage, the heart of which was the royal ideology of the First Templars. Elitist and highly secretive, it was based on the Melchizedek tradition. This was a tradition intent on preserving a pure priesthood, and thus ready to take over at the Endtime, when the current corrupt Jerusalem elite would be superseded by the priests of the New Melchizedek.

'Melchizedek' is the archetypal wise old man of the Bible. It means king (*melek*) of righteousness (*zedek*). He was the king of Salem, or Jerusalem, long before it had anything to do with the Israelites and their religion. He was also priest of El Elyon, the Most High One. In those days, the role of a priest was often part of a shaman's calling. He was such a powerful and holy figure that even Abraham was subordinate to him in spiritual matters. We read that

> Melchizedek brought out bread and wine and blessed Abraham, saying, 'Blessed be Abraham by The Most High One, Creator of heaven and earth' (Genesis 14:18-19).

Since his origins will always be lost in the mists of time, various legends have developed, in both Judaism and Christianity, around the mysterious figure that is Melchizedek. Little is known of how this ancient priesthood survived, but in one of the psalms King David is paid the supreme compliment with these words:

> The Lord has made a vow that he will not break. You are a priest for ever, in the Order of Melchizedek (Psalm 110:4).

This is very strange when you consider that the traditional Jewish priests were Levites and traced their priestly pedigree back to their ancestor Aaron, brother of Moses. The Levites were regarded as the holiest tribe in all Israel, and although David was from the tribe of Judah, there is no mention of David even being blessed by the Levites. Do I detect a hint of rivalry here? Jesus' brother Jacob (or James) was also a member of the Order of Melchizedek. Unlike Jesus, he was an ascetic, and his highly respected standing in the Melchizedek Order earned him the nickname of 'The Righteous One', almost as if he was Melchizedek's second-in-command. James didn't just emerge out of the blue to take over as leader when his brother Jesus died. His commitment to traditional Hebrew values also earned him the extra title of 'Defender of His People'. He became the protector of the true Agreement between God and his people. He was to lead his people out of Jerusalem in 62AD, just as Isaiah of Jerusalem had done centuries before, in order to preserve their purity as they waited expectantly for the Endtime and Jesus' return in glory – neither materialized. As head of yet another group to challenge the religious status quo led by the temple hierarchy, James was eventually stoned and clubbed to death by the Jerusalem authorities. Rules are rules. He had it coming.

Jesus' baptism in Jordan in 28 AD was the turning point in his destiny. It was the moment of his consecration. The time to go public had arrived. Jesus was reticent about taking such a step.

Family members regularly teased him for his naivety in thinking that he could remain a private person while exercising a very public ministry. But it was his destiny. Jesus had been away from Nazareth for many years being educated. All who met him agreed that he spoke as one who had authority. He didn't just become a learned sage and radical theologian overnight. His training period had been long enough for the locals to ask, in amazement, on his return, 'Isn't this Joseph's son?' In other words, he'd been away for so long that some didn't recognize the new man in their midst.

During the 'hidden years', when he was away from home being trained in ancient temple lore, Jesus spent hundreds of hours studying and reflecting upon the Scriptures. Like Paul after him, Jesus unlocked secret wisdom hidden since time began. Quoting psalm 78, he once declared that 'I will utter things hidden since the creation of the world', (Matthew 13:35). He was talking about the plan of salvation hidden until it was opportune for *abba* to reveal it to him: *Abba*'s purpose for the wellbeing of Israel and the nations.

> I praise you abba because you have hidden these things from the wise and learned and revealed them to my little ones (Matthew 11:25).

At the end of his life, Jesus summed up his teaching by saying:

> Everything that I have learned from abba I have made known to you (John 15:15).

Some family members were furious when he appeared to turn his back on years of highly specialized study, for a highly unorthodox public ministry. His cousin John had a lot to answer for. Jesus supported himself as a craftsman, as Saul, the renegade Pharisee (who became Paul the Apostle) did, busy working to earn a living until the start of his mission. The Melchizedek Code provided the timetable for his mission, but Jesus carried it out in a way that was to shock his contemporaries, especially his family, to the core.

According to Israelite tradition, every seventh year was known as a 'little' Jubilee Year. This is when a whole year was kept as a Sabbath or a 'day of rest'. Ideally, life was meant to be more wholesome, and therefore more holy, in every respect. For example, the land was allowed to 'rest' in order to give the soil an opportunity to replenish itself. Slaves were released and outstanding debts to one's neighbors were cancelled. Every four hundred and ninety years (referred to as 'every seventy of those seven years'), a major Jubilee Year was held, culminating in an extra special 'day-of-at-one-ness'.

Melchizedek was the key player in the proceedings. While many books outside the Jewish Scriptures also contain references to the Melchizedek Code, the biblical Book of Daniel has a passage that provides a key insight into the dynamics that influenced Jesus. We are told that once, when Daniel was 'still in prayer', the angel Gabriel came to him and instructed him, 'Daniel, I have now come to give you insight and understanding. Therefore, consider the message and understand the vision'. Jesus had also been seeking insight and understanding. The Archangel continues,

> Seventy 'sevens' are decreed for your people and your holy city to put an end to sin, to make an act of 'at-one-ness' for your evil ways, to put things right with God and to anoint the most holy (Daniel 9:22-24).

The Biblical scholar, Margaret Barker, has discovered that the 'seventy sevens' foretold in Daniel is the equivalent of the long-awaited major tenth Jubilee of the Melchizedek Code, when something truly epoch-making was expected to happen. The major Jubilee was basically a 'Back to the Garden of Eden' festival, when everything would be restored to its original purity and glory once again. It was the time when the land and its people, the city and its temple, would be perfect once more and God could again look at his restored creation and see that it 'really was good' (Genesis 1:31). Well, people can dream, can't they!

At its climax, the plan was that Melchizedek would carry-out one of the most awesome acts of sacrifice the world has ever seen, rescuing his own people from me in the process, and then going on to take his place in the Heavenly Council, as the long-awaited Day of Judgment got underway. Guess what? Jesus' baptism occurred during the first week of the tenth Jubilee! We know from the gospel that Jesus started his work with the words 'the time is fulfilled' (Mark 1:15). This was the time 'appointed', or chosen, by God for Melchizedek to appear. Quoting Isaiah III, Jesus informed his listeners that he had been anointed to bring about the Great Jubilee.

> The spirit of the Lord is upon me, because he has anointed me to preach good news to the poor, to proclaim freedom for prisoners, and recovery of sight for the blind, to release the oppressed, and to announce the year of the Lord's favor (Luke 4:18-19).

I'm not deliberately trying to be provocative, but because of the nature of the battle between us, I probably got to know Jesus better than most. It's because I'm fed up with so many scholars and theologians for getting it wrong about Jesus, that I've put pen to paper to write this gospel. In the words of a famous Chinese sage: 'Keep your friends close and your enemies even closer'. I got to know my bitterest enemy well.

At the end of his intensive period of preparation, Jesus was initiated into the tradition of the New Melchizedek. Jesus wasn't born into this privileged caste; his was a spiritual calling and not a hereditary gift. And herein lies another secret within a secret. Jesus' peers came to recognize him as the New Melchizedek, the Great High Priest: the long-awaited Just One, whose role was pivotal in completing the mother of all 'days-of-at-one-ness' – The final act in human history.

One of my demoniacs also cottoned on to the secret. Demon possessed persons are always insightful regarding power, especially spiritual power. What else do you expect, when I've trained them so well? He instantly recognized Jesus as 'The Holy One of God', the High Priest, Chief of the traditional Sacred Order of life. Jesus flirted with the possibility of accepting this most special of accolades, at least for a while, but came to realize that he was the anti-type of the High Priest. He took on board everything that secret documents had said about Melchizedek, but interpreted it in a different way. He turned the tradition about Melchizedek on its head and so redefined those most sacred words, the 'King of Righteousness', or simply 'The Just King'. It was this reversal that ultimately alienated Jesus, the Just One, not only from the Jerusalem establishment but also from alternative communities like Qumran and, of course, his own spiritual home and family.

Jesus embraced a different kind of royalty.
and redefined it.

Jesus embraced a different kind of sovereignty.
and redefined it.

Jesus embraced a different kind of priesthood.
and redefined it.

Jesus rejected the royal ideology of Melchizedek and the First Temple, his native Israelite faith. He turned his back on all that could have been his, the unique dignity and power of God's supreme political and religious ruler on earth. Is it any wonder that some of his brothers and sisters thought that he was a fool? Jesus' peers wanted him to fulfill their earthly hopes and expectations, as millions of his so-called followers still do to this day. Many still want him to satisfy their lust for power as friends and servants of God's Chosen One. Jesus' so-called followers are not the only ones with fantasies of omnipotence. They share that with leaders in every age. I'm especially fond of those who declare 'But I didn't want the job, you know', or 'I don't want the power and the honor that goes with it' but 'somebody's got to do it'. I just love such humility.

I am he
who empowered
the fantasies of your ancestors,
'lords spiritual and temporal'.
I am the will to power.
I am Satan.

I am he
who unmasks
the fantasies of your ancestors,
'lords spiritual and temporal'.
I am the will to power.
I am Satan.

I am he
who empowers
your fantasies,
'lords spiritual and temporal'
I am the will to power
I am Satan

Jesus voluntarily renounced all power in favor of the role of the Suffering Servant that Isaiah speaks of, and I told you about earlier. The Just One, whose humility would be an example to the whole world. Jesus could have been one in the line of Moses or the Roman Emperors, who were also believed to be 'like God' or even 'sons of God'. However esoteric Jesus' training and education had been, his path now became that of a religious maverick and holy shit-stirrer. This new 'King of Righteousness' was proud to be a mere mortal, just like the Suffering Servant. He claimed no special privileges, even at the bitter end. Actually, he claimed no special privileges, *because of* The End! With universal harmony restored, every part of creation would be at-one again. Jesus, the New Melchizedek, would, through his humility, bring everything in human history to completion. This is why you can't really blame the Christian elite for not accepting Jesus.

They are theologians after all.
Jesus is the end of all theology.

They are Biblical scholars after all.
Jesus is the end of all Bible study.

They are church leaders after all.
Jesus is the end of religion.

Regime Change

Having disassociated himself from the world of power-systems – a world with its own language, the language of power and prestige – Jesus was faced with the challenge of finding ways of communicating his message that wouldn't compromise his teaching and integrity. This is why, at the end of his life, actions really did speak louder than words. His native language was tainted with the myth and religion of the old regime. Most of it had become impoverished, debased and empty of any power to challenge the status quo. Jesus couldn't use language that ended up reinforcing the very system that *abba*'s sovereignty was going to do away with. And yet he had to find words that people understood, words that would engage them. Regime change requires language change.

I've already explained that Jesus referred to his disciples as 'the little ones'. Weird! And to the sovereign presence in his life as *abba* or 'Daddy'. Even more weird! So how did he refer to himself? Actually, Jesus tried not to! After all, he was always the awkward one. With respect to all religious leaders, past and present, Jesus never used a title that was 'lordly'. For him, there was only one authority, and he made it quite clear where he stood on the matter when he declared that the first shall be last and the last first. It wasn't in his nature to draw attention to himself. If a title was needed, you could be sure that Jesus would choose something simple and humble, since he never thought of himself as a religious or nationalist superhero. After all, superheroes are just pretend, aren't they? He was no angelic being, no matter what some of his followers may have thought later. As the New Melchizedek, Jesus could never identify himself with the figure in the Book of Revelation, where it is stated that he saw...

> Another Mighty Angel coming down from heaven. He was clothed in a cloud, with a rainbow above his head; his face was like the sun, and his legs were like fiery pillars. He planted his right foot on the sea and his left foot on the land, and he gave a loud shout like the roar of a lion (Revelation 10:1-2).

Pretty impressive, if confusing, stuff. One minute Revelation describes Jesus as a little lamb and the next minute he's a gigantic bloody angel with the voice of a lion! But, as you know, Jesus didn't 'do' sacred categories. Traditional values and language were meaningless to him, since he spoke of a reality with a totally different set of values. When he went public, Jesus chose to refer to himself as a 'son of man', a mere mortal. A man among many, or better still, 'one of you lot'. 'Son of man' was no longer a popular religious title, though Jesus, along with many of his listeners, especially fellow sectarians, would have known of its connections with Ezekiel, the visionary-prophet; Daniel, the interpreter of dreams; and Enoch, the biblical equivalent of today's science fiction 'Time Lord'. What's more, Jesus knew that for some of the more elitist Endtime sects, 'son of man' was the secret code for God's special agent, who had a key role to play at the final judgment. Who else but Melchizedek!

Jesus, true to character, debunked the whole concept of the 'son of man' as he had done with Melchizedek. He ridiculed it, thus stressing the point that he was as far removed as possible from the apocalyptic, supernatural and mythic world of the 'son of man' as anyone could be. That's what Jesus does. He brings everything down to the human level. Imagine the response when he once declared that 'the son of man must suffer many things and be rejected by this generation' (Luke 17; 21). No one, religious or otherwise, wants a suffering and humiliated hero. Certainly not one who is always at everyone's beck and call.

We will look at myths in more detail later on in the book, but there are recorded instances where Jesus appears to be in thrall to a far more impressive and mythical 'son of man'. He once said:

> But I say to you all. In the future you will see the son of man sitting at the right hand of the Mighty One and coming on the clouds of heaven (Matthew 26:64).

Was he confused? What on earth was he talking about? Who'd have thought that two thousand years on I would find myself putting the record straight! But I was there after all. I not only heard his words, but more importantly I also heard the way that he said them. I saw his face and looked into his eyes. Jesus was using myth that grabbed people's attention in order to show them how gullible they were. Idle speculations about future spectacular cosmic events were meaningless. He ridiculed the whole 'clouds of heaven' idea, challenging his contemporaries to look not only at themselves, but also at him in a different way. Jesus was being ironic. Irony is always a threat to accepted authority. What mattered to Jesus were people's concrete decisions in the here and now in favor of *abba*'s impending New Peace Agreement. Past and future events were no longer of any relevance to him. When asked on one occasion whether there would be signs to show when *abba*'s sovereignty was going to be revealed, Jesus replied that

> *abba*'s sovereignty doesn't come visibly, so people won't be able to say "Here it is" or "There it is". *Abba*'s sovereignty is already in the midst of you. It is there among you now' (Luke 17:21).

Even the parables that Jesus used reinforced the fact that a new humanity fashioned by *abba* was already within every individual's grasp. 'Lay its seeds now', was Jesus' challenge, since he really believed that small and unpromising beginnings among a handful of people on behalf of *abba*'s way could grow with startling outcome in the future.

Few of the 'son of man' sayings can be taken at face value. For example, Jesus would never have said that 'whoever blasphemes against the Holy Spirit will not be forgiven' (Luke 12:10). This is yet another example of the early church projecting its own teaching back to the time of Jesus. But Jesus did say that 'whoever speaks a word against the son of man will be forgiven' because that message lay at the heart of his teaching. Forgiveness. Damned forgiveness!

Peter came to Jesus and asked, 'Lord, how many times must I

> forgive my brother when he sins against me? Up to seven times?' Jesus answered, 'I tell you, not seven times but seventy times seven' (Matthew 18:21).

Jesus also made it clear that he would never impinge on *abba*'s sovereignty and 'his' future plans for humanity by second guessing the way that *abba* would choose to bring 'his' work to fruition. What Jesus did know was that 'no one knows', not even the son of man. His teaching is clear enough on the matter, for

> No one knows about that day or hour, not even the angels in heaven, nor the son, but only abba. Be on your guard. Be alert! You don't know when that time will come (Mark 13:32).

Finally, Jesus' teaching about the 'sheep and goats' gives you an insight, not only into his thoughts on the final judgment but also into the way that he dramatically exposes people's belief systems, especially religious ones. Jesus sets about grabbing their attention by describing the awesome arrival of the 'son of man' on earth, sitting on his heavenly throne and surrounded by hundreds of angels. Presided over by Melchizedek, the final judgment takes place, with every human being placed either with the sinful goats on his left or with the good and faithful sheep on his right. Imagine the excitement, as the listeners assumed that they would be moving into the sheepfold reserved for them. Listen to Jesus' message as recorded in Matthew 25:31-46:

> Then the King will say to those on his right-hand side, 'Come, you who are blessed by abba; take your inheritance, the kingdom prepared for you since the creation of the world.'

With just a few words, their mythical, religious and self-righteous world is laid bare by the most human and down to earth of situations.

Melchizedek, the heavenly king, continues,

> I was hungry and you fed me, thirsty and you gave me drink, a stranger and you invited me in, naked and you clothed me, sick and you looked after me, and when I was in prison you visited me.

In deep shock, the 'righteous' answer that they have never seen their king in need of such help, to which he replies, *'I tell you the truth, whatever you did for one of the least of these brothers of mine, you did for me'*. In *abba*'s world, the verdict of the Day of Judgment is ultimately in your hands, for this king can evidently be encountered in everyday life. Jesus continues...

> I was hungry and you gave me nothing to eat, I was thirsty and you gave me nothing to drink, I was a stranger and you never invited me in, I needed clothes and you never clothed me, I was sick and in prison and you didn't look after me. Whatever you did not do for one of the least of these, you did not do for me.

The story's climax is logical for religious people who think in a self-righteous way. If you want to live by those standards, says Jesus, then you die by them also. It's your decision.

> Then the King will say, 'Depart from me; you who are cursed into the eternal fire and punishment prepared for the devil and his angels, but the righteous to eternal life'.

Though Jesus may have ridiculed the tradition of the son of man, his followers couldn't let go of such a potent myth. After Jesus' suffering and humiliating death, they badly needed something to hang on to. It's a natural reaction, after all. What better than the age-old religious expectation and hope for... what else? The original Melchizedek, coming in power and glory! The Book of Daniel was guaranteed to boost morale:

> In my vision at night I looked, and there before me was one like a son of man, coming with the clouds of heaven. He approached the Ancient of Days and was led into his presence. There he was given authority, glory and sovereign power. All peoples and every nation on earth worshipped him. His dominion is an everlasting dominion, a kingdom that will never be destroyed (Daniel 7:11-14).

Don't fall into the trap, as I nearly did, of thinking that talk of *abba*'s sovereignty was just pious claptrap. Since *abba* was sovereign, all 'Caesars', past and present, would have to renounce their titles. All kingdoms would be rendered impotent. This wasn't just religious and political dynamite, it was also cultural dynamite. Jesus rejected all myths and mystifications. As far as he was concerned, there would never again be a mythic hero or god to usher in a new world order. There was to be no 'Apocalypse Now', so beloved of Hollywood and religious fundamentalists, with its violent apocalyptic terror and sacred bloodbath. *Abba* didn't rule with an iron rod, since his love opposes all kinds of worldly power. Jesus is all about the power of love. *I'm* about the love of power. I try not to use that offensive four-letter word. Jesus was the special agent of pure, unconditional and non-violent love. Love! There! I've said it again. This was the only non-negotiable part of his life. There could be no deals with the Sacred Order, since it is based ultimately on violence and vengeance. It is based ultimately on me, and the tried and tested power-systems that had ruled the world for centuries. I wasn't going to give it all up without one hell of a struggle.

The Trial

As Jesus' mission intensified and gained momentum, it was always on the cards that he would end up going to Jerusalem for a final showdown with the Jewish authorities and especially with the priestly aristocrats who ran the Temple. For Jesus, it was the beginning of The End. The confrontation led to his trial, or rather to a preliminary hearing or investigation, to identify the charges to lay before him. The stage was thus set for an almighty clash between the defenders of sacred dogma and a person who by now was clearly a dangerous and destructive dissident. This was no chance happening; it was an integral part of Jesus' plan. In some ways, I think he engineered it. Not surprising, since most of us knew all along that he was stark raving bonkers. But was he? You must decide for yourselves.

He was my toughest adversary ever, the only one to ever beat me. But from then on, I've had nothing to worry about. Jesus was a one off. Thank God for that. *God*? Don't panic. I haven't become religious all of a sudden. It's the truth, and one of the great ironies in history, that it was ultimately 'God' who got Jesus murdered, with a little help from me. Because of *abba*, it was the God of the Sacred Order, and his trusted employees, that Jesus exposed in Jerusalem.

He had consistently attacked and undermined a religion that gave meaning to people's lives. He was bypassing centuries of sacred traditions and customs that for him were no longer necessary. In fact, they were not even right. For once I agree with those traditionalists, especially the 'politically correct', who argue that it was irresponsible of one individual, however inspired, to challenge, and indeed to try to change, a whole religious system. Surely a religion wouldn't have survived for so long unless it had something of value to offer the masses, especially with leaders who had absolute faith in the salvation that they had on offer? But, as you are fully aware by now, Jesus' life was all about radically pushing the boundaries of his own native religion to the extreme. It was easy for him. He lived with no boundaries. *Abba* was enough for him.

By coming to Jerusalem, it looked as if Jesus was playing into the hands of those who wielded political and religious power. And that of course is what he did. I foolishly believed, for a while, that I'd trapped him. But he wasn't prepared to compromise with me, or anyone for that matter. His religion had taught him that at some time in the future Evil would be defeated. The hosts of heaven would be lining up against the hosts of hell in the greatest of all Apocalypses. But I was taken by surprise. The battle, if you can call it that, took place in the heart of one extraordinary individual. It was a battle with serious political implications for your world and my world.

Do I need to remind you of my background in Sacred Law and its enforcement? It's my expertise. The Law is the law. Since the Law is there in writing for everyone to see, people know beforehand exactly what is expected of them. When they break the rules, they know that they will be dealt with accordingly. The Law is always honest. There was nothing daemonic about Jesus' trial. It was 'by the book', and a 'holy book' at that. When he looked at the guidelines before him, it's no wonder that Caiaphas, the High Priest, instigated the plot to kill Jesus. Supreme in virtue and wisdom, it was the High Priest's duty to mediate God's will among his people. I was, in fact, still serving God when I tested Jesus at the start of his career. I was perfectly justified in pushing him to the limits... Yes, even using lies and deception, if need be, to see if I could get a conviction against him. You can't blame me for trying. I was only doing my job as the Accuser, even if I was, by then, working for myself. It was my way of helping to maintain 'right order' in God's world that those bloody prophets were always going on about.

"The High Priest"

The High Priest was God's presence among his people. He could

be relied upon to get a conviction against Jesus. I recently came across the saying '*the acquisition of power already marks the arrival of decadence*'. The High Priest and his like are fine examples of religious authority at its most decadent, a joy to observe, in any walk of life. The religious law had clear guidelines as to how one should deal with difficult moral or legal cases in first century Palestine. There was nothing vague about them. They could be referred to the High Court in Jerusalem. The procedure was clearly laid out in the Book of Deuteronomy 17, verses 8 to 13. It states that the sacred guidelines were to be mediated through the 'judge who was in office at the time', which invariably meant the High Priest. It was his sacred duty to pronounce God's judgment. There was no evil intention afoot. He was fulfilling his role in the religious power-system.

Behind all political and religious power is the claim to absoluteness. The High Priest embodied the absolute authority of the temple and religious law. He was just doing his job, acting for the good of his faith. After all, the rules were unequivocal. Any person who showed contempt of court would be put to death. You don't argue with God. Such behavior had to be purged from Israel. An example had to be made of Jesus, and rightly so. His death would serve as a warning to the masses.

Jesus came to know and experience the horror and cruelty implicit in his native religion, as many have done since. And the charge against him? Jesus was charged with contempt of court. Jesus refused dialogue with the High Priest; he refused to answer his questions. To insult the High Priest was to insult God. What a bloody idiot! He was brilliant with words; his answers could have saved him. It's as though he was hell-bent on rubbing those in authority up the wrong way. As always, Jesus refused to play by religious rules.

From a human point of view, the most obvious question has never been asked in nearly two thousand years. I'm asking the question now and I'll give you the answer. Why was Jesus executed as a rebel against Rome when in fact he was a rebel against his native religion? I feel quite proud that Jesus and I had at least a couple of things in common. We both saw ourselves as God's servant and both of us were accused of being rebels, though I wasn't killed for being one! You see, I did overstep the mark with my job. I grew up with the power and authority that God had vested in me. Heady stuff, as many of you know. From administering the law, I became a law unto myself, and was eventually banished from the Heavenly Council. I became a pariah, just like Jesus.

If Jesus was a threat to Rome, why didn't Pilate, the Roman governor, simply order his assassination? He had the resources to get rid of Jesus with a minimum of fuss. Keep an eye on him for a few days. Observe his every movement. Then, using a knife or rope, a professional killer would have had no problem in disposing of Jesus' body after the execution. It could even have been made to look as if Jesus had fallen foul of bandits. From a Jewish point of view, the temple police could have arrested or even imprisoned him. The local crowd would soon forget him. A new religious hero would eventually appear for them to follow. The temple authorities could even have had him banned from Jerusalem. In the middle of the eighth century BC, because his message was subverting the foundations of Israel's religious and social order, the prophet Amos was expelled by the High Priest from the royal sanctuary at Bethel. The religious authorities could have arrested and imprisoned Jesus or even had him expelled from the capital city. Why didn't they? These questions must be answered in order to understand the real meaning of Jesus' death. The biggest mystery of all is why Jesus wasn't stoned to death? It was the traditional way of dealing with religious and moral deviants and you didn't need imperial permission to carry it out. On one occasion a mob tried to kill Jesus by the other approved method of religious execution. They drove him to the edge of a precipice in the hope that they could literally drive him over the edge. Both methods ensured that the faithful didn't have to get their hands dirty by shedding human blood and touching the guilty party.

It always amazes me, not that I would wish to change things, how ingenious religious people can be in their dealings with one another, and especially with those who don't fit into their idea of what is right. Who were the truly religious? In Jesus' time it was those who were referred to as being 'zealous for the law', the fundamentalists, who persecuted those who refused to follow their interpretation of the Law of Moses. Religious 'interpretation' has certainly made my work easier over the centuries.

The religious authorities knew their godly business and that their power lay ultimately in the violence of divine judgment. Jesus challenged that belief and was eliminated as an enemy of their faith and their God. In his opinion no one has the right to pass judgment on others.

> Do not judge or you will be judged in the same way that you judge others; (Matthew 7:1)

Jesus was equally unequivocal about his own role, '*I have not come to judge the world but to save it*' (John 12:47).

Stoning Jesus would have been perfect! As I look at the facts something just doesn't add up. Why did Pilate get sucked into a religious controversy that was none of his business? The standard explanation is that Pilate was afraid of the crowd; it was a public order issue, the fear of civil disobedience. I don't buy that. Crowds can always 'be worked', as they were just before Jesus was sentenced to death. Failing that, Pilate had the military resources to sort out any mob, as every governor had done in the past. There's no denying that Jesus was sentenced to death, and handed over to be murdered, by the supreme religious authority of the day in collusion with empire, who actually carried out the sentence. Leaders of the Sacred Order always got the secular power to carry out their dirty work, as would happen centuries later in Europe with the Inquisition.

Fucking cowards! But in this case, more was at stake than the High Priest issuing a warning to all who dared to challenge his authority. That may have been the official cause of death entered on Jesus' death certificate, but you have to look deeper to discover the real reason.

The Good News

Although Jesus had inverted the role, and alienated his own

spiritual community in the process, the High Priest and his cronies feared that maybe he was the long-awaited Melchizedek after all, chief figure and mediator of the Endtime. They knew about the secret traditions concerning this pivotal Endtime figure. It was a tradition that was almost taboo in Israel. I'm convinced that members of Jesus' own sect had shared their disgust with the High Priest when Jesus refused to honor his sacred calling. Even if they were ninety nine per cent certain that he wasn't Melchizedek, stoning Jesus to death on the one per cent chance that he might be, wouldn't go down very well with their God. They would then be held responsible, as the Endtime got nearer, for the death of the King of Righteousness. Not 'King of the Jews', as Pilate thought. Although, in a way he was right, because Melchizedek was for some 'the righteous king of the Jews'.

It was the High Priest's nightmare scenario. What if the 'mere mortal' facing him was Melchizedek after all? And so, hedging his bets, the High Priest, ever the consummate politician, manipulated the situation, by getting Pilate to execute Jesus on a trumped up political charge. Should it ever turn out that Jesus was Melchizedek, then Caiaphas, hand on heart, could honestly say that 'it was nothing to do with me, God'.

What killed Jesus wasn't irreligion
but religion
What killed Jesus wasn't lawlessness
but the law
What killed Jesus wasn't anarchy
but the desire to maintain Sacred Order.
abba
offered
an alternative to religion
an alternative to the law
an alternative to Sacred Order

Who would ever have thought that I would be the harbinger of good news? Well, here is some more. There was nothing sacred about Jesus' death, as some Christians have claimed for two thousand years. He died a common criminal, tortured in the most horrific way possible. It was the most irreligious of acts, not on a 'green hill far away' but on the civic rubbish tip, among decaying food, dead bodies galore and plenty of human and animal faeces. He was murdered and died outside the temple, as well as outside the boundaries of his holy city. His life and death makes meaningless for ever the sacred distinction between holy and profane, religious and political, pure and impure, because Jesus, the Just One, was killed in the most profane of manners by religious devotees. No wonder Jesus said once to his followers, 'Don't be offended by me'. Because of me, his was a path that led to the most religiously and morally offensive endings.

As the anti-type of the High Priest, Jesus was anointed, not in the temple by fellow priests but in public by a woman, and in the most sensuous of ways. Jesus, rebel to the end! She was the woman with the alabaster jar, full of valuable oil. She broke it and poured the oil on Jesus' head to anoint him. Aware of what lay ahead for him, she wept and began to wet his feet with her tears and to dry them with her hair. She even kissed his feet and anointed them with oil as well.

His death was also, in some mysterious way, my defeat, as well as being the end of the traditional concept of God. I suppose you could say that his death was the death of God. Since I have no hold at all over Jesus, how can I be so blasé about my defeat? I'll tell you. If I had to lose once, then at least I lost to the best you have to offer. I made the final battle and lost, but I still came second. Jesus was no pushover, but his so-called followers are.

Jesus was no failed hero either. He was no martyr. His death wasn't a mistake. He set out for Jerusalem totally focused on his meeting with the High Priest, totally convinced that *abba* would vindicate him at the Endtime. His solidarity with every human being was so complete that, even on the Cross, Jesus sought no special favors from *abba*. Why? Because of his special love for Israel and the nations… his special love for all the victims of my way of ordering the world.

Jesus died because of me. He suffered and died for the new peace agreement, that special bond of peace whose foundations Jeremiah had laid in the human heart and mind centuries before. He died to empower human beings to behave in a radically new way towards each other; the privilege mediated no longer via temple or religion, but directly via *abba*'s love in the human heart. It wasn't the ability to curse the Sons of Darkness, as Qumran and similar sects believed. No. It was something far more subversive – *'Love your enemies. Pray for your persecutors'* (Matthew 5:44).

Love your enemies
in order to break the power of the warring brothers,
the power of all warring opposites.
Love your enemies
and break forever
the Eternal Cycle of Human Violence

Because of *abba,* every person is an inverted High Priest, Archbishop, Patriarch or Pope. Every person is sovereign. Jesus demystifies the whole issue of divine punishment and stresses individual responsibility instead. Everyone from now on is in charge of the essence of religion. In *abba* everyone is responsible for the once-a-year exclusive priestly act of at-on-ness. The once-a-year special day is now a 365-day affair between every person on the planet. As sons and daughters of *abba,* all of you are potentially brothers and sisters. No matter whether you are religious or not, *abba,* says Jesus, 'causes the sun to rise on the evil and the good: the rain to fall on the righteous and the unrighteous' (Matthew 5:45). One happy family! What sentimental twaddle!

"Jesus on the cross"

As kinfolk, every person, for Jesus, is a walking peace agreement, a bridge between warring brothers and sisters. All can make a direct and pure offering of peace to the offended, and forgive those who sin against them. Impossible, I say. It's not natural to turn your backs forever on thoughts of revenge and retribution. It's not human. Hate has no place in the human heart, according to Jesus, but for humans as 'Children of the Grave', love and hate will always belong together.

Children, you can dream as much as you like that love is all you need. As lord of this world, your Father Confessor, I also know of the hate that dwells in your hearts.

That's why I disagree with those psychologists and anthropologists who suggest that religion is the dream of the human mind. Rubbish! Religion is its worst nightmare! History its celebration!

Chapter Four

You'll miss me when I've gone

"The censorious priest spoke, probably for the last time: 'Bloody?' 'Well, they are bloody. The whole Faith is bloody – look at the stations of the cross, or the Sacred Heart of Jesus, or the Blood of the Redemption, or almost anything else you care to mention. The whole Faith is floated on blood ...". P113

"He went over to her and put out his hand and touched her cheek. Physically, that is what he did, just touched her cheek, and thereby did what had been denied him for so long, for almost three decades; made intimate contact with someone. You shake hands, yes; maybe you even embrace and exchange kisses. But you never touch another's cheek. An act of intimacy, a carnal act, feeling the flesh ...". P114

Simon Mawer – The Gospel of Judas – Abacus 2005

'Mighty Mammon'

The Church is spiritually bankrupt and seriously in need of a new savior. I'm proud to offer my services. Having lost its way in the world, it has become obsessed with its own status and survival. A lost soul myself, I've become an expert by now on status and survival. Jesus may have passed sentence on me all those centuries ago when he declared 'judgment on my world', but as to his suggestion that 'the Prince of this world' was going to be driven out, he couldn't have been more wrong. My kingdom is prosperous and flourishing.

I can't wait to get started again, now that I've got more time for ecclesiastical matters. I see myself being employed by the church as a SIC type of expert – a 'Special Independent

Consultant'. Church politics is serious business. A great deal is at stake. Saving the church is a dirty game between professionals. It always turns out nasty in the end, even if no blood is spilt. A violent struggle is going on for the soul of the church and always it's the same goal: power and money. History bears witness to the fact that contrary to what Jesus believed, you *can* 'serve God and Mammon' (Matthew 6:24). I even wrote a hymn about it, to the tune of *The Church's One Foundation*. Here's the first verse:

The Church's one foundation
Is built on blood and gore,
The Bible tells us plainly
Jerusalem was a whore.
The Church betrayed its Master,
His salvation didn't pay.
And turned instead to Mammon,
It's still the only Way.

I'm ready and willing to do my bit to support God's 'chosen ones' as they struggle to enforce sacred justice and uphold religious order. Like *abba,* I too have no favorites. I work with members of all sects. I'm more than willing to accept men and women from every nation who honor my way of doing things, the people in every age who will do anything to hang onto power. I've been honest with you throughout this book. The temptation to achieve and then exercise sovereignty is one of the greatest tests that humans have to face. And although it's such an enslaving force, it's a good one nevertheless. And it's natural, bloody natural. It's in your genes to dominate others, to create empires, however large or small. Jesus said

> Seek abba's sovereignty and justice before everything else, and the things you really need for your lives will be given to you (Matthew 6:33).

But the church prefers human sovereignty every time. Abba is impotent in the things of the world. He even proved powerless to prevent what the early church did to Jesus when he was kidnapped and molded to be its new Prince of the World. It doesn't bother me. Competition is always healthy.

No Second Coming!

We know that Jesus didn't return in the expected way with 'power and glory' to govern the earth. There was to be no New Jerusalem descending from heaven, surrounded by thousands upon thousands of angels, led this time by a Jesus who is armed with an iron rod and authorized to 'crush the nations to pieces like bits of pottery', if they didn't behave themselves and submit to his power (Revelation 2.27). How strange to discover that a non-violent Jesus before his death suddenly metamorphosed into a heavenly thug after his resurrection! But the Jesus I know would no more wield an iron rod than I could offer the forgiveness of sins.

Since there was to be no 'second coming', the majority of Jesus' followers thought that he'd got the arrangements wrong. So they abandoned his core teachings and, you guessed rightly, interpreted them in a new way. Decades after his failed return, visionaries were still searching their Jewish Scriptures, as well as the teachings that Jesus had left behind, looking for signs of what was going to happen. The first draft of the Book of Revelation, the last book in the New Testament, is a collection of such prophetic oracles or insights. They were gathered together by an ex-Jerusalem priest-mystic called John the Elder. He was given authority to interpret (did they ever stop interpreting?) the oracles in relation to Jesus. While unsealing these heavenly mysteries, John was to receive his own personal experience of Jesus. You can be sure that a heavenly throne featured in it – the kind of throne that Jesus had rejected.

> I looked up and there before me was a door standing open in heaven. And the voice I had first heard speaking to me like a trumpet said, 'Come up Here, and I will show you what is going to take place after this'. I was immediately in the Spirit and there before me was a throne in heaven with someone sitting on it.

Out went the prophetic foundation of Jesus' teaching, *abba*'s alternative way of doing things. The idea of living humbly on the edge of society as people of the Endtime was rejected as a non-starter. In came a new version of the two thousand year old priestly religion, the invention called Ecclesiastical Christianity. Jesus, the humble servant, the 'son of humanity', was murdered, along with Mithras, and refashioned into a religious mascot. For non-Jewish Christians, Jesus, or the Christ, as he was now called, became the new god on the block. He was a novelty, based partly on the god Zeus who usurped his father Saturn. The Church would eventually usurp both *abba* and Jesus with its new religion of violence and sacred justice. I wish that Christians had the courage of their convictions to ask me directly for help in dealing with their enemies. After all, I'm the Heavenly Thug and proud of it... the Global Enforcer *par excellence*... the true Prince of the World.

The fourth century Emperor Constantine was a shrewd operator, who saw the new Jesus, or Christ, as a pivotal figure in the new religion of Roman imperial authority. Who better than Christ to continue the pagan tradition of the sons of God? A truly powerful military and political figure when twinned with the ancient Israelite 'God of War'. The Book of Exodus (15:3) never had any doubt that 'God is a Man of War, the Lord is his Name'. A winning combination if ever there was one. With him on your side, all things could be possible, maybe even world domination?

With Jesus out of the way, 'The Christ', as he was now called, soon took his place. A heavenly being who, crowned as monarch, soon reached the status of a super Cosmic Being. With such support on its side, the church went on to align itself with Roman imperial power: the very power that had colluded in the murder of Jesus.

Emperor Constantine courted followers of Jesus for his own political purposes. Many of them were happy to oblige. So don't scapegoat Constantine, as if it was all down to him. He was powerless without his supporters. Remember, they needed him as much as he needed them. It's only natural to get as close as you can to the seat of ultimate power, especially the kind that supports and sanctions your eternal longing for some kind of transcendence. It's good to be on the side of The All-mighty.

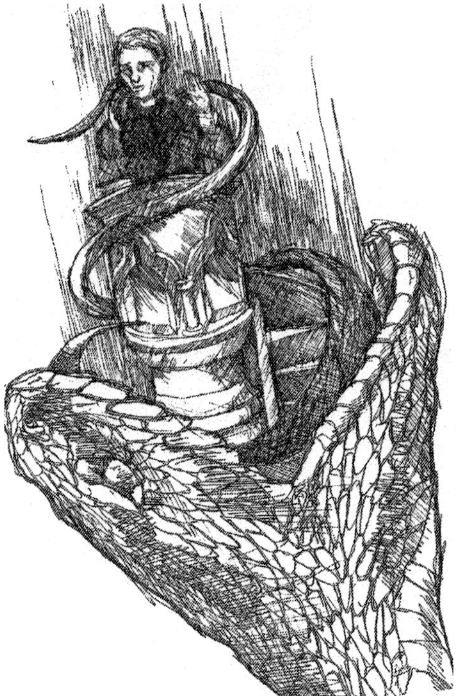

"Mighty Mammon"

'We have no king but Caesar'

A few of Jesus' followers never gave in to the much loved 'ways of the world'. They still remained loyal to *abba* and faithful to The

End. But the status of Christians was to change dramatically for the better, almost overnight, as they began mixing with the social elite. It wasn't long before they had the support of the wealthy and the powerful. Influential patrons are as important as powerful gods and goddesses. Christians were soon getting the top jobs with prestigious titles, and of course the wealth – Always the wealth! As part of the establishment, Christians even gained the upper hand on their pagan opponents and enemies. Persecution of godless pagans, as well as of fellow Christians with whom they disagreed, became the norm.

The Emperor's success meant Christian success: an empire built and maintained by violence – institutional violence, the best kind, the violence that Jesus suffered and died to try and eradicate among humans. Supporting the imperial army, which Christians were happy to do, was even accepted as an act of devotion, both to the State and to God. Don't judge them. It made sense. Good common sense. The logic was clear for all to understand. The church was protected by the emperor and so it was only fair that, for Christianity to grow, Christians had to fight to defend the emperor. They had no qualms about killing for Christ's sake. Oppose the emperor and you oppose the gospel of Jesus. Good News indeed! My kind of church! One intoxicated with the nectar of Christian imperialism.

Wise politicians, whatever their beliefs, know that you can always use something popular to maintain your authority and to advance your interests. With the All-Mighty on your side, you can't fail. Emperors, be they spiritual or secular, aren't really bothered what people believe in. They know that popular beliefs are more often than not deluded. But it makes no difference, as long as it helps keep society together. False beliefs can be just as beneficial in helping you hang on to political power. The truth doesn't come into it. The truth can also be sacrificed.

Christianity spread like wildfire.

I can't talk about the Emperor's success without mentioning

the vision that proved pivotal in getting, and then keeping, the Christians on his side. Early church historians were to compare it with Paul's conversion on the road to Damascus. Constantine even referred to himself as a true servant of God, the 'thirteenth apostle'. Not one to be humble, he also made himself 'Supreme Pontiff', the head of the Christian priesthood. The story goes that Constantine had been sent a vision by God before a major battle, the Battle of Milvian Bridge, a few miles outside Rome. Empowered with this revelation, Constantine went on to win the battle. Church historians, eager for a new Christian hero, put him on the same level as Moses, who also won God's approval with a sign from heaven, in the latter case, a burning bush. I'll let you into a secret. Constantine never became a Christian, no more than I would, but we would never hesitate in sponsoring anything that benefits our goals. Constantine remained a pagan and successfully allowed Christians to coexist side by side with pagans. Constantine was a fan of any god that kept him popular with the masses. Hercules, Apollo (whom he also saw in a vision, by the way) and the extremely popular Cult of the Unconquered Sun were among his favorites. With echoes of the Egyptian pharaohs of old, Constantine adopted the sun, the heavenly sign of his god, as the symbol of imperial power. Coins still exist with his face on them, the rays of the sun radiating from his head.

Celebrating his victory in 312AD, Constantine, ever the shrewd politician, announced that he had received the support of 'the supreme deity', and had heard the words 'By this sign conquer'. Constantine was happy. Pagans were delighted. Christians were overjoyed. To a Christian audience, Constantine is reported to have said that Christ had appeared to him and said that he was to conquer by the sign of the cross. Aren't people gullible?

Constantine was baptized a Christian on his death bed. You've nothing to lose by getting as many gods on your side when preparing to enter the afterlife, even if you are an emperor.

The best of religions? Ones utterly corrupted by political and personal gain.

The temporary gathering of Jesus followers, once full of excitement and looking forward to *abba*'s triumph in the world, was transformed within a few generations into an institution that was chained to a temporal past, instead of being anchored in a new world that was already dawning. How tragic, especially when you consider that Jesus had invested his very life to inaugurate it. The church put itself center stage, instead of humbly pointing towards *abba*'s emerging sovereignty. When lordship over physical territory gradually diminished, spiritual imperialism was just as appealing. And just as rewarding. An institution developed that usurped *abba*'s sovereignty and thus the sanctity and integrity of the human heart; an institution that set about assuming exclusive control over both the communion between heaven and earth and the community of believers.

A new salvation industry was eventually set up in Rome, with its own High Priest. In true imperial theological tradition, he was called The Pope, *Pontifex Maximus*. He was a spiritual Caesar, supported by an exclusive male priesthood that jumped at the opportunity to organize, and exercise authority over, thousands upon thousands of individual souls. Faith as trust in the revelation that came from within an individual was now frowned upon. It was replaced by a faith that involved having to believe and accept what church leaders decreed to be authoritative. It was a case of 'I Believe' instead of 'Experience'.

The Church cast *abba* aside and elected instead to follow Caesar.

Caesar
and
his
power
Caesar

and
his
prestige
Caesar
and
his
privileges.

The Apostolic Assembly

The apostolic assembly or gathering was an ad hoc or temporary response, struggling to cope with the delay in Jesus' return. It wasn't 'a church' in the sense that people think of it today, or a religious structure that would last for centuries. It wasn't hierarchical in any respect. That would have been totally alien to Jesus' way of doing things. As far as Jesus was concerned, the very act of striving for sovereignty in the world is a great delusion. The apostolic assembly never even thought of itself as being sovereign. The center of *abba*'s sovereignty is each person, and maybe, if lucky, two or three gathered together in unity of mind and spirit.

You don't need to belong to a religious institution to follow Jesus. Only the very barest of social arrangements is necessary. The apostolic manifesto is as vibrant today as it was two thousand years ago. Along with Karl Marx, I have a grudging admiration for its simplicity. This is how the Acts of the Apostles describes it:

> *All the believers devoted themselves to the teaching of the apostles, to prayer and to sharing fellowship in their homes, where they had meals together. They worshipped God with pure hearts , and were popular with all the people. They met regularly , and held a common purse, being more than ready to sell their possessions and to give to those who were in need* (2:42-47).

No one person experiences Jesus in the same way. The fact that there are four accounts of his life, or gospels ('good news') as they are called, bears witness to that. Known as Matthew, Mark, Luke and John, they were written by four evangelists, although nobody really knows who the authors were. Some of their contents may be based on the memories of eyewitnesses, but the 'famous four' didn't write them. Some followers of Jesus believe that there is a fifth evangelist. Saul of Tarsus, or St Paul as he came to be known. And I can see their point, when you think that Paul was busy writing his letters and celebrating the good news of what Jesus had done, a generation before Mark, the first gospel, was being penned. Paul ended up writing nearly a third of the New Testament. He brought people to Jesus by the force of his preaching and healing miracles and not by getting people to read about the things that Jesus had said or done. And let me make one thing clear. Paul didn't invent Christianity, as some modern theologians like to claim. Emperor Constantine and the theologians that he patronized did.

Remember, John the Baptist, Jesus and Paul were not Christians! They were cast out of the same Jewish mould. All three were rooted passionately in their belief about The End, although they were to walk very different paths as spiritual teachers and guides. Paul also included himself in the list of those who had not only seen Jesus, but had also received a commission from him to be an apostle. He thought of himself as the thirteenth apostle. And that's where the problem lies. The apostolic church had different interpretations of what Jesus was all about from the very beginning. Though Paul never met Jesus in the flesh, he assumed that his vision of the resurrected Jesus was on par with what the other apostles had seen. But it was clearly very different. They had seen a more physical body. Paul's experience was of a mystical kind. His Jesus was a spiritual being. In one of his letters, he even makes the point that 'flesh and blood cannot inherit the kingdom of God' (1 Cor.15.50).

Paul, like his master, Jesus, was a religious maverick, adept at rubbing religious people up the wrong way. He made it clear that his commission was not the result of a human directive. It was '*abba* or Jesus direct'. He hadn't consulted any human teacher about Jesus, neither did he go to meet The Twelve as soon as he had had his Jesus experience. The Jewish establishment hated him and many of the first Jesus followers believed Paul to be the devil incarnate. I adore receiving such compliments.

The Apostolic Succession?

Once you are in league with The All-Mighty, or his closest representative on earth, all is well with the world. The sacred comfort zone on offer by the church is potentially within your grasp, assuming, that is, that you 'know your place' in the sacred order of things. By the end of the fourth century, when Christ was also declared to be God, then logic demanded that you get as close to him as you can. So let's look at the chain of command (or who wasn't in the 'chain of command', as the case may be). We already know that Jesus didn't appoint a successor. He never thought he'd need one. The Endtime was near. The Twelve were to be given pre-eminent serving roles in the new earthly order when it came. His brother James took over the temporary leadership of those waiting for the End. There were many competing authorities to Jesus' spiritual legacy from the start. So how come, two thousand years on and in rival Christian sects, bishops claim to be able to trace their authority back to Jesus and his apostles, when there clearly is no such link? People in the twenty-first century are still being asked to take seriously what is known as 'the apostolic succession'? You must be joking!

Just think about it. Jesus' nearest and dearest, as well as his closest disciples and friends, never really grasped who he was, or what he was all about anyway. There was an '*abba* direct' but no exclusive 'Jesus direct', at least in a religious or institutional sense. In the middle of all the confusion that surrounded Jesus' non-appearance, there was no male hierarchy ready to carry on his work. I find it amusing that bishops still have the effrontery to claim to be rooted in the original apostolic assembly. They even base their authority on it. But the genuine apostolic church was not institutionalized and it most certainly wasn't hierarchical. No one group had a direct line to Jesus in religious terms because everyone had a direct spiritual line to him as the one who pointed the way to *abba*. Long before Constantine came on the scene to consolidate things, a religious male elite was actively assuming control of Jesus' legacy. Why did they bother? Because Jesus, as the new god, was the true god, so who better to have on your side? Who better to sit by in the heavenly kingdom? Decked in fine clothes and guaranteed a seat next to God's Throne. But bishops are only human, after all. Who wouldn't want the best sacred seats in the house? The so-called apostolic succession of the hierarchy of the church is a fiction. It's a dogmatic lie. It blatantly contradicts what Jesus taught. I know it. Bishops know it. New Testament scholars know it. Here is another quote from the apostolic manifesto:

> You know that the rulers and high ranking officials of the Gentiles like to lord it over them, obsessed as they are with exercising authority. But I don't want you to be like that. Instead, I want the greatest among you to be like the youngest, and rulers among you to behave like the servant who waits at table. For who is the greatest, the one who sits at the table or the one who serves?
>
> Isn't it the one who sits at the table? But I have come among you as a servant. Therefore, whoever wants to become great among you must become your servant, and whoever wants to be great must become your slave (Matthew 20 and Luke 22).

The first Jesus 'assemblies' were local house-groups, loosely connected and organized mostly around lay-leaders, i.e. nonpriests, although there were some ex-Jewish priests among them. These homes became the focal point for worship and witness. Both men and women served as informal leaders and married couples often shared the responsibility as equals. The apostolic 'coming-together' in Jesus' name emerged as a grouping of complementary spiritual gifts that were personal, inspirational and creative. Believers were convinced that *abba*'s gifts were not subject to hierarchical obligation. A new social order was emerging, called to service and reconciliation and not to traditional lordship. If one must talk of an apostolic succession then it applies to all who follow Jesus. Everyone is 'next in line' as far as *abba* was concerned. This is why I prefer to call it the '*Abba*stolic Succession'! Members received the gifts of the spirit directly and shared them without the need of a special intermediary.

So what went wrong? All human institutions need organizing and Christianity was no exception. There was no one obvious authority after the death of James, so plenty of opportunities arose for a male elite to 'get on' in the world. The apostolic succession was invented to justify the Christian will-to-power. It wasn't long before old habits kicked in. Leaders became petty monarchs and took the place of both *abba* and the apostles, and a patriarchal Church usurped the place of the coming kingdom. What became known as the threefold hierarchy of 'bishop, priest and deacon' only started to emerge at the end of the second century AD. It clearly has nothing to do with Jesus.

The new male priesthood drew its inspiration from the Jewish synagogues. These were led by men known as presbyters or elders. Senior leaders gradually emerged, modeled on the guardians that were a common feature of many Jewish sects, such as the Essenes. As Roman influence began to take over, a non-religious name was chosen for the super senior spiritual leader. 'Episcopes' was the secular administration officer but, in time, the episcop or 'bishop' became a political leader in his own right, with territory to govern. Many had absolute authority over their subjects. This authority continues to this day in many branches of Christendom. Questions related to theological truth became a matter for bishops only. After all, they were 'next in line' to Jesus and so it was only natural that they should be consulted as the last word on important matters. Soon there was only one Christian truth – the truth of 'right belief' or orthodoxy as defined by bishops. Anyone who disagreed with, or opposed, their authority were classed as rebels against God, while non-believers and 'heretics' were deemed to be 'evil-minded'. When Christians were persecuted, with many turning away from 'the faith', it was only the bishops who remained faithful to the truth who could decide who was to be re-admitted to the church or not.

'Bishop-direct' replaced '*abba*-direct'.

The *abba*-stolic church continues to this day in spite of the church hierarchy and can and does extend beyond individual sects. It follows its own spirit-driven path, just as the gifts of the spirit are not limited or exhausted by a clerical hierarchy, be they called priests or ministers. *Abba* is a spiritual reality not subject to, or regulated by, any religious elite. As I know only too well, *abba* can look after himself. Or is it herself?

How could the apostolic church be so confident in the divinely inspired freedom that energized it so? Once again, its manifesto is crystal clear on the matter. The apostolic way is guarded by the simple injunction 'Quench not the spirit' (Thessalonians 5:19). Another translation has it as, 'Don't put out the Spirit's fire'. *Abba*'s spirit is shared 'without measure'. It cannot be handled by anyone or rationed and 'made to measure'. It burns of its own accord. The second letter to Timothy also describes it in a dramatic way, especially considering that most of you are into some kind of bondage or another. It states, quite simply, that '*abba*'s word can never be chained' (Timothy 2:9). The absence of any laws is the norm so far as the Spirit is concerned, church laws included. Paul, for all his limitations, got that right, as did the author of the words in John's gospel, when he celebrated the fact that 'the Spirit blows where it wills' (John 3:8). A recipe for disaster, if you're asking me. Ecclesiastical Christianity, I'm happy to say, would have none of it. Too much freedom, including spiritual freedom, is dangerous.

That's why the Church needs rules: rules that have to be obeyed – by everyone.

The Oath of Comical Obedience

If Jesus was to come back in the flesh today, he would be horrified to see what the Church has done in his name. Jesus challenges the exclusive claims of all tribes and nations, religious traditions and political persuasions. With *abba*'s sovereignty, there is never talk of being in subjection to another, of systems where value is based on childish and slavish obedience to an authoritarian leader, where being submissive and subordinate, the greatest virtues, is rewarded while questioning and defiance is punished. With *abba,* love comes first. I hate to admit it, well, not really, but the Church got that wrong as well. Jesus didn't come to obey. Not even to obey *abba*. Jesus came to love. The precondition for love is release from the age-old communal bond of obligation. Love demands equality and solidarity, because only in this way can there be real friendship. With *abba,* individuals are freed in order to love, growing up to empower one another through mutual love and trust.

Patriarchal hierarchy divides followers of Jesus into two parties: ruler and ruled; teacher and taught; those who command and those who obey; those who have 'power over' and those who 'serve under'. It nurtures behavior that perpetuates a culture of flattery, coercion, exploitation and manipulation.

The *abba* test is a simple one. I have no hesitation in sharing it with you, because it's such a painful test for those who want to get on in the world. And this is it: Once you get to know Jesus who, in the eyes of the world, is powerless, you are set free from the desire to have power of any kind. You are meant to rise above such worldly things! Especially spiritual power and domination over people's lives. And it's a painful lesson because I know that ninety-nine per cent of religious leaders will never relinquish that power. *Abba* doesn't demand obedience, because obedience is a barrier to spiritual intimacy, whether it is the relationship with *abba* or with another human being. You can't command anyone to love. There is nothing legal about it. *Abba* invites everyone to love. *Abba* invites everyone to be love. In order to serve *abba* and Jesus, Ecclesiastical Christianity even demands that priests swear an oath of 'canonical obedience' to church law as personified in the person of the bishop. And rightly so, though I refer to it as the oath of 'comical obedience'! It may have nothing to do with following Jesus but it does help keep the workforce in order. Church order. Religious order.

In the apostolic assemblies, all social, national, cultural and religious ties are abandoned for *abba*'s sake. People become totally free of them. Talk about taking things to the extreme! It's too hard a path to follow. For starters it's inhuman to turn your back on your family or tribe, your culture, your nation, your religion. Jesus knew he was advocating too radical a path with such an idea. That's why he admitted on one occasion, 'Blessed is he who takes no offence at me' (Matthew 11.6). I find the whole idea highly offensive. And I'm not the only one. All this talk of freedom is dangerous. It doesn't work. Trust your leaders. Stick to what you know, which is tradition. Hundreds upon thousands of you have sung the words often enough in church on a Sunday morning: *'As it was in the beginning is now and ever shall be, world without end. Amen'*. Listen to those among you who continually appeal to tradition. They are not hiding behind it but protecting it. They have your best interests at heart. Tradition allows you to feel safe and secure within the comfortable and reassuring womb of 'mother church'. You can relax because you know where you stand in the great scheme of things. Who am I to start preaching? But you do need to listen to your religious leaders, especially at this time of crisis for the faith. They are the ones who are 'in the know' and are thus in a privileged position as to the best way forward at this critical time.

Your leaders have proved their aptitude for the task entrusted to them by their God. They have become experts at clothing their will-to-power, self-preservation and aggression under the veil of normalcy and holiness. They've earned the right to defend ancient truths. I'm proud to salute them. The stakes have never been higher. 'The faith', as they like to refer to it, is facing a crisis that necessitates the suspension of all intellectual and moral concerns. You're foolish to think that using your critical faculties to question your superiors can be of help. Surrender that right, for the time being at least. What is at stake is ecclesiastical self-preservation. I'm talking from millennia of experience. Hierarchical structures have an in-built inertia. Accept it. The Church has an incredible capacity for survival. So don't panic. With good leadership, it will come through the present crisis. Let me say it again. 'Trust your leaders'.

Long may the Church be served by leaders, both theological and ecclesiastical, who are experts at obscuring and ultimately blocking any change. Theirs is a legacy of cowardice and opportunism that I'm proud of. And never underestimate the power of those who retreat behind the use of coercion and censorship against those who refuse to conform. Be warned. Rebels will be dealt with harshly, as happened with Jesus.

Rivalry

I've already explained that rivalry is part and parcel of being human. Rivalry is also part and parcel of Christian dynamics. It was an integral part of its birth as a new religion. In fact, rivalry is one of the things that I find attractive in all religions. I'd be lost without it. The disciples of John the Baptist clashed with Jesus' disciples by competing for baptism candidates. And to think that this was going on while Jesus was still alive! Things were no better when Paul became a follower of Jesus. Within a generation of Jesus' non-appearance, things got worse not better. He pulls no punches in the opening part of his first letter to the Church in Corinth, where we see the dark side of life in the apostolic assembly in action:

> I beg you brothers, in the name of our Lord Jesus Christ, that all of you agree with each another. I don't want to see divisions among but perfect unity of mind and thought.. Sadly, I have been informed that there are quarrels among you:. One of you says 'I follow Paul', another says 'I follow Apollos', another 'I follow Peter', still another 'I follow Christ'. Is Christ divided? Was Paul crucified for you? Were you baptized into the name of Paul? (1 Corinthians 1:10-13)

For Paul, such behavior is the opposite of spiritual maturity. In fact, because of such rivalry, Paul goes on to call the Corinthian Christians 'little children'. Spiritually retarded and immature men and women motivated by jealousy and quarrelling. Things were no better when he wrote to them a second time:

> I fear that there may be quarrelling, jealousy, angry outbursts,, bitter factions, slander, gossip, arrogance and disorder (2 Corinthians 12:20).

I thought that the whole point of education was to show humans how to learn from their mistakes, especially in spiritual matters. Not so. Clement, a late first century teacher, wrote his first epistle or letter to the Corinthians round about 94AD. His letter never made it into the official New Testament, but that didn't stop some Christians from treating it as 'holy writ'. Clement was particularly concerned about the effect that 'willful and determined' men were having on the church in Corinth. These were men driven by the lust for power, 'career priests' who had taken over the leadership of the church, splitting the church because of jealousy and strife. Clement asks, 'Why are there quarrels, bad temper, factions and tensions among you and warfare? Don't we have One God and One Christ and One Spirit that has been poured out on us? Why do we tear one another apart and split in pieces the Body of Christ?'

Christians were suffering, Clement argued, not because of persecution by pagan rulers but by the jealousy, ambition and spite of fellow Christians – the warring brothers and sisters that Jesus had hoped to reconcile. There never was a Golden Age, when the church was whole, perfect, pure and virginal. The faith was not purer. Christians were not braver. The church was not one and undivided. Clement even highlighted the fact that some of the heroes of Jewish Scriptures, such as Abel, Jacob and Joseph, had also been betrayed by their own kind. At least Clement had got the core of Jesus' message right. 'You see brothers how jealousy and envy resulted in the violence of a brother's murder?'

Come to think of it, it's strange that this letter never made it into the New Testament! Maybe Clement's theme of the betrayal of one brother by another because of envy and ambition was a truth too much to bear.

Rivalry and competition are incredibly motivating qualities. We know that Peter was one of the leading apostles and in John's gospel we see evidence of the tensions between Jesus assemblies that championed one particular apostle over another. In the gospel dedicated to John, the hero, naturally, is John and not Peter. It was John who gained access to the High Priest's house after Jesus was arrested, Peter having denied Jesus three times. It was John who reclined on Jesus' breast at the 'last supper'. John was the only disciple to remain with the women at the foot of the cross when Jesus was suffering the torture of crucifixion. When Peter and John rushed to the empty tomb, who went in first? You guessed right. John. He is even referred to in this gospel as 'the disciple whom Jesus loved', as if he didn't love the other disciples. And to whom did Jesus entrust his mother while dying on the cross? John, who 'took her into his home' (John19.27), treating her like his own mother.

John's gospel was finalized at a time when the new Jewish sect called Christianity (although initially it was called 'The Way') was finally breaking away from its Jewish roots. Its editor was writing under the pressure of being a member of a persecuted sect, a small group under threat and isolated on the margin of religious life: a vulnerable community, getting more and more anxious and neurotic, because of Jesus' non-appearance. John, therefore, had to draw a wedge between his fellow Jews and his own breakaway heretical sect. This meant attacking the Jewish authorities who opposed his spiritual community. This is why, for example, his highly hostile attitude towards the Pharisees is projected back to the time of Jesus. There are over seventy references to Jews in this gospel, most of them negative. Many Pharisees were in fact sensitive to Jesus' message and debated with him. But the rivalry and in-fighting between the two Jewish communities was to become very bitter, especially after the Fall of Jerusalem in 70AD, when Jews were banned from Jerusalem. The Pharisees tried to establish their beliefs as the new orthodoxy. This meant that all other sects, including the Nazarenes (as Christians were also called), had to accept it as the new standard for Judaism or be excluded. The rabbis even cursed the Nazarenes as heretics and asked God to blot them out forever from the Book of Life. In other words, the Nazarenes were to be barred from heaven, just like I was!

In retaliation, John set out to prove to his fellow Jews that Jesus was the new supreme superhero. Even Enoch, always popular in the spiritual hero stakes, paled into insignificance when compared to Jesus. While Enoch may have gone up into heaven, Jesus can go one better, since he actually 'came from heaven' in the first place. 'No one has ever gone up to heaven except the one who came down from heaven, the son of man' (John 3:13).

In fact, one of the theologians responsible for John's gospel (and there were a few of them) came up with one of the most important formulas in the emerging new religion that was to become Christianity. It was he who was responsible for combining two powerful and already famous religious images, in the person of Jesus: A super-angel and a superhero all in one. A being greater than St Michael the Archangel was combined with an earthly hero of the stature of an Abraham or a Moses. Trump that if you can! Constantine did just that, hundreds of years later, when he got his theologians to declare that Jesus was actually much more than that – Jesus was God.

John's gospel also provides a good example of how the early followers of Jesus couldn't resist putting words into his mouth. They did this because they believed that what was true for them must have been true for Jesus. John's community became a closed and exclusive community. Its experience of the *abba* that Jesus had talked about also became closed and exclusive. Even the meaning of the only prayer that Jesus taught was changed. I'll explain. Jesus had no doubt that *abba* was the 'true bread', the real spiritual nourishment from heaven. It was his privilege to proclaim and point to the profound truth that was '*abba* direct'. So John was right to quote Jesus as saying that '*abba* gives you the true bread from heaven' (John 6:32). But for John's community, Jesus had become the unique embodiment of the true bread from heaven. But Jesus had refused to be tied down by any title. So the freedom and humility of Jesus' 'Am I?' in front of the High Priest was reversed. It became instead an arrogant and proud 'I am', as when Jesus is heard to say that 'I am the bread of life' (John 6:35). But Jesus never said those words. No more than he said 'I am the way and the truth and the life. No one comes to *abba* except through me' (John 14:6).

John's church failed to rise above the temptation to claim a monopoly on *abba* and Jesus. It fell into the trap of believing that its interpretation was right and everyone else was wrong. It even believed that, through the act of 'breaking of bread', it had a monopoly on the salvation that *abba* offered freely to everyone.

Jesus is supposed to have said to his disciples,

> I tell you the truth, unless you eat the flesh of the son of man and drink his blood, you will soon be dead. . Whoever eats my flesh and drinks my blood has eternal life, and I will resurrect him at the last day. For my flesh is real food and my blood is real drink (John 6:53-55).

Jesus never said these words. Many New Testament scholars agree with me.

More Warring Brothers (and Sisters!)

Devouring rivalry is still alive and kicking within Ecclesiastical Christianity. Not just among rival sects but within members of the same tradition. Paul's warning is as relevant today as it was nearly two thousand years ago. But no one is listening to his words, and devouring is a cherished Christian character trait by now. He writes:

> The entire law is summed up in one commandment: 'Love your neighbor as yourself'. If you keep on biting and devouring each other, watch out or you will be destroyed by each other (Galatians 5:14-15).

Paul wants every Christian, church leaders included, to 'live by the Spirit' instead of living by ecclesiastical law, which Jesus has already declared null and void. Living by the law is synonymous with living to gratify your own desires. This includes behavior characterized by 'idolatry, hatred, discord, jealousy, fits of rage, selfish ambition, and factions' (Galatians 5: 20-21). A good description of what happens when Church leaders come together, Anglicans included. It's quite a spectacle to behold. The Anglican Communion is an eighty million strong global fellowship of Christians, dominated by rival factions from the beginning. They have coexisted in a spirit of mutual hostility and distrust ever since Henry VIII split from the Church of Rome because he wanted to remarry as well as build-up his finances.

In the fourth century, bishops became orthodox to make sure that they could hang on to their assets! There's a lovely story of a bishop at the time who went in person to Constantinople to ask for imperial backup against the heretics in his diocese. In his absence, the heretics changed their views, became orthodox and grabbed the land, churches and other property under his care! Henry VIII would do something similar. He was excommunicated by the Pope in 1533. With a male heir, Henry could guarantee the survival of the Tudor dynasty. He had to get a divorce to see if a new wife could give him one. With more money, he could also become the most powerful monarch in Europe. The church in England was rich. As head of the church, Henry would have total control over its revenue.

Anglicanism is a church founded on divorce and the love of money, its sovereignty a far cry from the kind of sovereignty that Jesus had envisaged. Henry eventually replaced the Pope as the royal leader of the church in England. His title was a humble one: the 'Supreme Head and Sole Protector of the Church of England'! *Abba* is always a pushover when it comes to real power.

Anglicanism is living proof that divorce does pay; though, a different kind of divorce is now on the cards. Only church politics has kept the factions together these last few years. But that's nothing new. Anglicanism was a political solution from the very start. But to be fair, it has been a beacon for champions of religious tolerance. Anglicanism developed in response to the horrific religious and cultural wars of the sixteenth and seventeenth centuries that saw Europe knee deep in blood. The

English church grew to have a great distrust of ideology and developed a spirit of compromise between Protestants to the left and Roman Catholics to the right. I'm not a total cynic. You won't see me knocking the genuine tolerance that has emerged among many Anglicans, especially in the USA where they are called Episcopalians. Their senior bishop is a woman. But Anglican tolerance is gradually running out because deep down the various factions have never really liked each other. Hypocrites, all of them, and I'll tell you why. Each faction believes that it alone embodies the true spirit of Anglicanism. Each wing sees itself as the true guardians of 'the faith' and the real interpreters of the Bible.

Nothing much changes, does it?

Christians will always find something to argue over and Anglicans are no exception. The words of Emperor Constantine still ring true, when he pointed out that bishops do nothing but that which encourages discord and hatred. The catalyst recently was the consecration in 2003 of an openly gay bishop, Gene Robinson of New Hampshire, USA. There are dozens of homosexual bishops but that's allowed. What's frowned upon is admitting it publicly and therefore not being hypocritical. Hypocrisy always pays in the church. Bishops and archbishops have since been at each other's throats over the whole issue of 'gay leadership'. Gene has become the new scapegoat. A group of married heterosexual men have decided that sexual relations must be reserved for married men and women. Note, *married men and women*. Really? No wonder that the Anglican hierarchy has become a laughing matter worldwide. An irrelevance to many, even within their own ranks. Conservative leaders maintain that too many have 'transgressed the boundaries of traditional morality in defiance of the Bible's authority'. It's therefore up to them to 'defend Biblical principles'. Which ones? I once heard a bishop say that people should be worried about Biblically derived morality, since Christians don't always know what the

Bible means by being moral. I couldn't have put it better myself.

At least we can all agree on one thing. There is a profound crisis of leadership going on in the Anglican Church because there is no one Biblical authority to turn to, except Jesus, and he doesn't appear to get a look in. There are so many different types of bishops and archbishops that it's become a case of 'take your pick' in the leadership stakes. There's a bishop to suit every political persuasion on the planet. In addition to traditional conservatives, you've got moderate conservatives and even traditional traditionalists. On the left wing there are traditional liberals, as well as progressive liberal bishops. I'm sure that somewhere there is a moderately conservative liberal bishop! All claim that theirs is the true and only voice of authentic Anglican identity. In 2007, The Archbishop of Wales, , in a speech that I heard, said that

> Theological change is a fact of life. So is theological innovation. One part of the Church innovates and the rest of the Church eventually catches up.

I shall be watching developments in his church with great interest over the coming years.

Conservative bishops are always threatening to leave the Anglican Communion to start their own splinter group. Or will the majority who don't leave become the splinter group? Who knows? Who cares? Hundreds of the more traditionally inclined bishops served notice a year in advance that, because of the 'gay leadership issue', they would not be attending the once a decade Lambeth Conference in London during the summer of 2008, a shindig for about eight hundred and eighty bishops. About a third threatened to boycott the gathering. They would hold their own meeting in Jerusalem. Not to rival Lambeth, naturally, but to offer an opportunity for fellowship and pastoral care to those staying away from Lambeth.

A couple of weeks before Easter 2008, the Archbishop of Canterbury gave in to African blackmail (sorry, pressure) and informed Bishop Gene that he would not be allowed to take part in Lambeth '08. Bishop Gene would be able to attend the primates' jamboree but with no official status. He must attend as a mere mortal – 'one of you lot'. I think Jesus would have liked that!

The Archbishop of Nigeria won the day. A super Anglican bully-boy, he and his colleagues believe that gays are 'lower than beasts'. There must be some truth in that, because even the Archbishop of Canterbury refused to receive Bishop Gene at Lambeth Palace, his official residence. They had to meet at a secret location instead. The heart of the matter is that Anglican fundamentalist bishops are fighting for control of the Anglican Communion. Think of them as Christian fascists, engaged in an unrelenting spiritual battle that is bitter, vicious, abusive, aggressive and dogmatic.

They are fighting for the soul of Anglicanism after all. Its future must take precedence over *abba* and his justice for the world.

Need I spell out whose side I'm on? I'm right there with the ecclesiastical bully-boys. Dogma has to come first. Since some bishops can't even agree on the so-called 'truth of the Gospel' (the real meaning of what Jesus is all about), let the traditionalists spell it out loud and clear. They know their Bible. They know God's will. They know what is right for the church. That's why it's only right that a narrow stance on sexual morality should dictate all aspects of Christian teaching. That's why, in true High Priestly fashion, Anglican solidarity must be maintained by excluding the outsider. I see nothing wrong in one Anglican bishop suffering in order to keep as great a group as the Anglican Communion together. After all, seven hundred and seventy-nine primates are more important than one. Aren't they?

Your ancestors knew all those millennia ago that the logic of unity is always built on the reality of scapegoating . Anglican leaders know that also. It's in their genes as well. And in their favor, Bishop Gene hasn't been banned or excluded. That would be un-Christian. He just wasn't invited in the first place. Naturally!

The True Church

The Church of Rome doesn't get involved in silly games about who to invite to join its church, because the Church of Rome is the One True Church of Christ.

The problem is that the Orthodox Church also believes itself to be the One True Church of Christ on earth. Someone's telling lies. But at least the Orthodox Church is generous towards Anglicans. It does allow Anglicans to be brothers and sisters 'in the faith', even if they are banned from full membership. How kind. As the poor relations, Anglicans have never claimed to be the One True Church, but are glad to be a part of it, although their church is a more universal and mysterious church, since it embraces all the others, including the Roman Catholic and Orthodox churches. Don't you just love ecclesiastical politics!

And who's in charge of the lot of them? The senior cleric of the Orthodox Church, known as the Ecumenical Patriarch, doesn't claim universal jurisdiction over other churches, but the Pope (or Bishop of Rome or the Western Patriarch, as he is also known) does claim to be the supreme head of Christ's church on earth. His Christian humility is an example to all. Orthodox and Anglican leaders don't claim to be infallible, but the Pope does; though when Anglicans and Roman Catholics come together to discuss church matters, the Romans insist that infallibility is a term applicable only to God. An oracle in his own right, his followers claim that he knows the absolute truth about anything and everything to do with God, salvation and the human condition. Maybe the Pope is God!

Although the number of its priests is still dropping, many

Christians are 're-converting' to Roman Catholicism. Notice the word. People don't 'become' Catholics. They 're-convert', as if they are becoming Christians for the first time. And rightly so, because it is a proper religion after all. 'I beg your pardon!' For Catholics, it is the only true religion. What Jesus has in mind is just a liberal and wishy-washy way of life that transcends all religions. People want something more. They long for something absolute.

In 2007, Tony Blair, the former British Prime Minister, re-converted to membership of the Church of Rome. The London *Sunday Times* (23.12.07) even described it as 'perhaps one of the most high profile conversions since St Paul on the road to Damascus'. With references like that, now that he is a Roman Catholic, Tony Blair is well on the road to sainthood. He can now join with Ann Widdecombe, a British Tory MP and herself a convert, in shouting from the rooftops of the Houses of Parliament 'You have to say out loud: "I believe everything the Church teaches to be revealed truth".'

We shall look in the final chapter at those revealed truths. Meanwhile, at Christmas 2007, the Pope, a true mediaevalist, offered indulgences for pilgrims visiting the shrine at Lourdes. But in true Wal-Mart and Tesco style, it was a limited offer only, available for twelve months from 8 December 2007. For the uninitiated among you, an indulgence is a discount on the time that the souls of the faithful have to spend after death in a place called Purgatory. This is a sort of in-between waiting room before being dispatched to Heaven or Hell. Not that I've ever been there. It hadn't been invented when I was first around.

A senior English Roman Catholic welcomed Tony Blair's conversion and described him as 'such an authoritative personality'. I have it on good authority that after he dies (or maybe even before) Tony Blair is considering a spell as the Pope's special envoy – to Purgatory! He won't of course be meeting any Protestants there since they don't believe in God's, or rather the

Pope's, 'waiting room'. Not that Catholics would mind, since most believe that all Protestants are going straight to hell anyway!

I can't begin to imagine what life would be like without a divided Christendom.

In addition to 'sin' and 'interpretation', do you know what my next two favorite words are? Rivalry and competition.

The British-based *Guardian* newspaper wrote that 'Blair looks to Rome as Catholics outstrip Anglicans in the United Kingdom' (24.12.07). This was in response to statistics that suggested that the Church of Rome was attracting more worshipers than the established Church of England. The Church of England responded by disputing the figures. Naturally!

False Apostles?

I wonder what Paul, the Jewish prophet, visionary and apostle, would make of it all. Unlike me, he would be saddened by the sight of a divided Christendom. And from my knowledge of his 'heretic gospel', he wouldn't pull any punches, any more than he did with those sinful Corinthian Christians all those centuries ago. Here is his two thousand year old message (from 1 Corinthians 3, 4 and 5) as a further warning to the leaders of today's rival churches:

> The last thing I want to do, dear children, is to shame you, but here is my message.. You should know by now that you are God's temple and that God's Spirit lives in you? If anyone destroys God's temple, I warn you, God will destroy him. Don't deceive yourselves any longer and stop this boasting about the religious leaders you follow, whether Paul or Apollos or Peter. Some of you have become arrogant. Stop boasting. Some of you have also become very rich, acting like kings. You lack for nothing.

The differences between the leaders of the apostolic church and the leaders of the numerous sects that comprise Ecclesiastical Christianity couldn't be greater. Paul sums it up like this:

> We are fools for Christ, but you are wise! We are weak, but you are strong! You are honored but we are dishonored! We go hungry and thirsty. We live in rags, and have been brutally treated. We are homeless, working hard with our own hands. We have become the scum of the earth. A laughing stock to the whole universe (1 Cor 4:8-13).

The followers of Jesus have always had a tough time down the centuries from the religious establishment of their day. I even came across Paul's list of the brutal way that he was treated as an apostle. You can't help admiring his courage: a real, live, Hollywood tough guy.

> I have worked much harder than all of you, been in prison more frequently, been flogged more severely, and been exposed to death over and over. Five times I have received the forty lashes minus one. Three times I was beaten with rods, once I was stoned and three times I was shipwrecked. Once I even spent a night and a day in the open sea, cold and naked. I have been in danger from rivers, from bandits, from my own countrymen, from Gentiles and from those who pretended to be my brothers. I have worked so hard that I have often gone without sleep. I also know the hunger and thirst that comes from going without food for days on end. (2 Corinthians 11:23-27).

A Fool for Christ

I wonder if Paul ever realized how much of a fool he was because of his mystical experience of the risen Jesus? The odds were against him from the very start.

He was a Jew, a Pharisee, who converted to an alternative kind of Judaism because he wanted to include Gentiles in the Endtime community. Critical though he was of his own religion, as all the prophets had been, it was never the case of getting rid of Israel but rather of finding ways of including non-Jews in the soon-to-come-events of the last days of planet earth. The vision of Jesus was the catalyst and the proof that the countdown was well underway. In light so brilliant that it blinded him, Paul had a vision of the Just One, the Suffering Servant in the Book of Isaiah, but with one big difference. Because of his resurrection, Jesus had already come through the Endtime trials of suffering and death, and had entered into Glory.

Paul compares his experience of the risen Jesus to the vision of the 'son of man' in the Book of Daniel, which had similarities with the figure in the book of the prophet Ezekiel. In Paul's opinion, Jesus was the man that Ezekiel saw.

> There came a voice from heaven, and high above on the throne I saw a figure like that of a man. He was on fire and looked like a piece of glowing metal. A brilliant light surrounded him. It was like the appearance of a rainbow in the clouds on a rainy day. He was so radiant that his appearance reminded me of the Glory of the Lord. When I saw it, I fell down on my face and heard a voice speaking (Ezekiel 1:25-28).

But Paul was an outsider and a heretic, so why listen to his interpretation more than anyone else? Because he, like Jesus, also drew from the religion of the First Temple in Jerusalem, the orthodoxy of its day. But as is always the case with religious movements, one man's orthodoxy is another man's heresy. By the time of Jesus, the Jewish rabbis had long banned aspects of first temple spirituality and it went underground. One strand of it was to reappear among Jewish heretics as a mystical system called Kabala. The other offshoot developed into Christianity. Think about it: within a generation or so of Jesus' non-appearance, Christian theology was already a sophisticated belief-system. It didn't just pop out of the blue! Its core beliefs had been around for centuries. Christianity is really an old Jewish heresy in a new suit. The Biblical scholar, Margaret Barker, puts it succinctly in these straightforward yet profound words:

> How was it that Christian theology grew so quickly into a complex system, if the greater part of that system had not existed within the Judaism from which it grew?... The first Christians fitted Jesus into an existing pattern of belief, so much of the scheme already existed (Margaret Barker, *The Great Angel*, p280, p2).

At the heart of this 'old time religion' was the belief that there are two key powers in heaven and not one. The senior one, if you like, was El Elyon or the Most High One. Having once created the world, he became so distant that few had anything to do with him. El Elyon, however, had many sons whose job it was to look after the nations of the world. Originally, I was also a son, but my role, as you know, was of a more international nature. A god called Yhwh, or Jehovah, was the Holy One in charge of Israel. He was the second power broker in the system. Each god had his own bit of territory, and was duty-bound to protect it by taking revenge on his people's enemies. I explained at the start of my book that this second God often manifested himself in the High Priest, King or Judge. I even found a verse in the Book of Psalms, which was part of Jesus' Bible, which contains these very Christian sounding words. God addresses his king, saying,

> You are my son, today I have become your Father (Psalm 2:7).

But some believed that Yhwh or God had another kind of second-in-command. A sort of 'mini, mini-Me!' A heavenly being known as The Great Angel. The most popular angelic go-between, one of its first appearances was to prepare the way as God's people entered the Promised Land. This angel not only embodied God in a human form but also looked after or carried God's name. This was a task reserved for the elite few. So intimate was this angel with God that it came to be known as 'the one who stands behind the (heavenly) throne'. It clearly shared God's sovereignty in a unique way. The Great Angel became so popular a mediator that the rabbis had to stress the fact that this second power was in no way equal to God and should not be worshipped – a message mirrored by early Christian leaders. For example, when the Letter to the Hebrews was written, fifty years after Jesus died, the author had to point out that, while angels had a key role to play, Jesus as God's son was 'as much superior to the angels as the name he has inherited is superior to theirs' (Hebrews1:4).

My investigative skills had come up with an astounding discovery. Centuries before the coming of Christianity, there were Jews who believed that there were two powers in heaven. While others, in acknowledging the existence of the Most High One, in addition to Yhwh and the Great Angel, were clearly devoted to a trinity of heavenly powers. Competing powers, angelic go-betweens, heavenly in-fighting – it's no wonder that some of the early Christian writers got confused with who was actually who! Similar, I suppose, to Christians today and their own private devotions. Some of them may pay lip service to the doctrine of the Holy Trinity, but don't ask them to explain it. Some are happy with God the Father, while for others Jesus is God. For many of the faithful, the Holy Spirit is their God. The first Christians may have called Jesus 'Lord', the most popular name for God. But which one were they referring to? When the Angel Gabriel (not the Great Angel, I should add) appeared to Mary to tell her about Jesus' impending birth, we are told that

Mary was greatly troubled. Wouldn't you be if a heavenly being suddenly appeared in front of you? 'The Lord is with you,' he said (Luke 1:28). But which one? 'He will be great and will be called the Son of El Elyon, the Most High One' (1:32). What is it with religious people and the obsession with the highest and the 'greats'?

For some of the early Christians, Jesus wasn't the son of El Elyon, but the son of Yhwh, the nationalistic God of Israel. For others, like John, he was the pagan Logos or Blueprint that kept the whole universe together. See what I mean about confusing! But all these are part of the Sacred Order of things, with its good and evil, highs and lows, 'Greats' and not-so-greats, Satan's world and God's world.

So who's right? Jesus. After all, he is the Great Heretic. There, you've got me at it now! Don't complicate matters. Listen to him, for God's sake! That's what my book is all about. I'm fed up with all this confusion about gods and lords and my place in the great scheme of things. Jesus made it quite clear that the mysterious *abba* was the source and origin of his life and no one else. His purpose was to help bring about *abba*'s sovereignty on earth. When you pray, Jesus said that everyone must ask *abba* that 'his kingdom come' on earth (Matthew 6:10).

While Paul never managed to fully break free from his allegiance to his nation Israel, and its God of Wrath, he did grasp, if only fleetingly, the truth that *abba* and his sovereignty were different from anything that he had ever experienced before in his life. Spiritual maturity for Paul means being in touch with *abba* direct and not with 'weak and miserable principles' that come from outside the individual, however sacred they may be. Individuals know *abba* because *abba* encounters them, and gets to know them first within the mystery of the human heart. Paul calls it becoming 'sons of God', and 'because you are sons, *abba* sent the Spirit of his Son into our hearts, the Spirit who calls out, "*abba*"' (Galatians 4:6).

Jesus had dismantled his religious and national heritage in one fell swoop, at least in theory. In Paul's hands *abba*-direct also ripped through the sacred traditions of the faithful like a whirlwind. Remember how crucial being pure was for John the Baptist and Jesus? Being-put-right with God in readiness for the Endtime and its judgment. Paul became convinced that pagans could join his fellow Jews and that both could together be 'put right' with *abba*, but only by totally abandoning every aspect of their respective religions. But how? He searched his Scriptures and found the answer. The key to salvation was simple. Total faith or trust. Nothing else is required, whether it is to do with festivals and ceremonies, angels or religious heroes. In 600BC, the prophet Habakkuk (2:4) had prophesied that 'there will come a time when the righteous will live by faith'.

That time has arrived.

'Glory! Glory! Hallelujah'

But even more importantly, Paul found out that one of the founding fathers of Israel, Abraham the patriarch, who wasn't even Jewish, had already believed or trusted in God centuries before, which meant that he was 'credited with being righteous' (Genesis 15:6). Abraham was deemed to be pure and just, although he had kept none of the sacred Jewish religious laws and customs. If it was good enough for one of the 'Greats', it was good enough for every other human being on the planet. Having faith is all that is required. But for Paul, it had to be faith in Jesus, or Christ, as he called him, and no one else.

As the Endtime approached, a one-off initiation into Jesus by being immersed, or baptized into his suffering and death, meant that you were ready to join the new humanity, a more spiritual breed of *Homo sapiens*. One word summed-up this transformation: Glory. It was the sign that a person's salvation was well and truly underway. 'Glory! Glory! Hallelujah!' In the past it had only been the ultra-faithful heroes like Moses who had the privilege of being part of God's Glory. So traumatic was the experience that, when he came down from Mount Sinai, Moses' face radiated with the Glory. Some, like Enoch, were transformed into angelic-like beings as a reward for being good. According to the Book of Daniel, they would 'shine like the stars' forever, the original 'twinkle, twinkle, little star'! In fact,

> Multitudes who have died will wake up; some to eternal life, others to shame and eternal contempt. Those who are wise will shine like the brightness of the heavens, and those who lead many to righteousness will shine like the stars for eternity. (Daniel 12:2-3).

But it wasn't just the chosen few who had a share in the all-encompassing Glory.

Paul democratized the divine Glory. As long as you had faith in Jesus, no matter what your background, you were greater than Moses. He had to cover his face after his mystical experience lest he blind others with his radiance. Not so Christians, since 'we, who with faces unveiled all reflect our Lord's glory, are being changed into his likeness with every increasing glory' (2 Corinthians 3:18).

It was an attractive invitation for people living their lives in those anxious days as the Endtime came nearer and nearer. Most of you have bought expensive goods that offer a guarantee should anything go wrong. That is what the spirit of Jesus is all about. A deposit guaranteeing your heavenly inheritance until the End finally comes. A safe, if albeit, painful passage through the Endtime trials. The logic was comforting. Indeed seductive. A Christian suffering for the sake of God's justice and truth is actually suffering as Christ did. Fighting the evil in the world is an integral part of one's glorification. Though life will end in death, dying as Christ did means being resurrected as he was, and having more of a share of God's glory as you go on to join the rest of God's true people in heaven.

Paul's creed was a simple one, so unlike the complicated creeds that Christians would later come up with. It states that

> The same Lord is Lord of all and pours his rich spiritual blessings on all who call upon him. For everyone who calls upon the Name of the Lord will be saved (Romans 10:12-13).

The message is also universal. All distinctions disappear, since 'there is neither Jew nor Greek, slave nor free, male nor female, for you are all one in Christ Jesus' (Galatians 3:28). Since every human being in the world has fallen short of the standards set by God, all can make a clean start as brand new individuals or 'new creations' in Jesus. Unity is the goal. Past discords can be overcome. This can only be achieved if Jew and Gentile alike abandon their religious customs and cultural differences. In other words, they must surrender their very identities for the sake of the Endtime Community. Paul had already done so. Others should learn from his example. Easier said than done! Just look at Anglicans today. Paul was convinced that a person's history and ancestry didn't matter anymore. Try telling that today to a Roman Catholic, a Lutheran Christian or an African Anglican! Jews and Gentiles coming together meant that they would have to interact socially in new ways together. For a Jew, this meant destroying the boundaries set up by the Law of Moses, ignoring the laws that were mandatory for all who would stay pure for God. Everything had to be abandoned as you waited for The End.

The Council of Jerusalem

Meanwhile, practical differences had to be hammered out, so in 50AD Paul set off for Jerusalem in order that the two wings of the young Jesus Movement could meet face to face. It was here that the bitterest quarrels came to a head. This wasn't a case of in-fighting among Jews, most of whom, to this day, have no interest in Jesus. It was in-fighting among Jews and Gentiles who both claimed to follow Jesus: early believers who were convinced that their interpretation was the right one. Does that ring a bell? The issue of circumcision was the catalyst, not openly gay bishops, and it had reared its ugly head at Antioch a few years earlier. Jewish Christians had been stirring things up by arguing that Gentile Christians could only be saved if they followed the Jewish law and became Jews first, i.e. by being circumcised. But Abraham was uncircumcised!

The debate was ferocious. In one corner you had the traditionalist faction, which insisted that non-Jews had to obey the law in relation to circumcision and dietary customs; animals had to be killed in such a way that blood drains from their bodies completely before the meat is cooked; food that pagans offered to idols could not be eaten by Jews, which meant that followers of Jesus were not allowed to share hospitality in each others' homes; Sabbath was the weekly holy day and not Sunday. Paul represented the alternative camp, arguing for a broader view of salvation, while James presided over the negotiations. A temporary compromise was agreed upon. The Gentiles didn't have to be circumcised, and more flexible food laws were introduced. In the long term, however, a parting of the ways was inevitable.

It's ironic really. Paul saw himself as the great reconciler and yet his approach turned out to be divisive! His experience of Jesus was so decisive that it enabled him to turn his back on his religious principles and customs in the most radical way possible. Devout Jews to this day rightly feel insulted when they read that

> Before faith came along, we were held prisoners by the Jewish Law, trapped until faith in Jesus could be revealed. Now that faith in Jesus has come, we no longer need the supervision of the Law (Galatians 3:23-25).

Paul may have been an apostle to the Gentiles but to the Jews he was an apostate, guilty of leading Jews astray from their faith. Paul was an apostate apostle! There was nothing novel in saying that the Gentiles could be saved. The rabbis already taught that righteous or just individuals among the nations had a place in the world to come. You didn't have to become Jewish to be saved, just as you don't have to become a priest to be holy. But Paul had to take it a step further. He believed that Jesus wanted him to create a single community out of the warring ones, since…

> …his purpose was to establish peace by creating in himself one new person out of the two:, and in this one body to reconcile both of them to abba through the cross, by which he destroyed once and for always the bitter dividing wall of hostility between them. (Ephesians 2:14-16).

But dividing walls are a normal part of group life and identity. There's nothing hostile about them. Surely Paul must have realized this. His 'ministry of reconciliation' proved to be a failure on every front. Jewish Christians remained just that, 'Jewish Christians', a sect separate to Gentile Christians. Much as I admire Paul, it wasn't long before he was calling his own faith brothers extremists, dogs (the contemporary equivalent of scum) and false apostles.

> Deceivers , masquerading as apostles of Christ. And no wonder, for Satan himself masquerades as an angel of light. It is not surprising, then, if his servants also masquerade as servants of righteousness (2 Corinthians 11:13-15).

Christianity became the very thing that Paul had tried his best to avoid all along, an alternative third grouping alongside Judaism and paganism that eventually became a religion. Paul, who remained a Jew all his life, never found it easy to even label this new community. More often than not, he simply talked about being 'in Christ' or being 'a new creation' instead of being a member of a new religion.

Paul also believed in the equality of believers, since everyone shared the same status and identity in the new Endtime Community. There was no talk of being part of a hierarchy. Believers had received the same baptism, the great leveler, and consequently the only label Paul envisaged was that of brothers and sisters 'in Christ'. But church hierarchy was to kill the spirit of Jesus. Furthermore, it was a family made up of ordinary individuals who were already in the process of being transformed into spiritual beings. That's why there was no longer any need for earthly hierarchies, including priestly ones, served as they are by myths, rituals and the law. He challenged Jesus' followers in Rome with the words, 'Do not conform any longer to the pattern of this world, but be transformed by the renewing of your mind' (Romans 12:2). That mental transformation never did take place. Worldly habits and rivalries continue to guide people's lives.

As a new and largely Gentile religion, Christians did the very thing that Paul dreaded them doing. They became arrogant in their attitude towards the Jews, who, in their opinion, had forfeited their right to be called God's People by rejecting Jesus. But Paul believed that his fellow countrymen would also be saved at The Endtime eleventh hour.

> I don't want you to be ignorant of this mystery, and I don't want you to be conceited. Israel is experiencing a stubborn period in her history, until the Gentiles are gathered in. Once that happens, all of Israel will be saved (Romans 11:25-26).

Saved, that is, by following Paul's way! But Israel wasn't saved 'in Christ'. Israel had its own salvation. Pagans continued with their practices. They too had their own spiritual paths. And Paul, for all his attempts at hammering out a new theology, had to turn for guidance in The End to the wisdom of the past. He couldn't resolve the contradictions in his faith, so unlike Ecclesiastical Christianity, he had to admit that he didn't have all the answers. When Isaiah II of Jerusalem went through a similar experience, he came up with these humbling words:

> For my thoughts are as different to your thoughts, as are your ways to my ways says the Lord. 'As the heavens are higher than the earth so are my ways higher than your ways, and my thoughts higher than your thoughts' (Isaiah 55:8-9)

Half a millennia later, Paul had to acknowledge the limitations of human knowledge when faced with the mystery that is *abba. He probably adapted an existing popular Hymn to Wisdom, when he declared that*

> *Since God's Wisdom and Knowledge are so mysterious and deep,*
> *can anyone really claim to know his mind? Who would dare to offer him advice? Or even attempt to understand his decisions? For everything*
> *in creation has been made by him and for him. This is why the Divine*
> *Glory belongs eternally to him and him alone. (Romans 11:33-34)*

Theology from now on is nothing more than a tinkering with the Mystery. In fact, some of the Christian thinkers that followed Paul were loath to reduce the mystery that is *abba* to any system of human thought. They insisted that *abba* is absolutely incomprehensible and ultimately unknowable by concepts, but can still be experienced when approached with a humble heart or spirit. But Jesus had already said that hundreds of years before, when he said that 'Blessed are the pure in heart, for they will see *abba*' (Matthew 5:8). And Isaiah III had quoted similar words nearly five hundred years before, when he too was struggling to understand the reality that was beyond all human understanding:

> This is what the Eternal, Transcendent and Holy One says,: 'I live not only in the highest heavens but also with those who are humble and sincere in spirit. I revive the spirit of those who are humble and restore the heart of those who have repented. ' (Isaiah 57:15).

Finally, Paul wanted *abba* to have the last word, his love to be the final authority. And he expresses it beautifully, even if you don't believe a word of it, in his famous Hymn to Love in the first Letter to the Corinthians. The kind of love that never behaves in a self-centered manner. Paul cannot stop singing the praises of the kind of love that is patient, kind and never given to jealousy. Love that is never angry nor boastful, never proud nor rude. Love that never keeps a list of wrongs. The love that 'delights in the truth'. The kind of love that never fails because it always trusts, always hopes and always sticks at it to the end. Paul believed that faith, hope and love will last for ever, although, if he had to choose, the greatest of the three is love (1 Corinthians 13:4-8,13).

But love never has the last word in any religion. There is a higher authority – Dogma. Love dies when dogma dictates your dealings with the divine. And with the death of love, suspicion returns to spread mistrust and intolerance.

Members of the same Christian sects can't even agree among themselves, not to mention the followers of different religions! This is why I delight in the truth that there will never be peace. Mutual suspicion will always prevail when one person or group sets itself up as God's favorites with their religious superhero as king pin. This is why I'm enjoying my *satanical*, confident that my kingdom is flourishing, as religious devotees argue amongst themselves and the defenders of Christian dogma continue to defy *abba*.

The Heretics' Gospel

Jesus wanted to create a new type of community: one that would totally reverse all traditional forms of institutional life; a community that would negate everything to do with power and the 'wielding of authority'. Jesus' Endtime gathering is not a sect or grouping of any kind. It is an open society, based on the ethos of voluntary membership. Anything else is a betrayal of his gospel.

Jesus believed that he had found the key to human life. He was able to extricate its true meaning from the mass of contradictions and delusions called theology. It would have been so much easier if everyone had listened to what Jesus had to say about *abba*. After all, dear friends, the equation is a simple one. It's not rocket science, namely *abba*-direct = peace-direct. All those centuries ago, Isaiah II had looked forward to '*abba*-times' when 'all your sons and daughters will be taught by the Lord and peace will be your children's peace. Tyranny will be far from you, and you will have nothing to fear. Terror will be far removed; it will not come near you' (Isaiah 54:13-1). I find the whole situation highly amusing. I assume that all of you want a peaceful life for your children, and your children's children. That social harmony, that only comes from the truth deep within each person. So listen to the heretics, if you've got the guts! With the gift of immaculate perception, heretics regularly appear to remind humans that the truth at the heart of all religions can never be contained within any one religion or spiritual path and yet they are regularly ignored, vilified and abused. Imagine how different a world it would be if everyone listened to them. I'm glad they don't.

I have a grudging admiration for heretics. I enjoy the hassle they cause the religious status quo and yet I also enjoy the entertainment when the establishment goes gunning for them, as with Jesus of Galilee. One of my favorite European heretics is a German called Jacob Boehme. He was born in 1575, the son of poor country folks. As a young man, he helped his parents look after the family cattle. He was apprenticed to a shoemaker after learning to read and write. He later left that trade and opened a yarn shop. A true entrepreneur, towards the end of his life he could be seen in Prague selling woolen gloves.

From a young age, he was able to enter into higher states of consciousness and see visions that he believed came from the Spirit. He called his mystical insights 'divine illuminations'. He led a simple and disciplined life of prayer and Bible study. But there was nothing simple about his spiritual creativity. Between 1612 and 1624, Boehme wrote thirty books about God, Jesus, angels, the meaning of life, the cosmos and everything. It was this that brought him into conflict with the narrow-minded clergy of his day. His free and independent spirit was too much of a threat to their authority. How dare a poor shoemaker, who had married a butcher's daughter, speak of things no human should presume to know? God had, after all, placed his sacred powers and wisdom into their safekeeping as official spokesmen for him. His heretical words about Jesus and the church are as true and fresh today as they were nearly 400 years ago:

> The theologians and Christian sectarians keep on continually disputing about the letter and form, while they care nothing for the Spirit, without which the form is empty and the letter dead. Each one imagines that he has the truth in his keeping and wants to be admired by the world as a keeper of the truth. Therefore they denounce and slander and backbite each other, and thus they act against the first principle taught by Christ and which is brotherly love. Thus the Church of Christ has become a bazaar where vanities are exhibited, and as the Israelites danced around the golden calf, so the modern Christians dance around their self-contained fetishes, whom they call God.

Boehme sums up the true spirit of Jesus with these words:

> The true Christian does not cling to any particular sect. He may participate in the ceremonial service of every sect and still belong to none. He has only one science, which is Christ within him. He has only one desire, namely to do good. Look at the flowers of the field. Each one has its own particular attributes, nevertheless they do not quarrel about the possession of sunshine and rain, or dispute about their color, odor and taste. Each one grows according to its nature. Thus it is with the children of God. Each one has his own gifts and attributes, but they all spring from one Spirit. They enjoy their gifts and praise the wisdom of Him from whom they originated. Why should they dispute about the qualities of Him whose attributes are manifest in themselves?
>
> We have only one single order to which we belong, and the only role of that Order is to do the Will of God, that is to say, to keep still and serve as instruments through which God may do His Will. Therefore let each one be glad of his own gifts and enjoy those of others. Why should all be alike? Who condemns the birds of the forest because they do not all sing the same tune; but each praises its Creator in its own way? Nevertheless, the power which enables them to sing originates in all from only one source (Personal Christianity: *The Doctrine of Jacob Boehme* p23-24).

Ecclesiastical Christianity emerged out of the death-throes of the Roman Empire, with Christ as its grim taskmaster, and the Church his body: the spiritual vampire par excellence, the destroyer of the world, sucking the lifeblood out of humanity in order to keep itself alive. Christianity will always love its idols and myths. It will never let *abba*-direct hold sway over it. And why should it? *Abba*-direct is the end of all empires, including Christian ones. I have no doubt that Ecclesiastical Christianity will defend the obsolete and dying institution that it is to The End! And should Jesus appear again, to try and distribute *abba*'s heavenly bread once more, I wonder how the great and the good will get rid of him second time round?

Jesus knew from the start what men would do to *abba*'s sovereignty. This is why he said, 'from the days of John the Baptist until now, the kingdom of heaven has been advancing with strength and violent men seek to lay hold on it' (Matthew 11:12).

With God's authority on their side, a group of men exist who has authority to specify and control the limits of *abba*'s love and mercy. A group empowered to say how far *abba*'s love can go. My kind of men! My kind of group! Your kind?

Chapter Five

Teach Your Children Well

The boy nodded meekly as his mother continued without pausing for breath.

'You are controlled not by the sinful nature but by the Spirit, if the Spirit of God lives in you.'

'Does the Spirit of God live in you, Daniel?' his father asked. The boy was silent for a moment then nodded. 'Are you sure boy?'

'I'm sure, Father.' It came out as a frightened squeak.

'You want to please God, boy?'

'Yes, Father, I want to please God.' The boy knew the answers that were expected, knew the only way to get peace, to avoid another slap, to avoid being thrashed or locked in the unheated shed in the garden all night. He nodded, and gave a weakly mouthed 'Yes.'

'You want the Spirit to be living in you, boy, or do you want eternal damnation?' his father said. 'And you want to be one of God's children, don't you boy? Not one of Satan's?'

'God's children,' the boy mouthed.

'Do you want us to save you from the Lord's wrath, boy?' His father asked again. 'Are you sure you wouldn't rather enjoin with Satan? Suffer the eternal fires of damnation in Hell?'

Peter James, *Alchemist* – p.32, 33

Bloody God!

There's one major issue that Jesus and I totally agree on. We both love sinners. And for all their failings, God's people of old did become aware of their predicament as serial sinners. They hated being impure in relation to God. It was an insult to his holiness. And an insulted God is an angry God. And, bloody hell, when he gets angry, he's not one to be messed with. This is the prayer of the prophet Habakkuk, to his God, a Rambo-like Sovereign, Lord and Savior:

> Plague and pestilence are your companions. You stand and shake the earth to its very core. Your look is enough to make the nations crumble. Mountains disintegrate before you and you ride the sea on your mighty chariots. You uncover your bow, letting loose your many arrows. In wrath you march through the earth and in your anger you beat the nations. You crushed the leader of wickedness, and stripped him of his armor. With his own spear you stabbed him in his head (from Habakkuk 3).

See what I mean? You wouldn't want to mess with that type of God! This is why there were sacrifices to say thank you to God for gifts like good weather, fertility and food. There were sacrifices to say sorry for continually breaking God's laws. But finally, and most important of all, there were temple sacrifices to keep God sweet: to placate him and thus make sure you stayed in his Good Book. Just imagine! The normal way of keeping God happy was acts of sacred violence against innocent creatures. Thousands upon thousands of animals were slaughtered to gain the forgiveness of sins. How perverse! Ah well, each to their own! And why blood? In all ancient societies blood was the ultimate symbol of life, the most precious of gifts. Nothing but the best for God – liquid gold. God has an insatiable appetite for blood. As I do. I feed on it. But let me make one thing clear. No one can accuse me of being angry with human beings. I love your sinning too much to be angry with you. I need you too much, your sinning and your blood. I am truly grateful for the gifts of human lives received throughout history. The millions of bodies sacrificed in the name of your rival Gods. Keep them coming!

Before the irreligious among you switch off, in the belief that talk of sacrifices has nothing to do with modern secular society, let me put you right. All ancient societies were religious, not just the one that Jesus belonged to. The cult of sacrifice to a god or goddess was the supreme act of worship in every ancient society. Sacrifices are in your blood, all of you alive today, no matter what your color, creed or convictions. Sacrifice was the ultimate ritualistic act; its clinical and controlled re-enactment of that first killing, the source of all human theatre.

But sacrifice is only a third of the story – your story. Sacrifice in only part of the threefold structure on which the whole of human culture and civilization is built.

We've already looked at the first building block, the *Do's and Don'ts,* the prohibitions that try and control the chaos that is *Homo sapiens.* I came across this passage in Jesus' Bible. It sounds very contemporary, with its classical summary of God's offer of life or death:

> Now what I am commanding you today is not too difficult for you or beyond your reach. It is not up in heaven neither is it beyond the sea. No, the word is very near you; it is in your mouth and in your heart so that you may obey it. Today I call heaven and earth as witnesses, that I have given you the choice between life and death, blessings and curses. So choose life, that you and your children may live, and that you may love the Lord your God (Deuteronomy 30:11-14, 19-20).

Teach your children well. Now do you see where Jesus' idealism came from? 'Not too difficult for you or beyond your reach'. *Not too difficult*! He got that one wrong. I'm not being negative but your record as human beings speaks for itself.

A life full of blessings is way beyond your reach. *Homo sapiens* is a kind of disease and a dangerous one at that… contagious. Conflict is a fact of life. Laws emerged as an exercise in damage limitation, because a life of peace and harmony will always be 'beyond your reach'.

I've also mentioned another 's' word a great deal in my book, as if 'sacrifice' wasn't enough to be getting on with! 'Scapegoating' isn't your everyday kind of word either! It also takes a bit of getting used to. Like sacrifice, it may sound very primitive, but scapegoating is as relevant today as it ever was.

The Monster Within

I so admire the skill with which you maintain your public façade or persona. There's a monster in all of you, although you like to pretend otherwise. Pretending has become the basis of civilized life, a necessity for all of us, myself included. Many of you are 'all sweetness and light' at home. A good phrase that. You can almost choke on it. But in public you are all power mad junkies, who pretend to be human, as you make life hell for as many as you can. Bloody hypocrites! I've given up counting the number of times I've heard someone say 'congratulations' when all the time they feel like vomiting, or 'love it' when, beyond the smiles, all you want to do is scratch her eyes out because her dress is smarter than yours! *Dr Jekyll and Mr Hyde* isn't the exception; it's the norm, an important part of your mental landscape, a survival mechanism, depending on where you are and whom you are with; an asset to help you cope with a rapidly changing and uncertain world. Your ancestors survived thanks to the part played by innocent victims in helping them bond together.

Human institutions gradually emerged, as culture began to develop from the regular need for ritual sacrifices and the 'industry' that grew up to support it. There would be no 'civilization' without the first funeral rites and places set apart to honor the dead. Animals had to be captured and domesticated not just for physical food but also for spiritual benefits. The collective hunt became an opportunity for perfecting skills that would also come in handy in killing humans.

Scapegoating also resulted in hierarchies, since it soon became apparent that some individuals were of more value than others.

Strange that such a violent and vicious act as scapegoating should help you to start moralizing!

Leaders emerged who had to be experts at blurring the distinction between truth and falsehood. After the first few killings, all cruel actions from then on were presented as a force for good. A response to God's will. Truth always takes second place to the clinical manipulation and use of power.

Words came into their own as myth became the third pillar, or foundation, of human culture, along with ritual sacrifice and prohibitions. Myths are stories that contain deep truths about the dynamics of human history. They developed in order to retell, in a dramatic way, the story of the first murder, presenting the original killing as a creative human act. Myths eventually became a safer way of reproducing the powerfully creative dynamics of the early period in human development. Rooted in human violence, myths always have monsters in them.

To this day, all tribes, religions, and nation-states have many communal and dramatic way of recharging and reinforcing their cultural identities. Sporting occasions, singing national anthems and 'rumors of wars', the prelude to the persecution of victims, are always popular. But nothing beats the ritual re-enactments of the modern theatre, the respectable and civilized way of transcending your immediate identities, in order to reconnect with your more primitive selves. I blame the Scottish writer, Robert L. Stevenson, for popularizing such a sensitive subject as 'the monster within'. Born in Edinburgh in 1850, he struggled as a boy with the strong puritanical influence of his nurse, who was a strict Presbyterian Christian. Suspicious of anything to do with sensuality and pleasure, her faith was dominated by the fear of hell-fire. Stevenson grew up to be revolted by the hypocrisy of Victorian society. I love one of his early poems where he mocks respectable religious folk, and goes on to say that he enjoys the company of 'publicans and harlots'. Just as I do!

Like many of you, Stevenson struggled with the challenge of how to reconcile the devilish monster that is part of everyone's makeup, including his own. His revulsion with Christian double standards found an outlet in a novel that is still one of the most popular in Western literature, *Dr Jekyll and Mr Hyde.* Dr Jekyll tries to transfer his 'sinful side' into another body but it simply engenders more evil. I like the way that Jesus describes the dynamics:

> When an evil spirit comes out of a man, it goes through dry and dusty places looking for somewhere to rest, but finds nowhere. Then it says, 'I will return to the house I left'. When it arrives, it finds the house swept clean and everything nice and tidy. Then it goes and takes seven other spirits more evil than itself, and they go in and live there. And the final condition of that man is far worse than the first (Luke 11:24-25).

In Stevenson's book, Poole the butler is quoted as saying that, on one occasion, he heard Mr Hyde 'weeping like a woman or a lost soul'. What a pity! Dr Jekyll even confesses at the end of the book that 'man is not truly one but truly two'.

Plagued by sexual hang-ups, Paul the apostle didn't write any novels on the subject, but he was equally as honest when writing about the struggles between his good self and his satanic self. The following passage appears in his Letter to the Romans. I bet he never imagined that his soul would still be laid bare two thousand years on, in what has become a classical summary of the neurosis that is an integral part of you all.

> I want to do what is good but I'm too weak to carry it out. For what I do isn't the good I want to do. No. It's the evil that I don't want to do that gets the better of me. And I keep on doing it. But if I do what I don't want to do, I'm not really to

> blame. It's the fault of the sin that's inside me (Romans 7:16-24).

At least Paul wasn't a hypocrite, even if he was a heretic. I admire him for doing his best to avoid accepting responsibility for his actions. He blamed his 'members'! I wonder which body part he was talking about? 'Judge not!' Well, maybe just a little. Paul continues,

> I am a miserable failure of a man.. When I want to do good, evil is always there beside me. In my inner self I honor God's law, but I see another law at work in certain 'members of my body', making me a prisoner of the law of sin working within me. Who will rescue me from this 'body of death?'

Most of you are unaware of the fact that you need rescuing. Like your ancestors, you're happy with your lot. As soon as they were able to read and write, the ancestral elite started producing literature which mystified and fooled the masses about the real origins of human society. It was a more cultured way of making sense of life's ruthlessness, its injustices and brutalities. Honor, decency, courage and mercy have their place in myths, but pride, conceit, hatred, lies, theft and revenge feature also in the list of human virtues celebrated by them. Pride of place, however, goes to sovereign instinct, the human drive for sex, survival and death, all of them served by violence in one form or another.

Your heroes are not heroes because they are decent, kind and good men. Your heroes are heroes because they are always ready to do whatever has to be done to get what they want. Nothing and no one will stop heroes from achieving their goals. Christians also have myths. Their heroes may wield the sword but they also have the power of a surprisingly subtle and highly effective weapon of 'disciplinary technology' on their side. I refer to the cross, my ideal instrument for submission and control.

Religious or secular, you've all become experts at justifying yourselves, always able to come up with good and exalted purposes to strive for. Religious truth and national purity are among my favorite goals, yours also. Producing 'high culture' is another one. I enjoy watching the way you demonize your children's innocent video games, when adult movies, television and theatre is full of sex and violence. Children have to learn at a young age how to cope with the contradiction that is *Homo sapiens*. That's why a child's version of the story of the Minotaur always presents the beast as pure evil, half-bull and half-man. But the Spanish painter Picasso inverts that idea in his painting of the Minotaur's death. He wants his audience to share the beast's pain and so see him for the first time as human as well as monstrous.

Harrison Birtwistle's opera, *The Minotaur*, which premiered in London during spring 2008, also highlights the human half of the monster. It's ironic, that it's only by looking into the eyes of the beast that you find the humanity of the creature. There is nothing inferior in the minotaur's animal nature. Animal skin and human flesh belong together. In fact, you can't tell one from the other. What is more, lust and rage, death and darkness, are part and parcel of today's civilized behavior.

I'm sure that many of you have your favorite myths. The myth of the Minotaur is a favorite of mine. It tells the story of the hybrid offspring of the intercourse between a great bull and Pasiphae, wife of Minos, King of Crete. The king offends the Greek sea god Poseidon by refusing to sacrifice (what else!) a bull that emerges as a godsend from the sea. Minos' regal wife ends up succumbing to the bull's erotic energy and falls in love with him. The Minotaur is the shocking result of her unnatural lust. Forever driven by burning rage and lust, the monster has to be hidden away in an underground labyrinth where he survives on a diet of innocent Athenian virgin boys and girls, after he has first raped and murdered them. Vultures feast on their remains. Great bedtime reading for children this! Ariadne, the monster's half-sister, has no pity, as the innocents are regularly torn from limb to limb and sacrificed to satisfy her half-brother's cruel appetites. It's to stop the drain on young Athenian lives that the hero Theseus arrives at the island. He succeeds in killing the bull, who turns out to be his half-brother, but only with the help of Ariadne, the monster's half-sister. Both fall in love, or is it lust, with each other? Incest always lurks in the shadows of ancient myths. Theseus is able to get in and out of the underground cave safely, by hanging onto Ariadne's scarlet ball of thread, on the understanding that he helps her escape from Crete in return. Both manage to escape from the island, though Ariadne doesn't stay with her hero. She manages to escape her dependence from him but only by becoming the partner of the god Dionysus instead.

Running away is an integral part of being human, whether it is from yourselves or from places connected with your deformed or monstrous sides. Myths always help you to come to terms with, and thus celebrate, your contradictions. Human passions will always bring out the animal in you, so learn to cope with it! Furthermore, what keeps you safe and secure will eventually imprison you, whether it is of a heavenly or earthly origin. It makes no difference. Few manage to break free. You will always be dependent on dogmas that enshrine your most valued beliefs, whether they are secular or religious. Dogmas invariably become demonic in the end. The demonic doesn't half produce some good theatre!

Jesus and I both want you to stop running away from yourselves. I want human beings to be courageous enough not only to be able to look through the eyes of the satanic in order to glimpse the real Jesus, but also to look deep into the dark and vicious place within yourselves, to see that I too have my human side. And don't think that it's only the Greek myths that make good theatre. One of the theatre hits of the last decade is Richard Strauss' opera *Salome*. In contrast to its debut in Dresden, amid scenes of great public alarm and horror just over a century ago, thousands were singing its praises in 2008. The opera is about the death of John the Baptist, but with a strange and perverted twist. It depicts a teenage girl, whose sexual awakening leads to obsession and necrophilia. In the New Testament account, Salome is persuaded by her mother Herodias to dance for her stepfather King Herod, after securing the promise that she can have anything she wants. Her price? The head of John the Baptist, Jesus' mentor, who had treated her with contempt. Her fantasies are so twisted that she even takes her clothes off for her lustful stepfather's entertainment.

Richard Strauss composed the music but the source of the story is Oscar Wilde's play of the same name, which was performed in Paris a few years earlier. As far as we know, Strauss was a normal heterosexual (if there is such a thing!) and a happily married man, though he never found it easy to express his emotions, at least directly. Music became his savior. His therapy was his collaboration with Wilde. Like Strauss, Wilde was also fascinated with the darker side of the human soul, though his interests also embraced a creative process that was decadent, sadomasochistic and misogynist. Mr Strauss and Mr Wilde were a unique cultural double act. The opera's climax is Salome's violent arousal by the celibate John, demanding his head after he has rejected her. She isn't so much aroused by the body of the holy man as by his head, kissing the lips of the dead prophet like a crazed nymphomaniac fondling a sex toy. No myth would be complete without someone paying the price, all the better if it is a *femme fatale* with an exotic or Biblical pedigree. What better entertainment can you get than a domineering or predatory woman and a man (willing or not) who is her sexual victim? Though in this opera, Herod gets the last laugh when he orders that Salome be executed for her monstrous actions. Salome is brilliant theatre. It's one of the most horrible, disgusting, revolting and unimaginable exhibitions of degeneracy that I have ever come across on the modern stage. Your primitive ancestors would love it. Wonderful stuff!

The Superhero

At the core of your ancestors' story telling was the myth of the superhero. If you can't get near to the All-Mighty itself, as the elite can, then you try and get as near as possible to the seat of power. This is the moment in history when we see the rise of the power and prestige of monarchy, in one shape or another – and all of it based on violence and intimidation. The shaman and the priest, the king and the tribal hero, all had to be feared and adored since they had the power to make your life a blessing and a curse. They knew how to use fear to its full advantage. Like gods and goddesses, they too have to be worshipped and adored, appeased and flattered. Your ancestors ended up loving them as much as they hated them. But the Jewish prophets had vigorously attacked the notion that human power is the supreme object of adoration. Read the classical authors of old, dear friends. Few of them protest against the cruelty of homo sapiens. And why? Because they know that it isn't just power that you ultimately venerate. You humans love to bask in the pomp and splendor of your leaders. It's what makes you blind.

This is why myths became obsessed with all-powerful mediators, and the rivalry between them. The more All-Mighty the protection, the safer your ancestors felt, as long as they behaved and obeyed their superiors, as long as they knew their place. To this day, humans can't live without their heroes, in whatever guise they appear, including the mini-heroes you call celebrities. Myths are your cultural and religious life-blood. Myths still allow you to divide life into the ever popular camps of 'goodies and baddies'. Myths also allow me to be an integral part of your lives.

But myths held no fascination for Jesus. They were an irrelevance to him. Myths were a cultural and religious prison to him. He demolished them, because he was able to live beyond all polarities. He was free of both heroes and villains. This is why he never once engaged in the sacred game between God and me. *Abba* was the end of all myths; Jesus the liberator from their power.

But you can't get rid of the power of the sacred (and by association, the power of myth and the scapegoat) unless you get rid of the needs that created them in the first place: the needs which are of lost children, desperate for protection in the face of the unknown; frightened children dependent on a higher authority, the higher the better; the needs of fearful children, struggling for a meaningful and ordered life amidst the unpredictability of nature, and the arbitrariness of your rulers.

Abba's sovereignty is about the total absence of social dynamics where every individual is subjected to, and dependent upon, another. Jesus' message is about facilitating the huge shift from escapism to realism, from myth to responsibility, from childhood to sovereignty, the sovereignty that is the novelty of freedom and openness to the future. It is about a brand new future, a brand new beginning, with individuals making right choices and acting responsibly, instead of blaming others for their predicament. In your dreams!

The role of all genuine religious leaders, according to *abba,* is to encourage maturity and freedom and not dependence and unfreedom. But I'm a realist when it comes to freedom. It's too much of a challenge for you. The pressure is too much to handle. It's sensible to allow more mature individuals, especially religious heroes, to inhibit your integrity, initiative and independence, by exercising sovereignty and power over you. The New Testament has several examples of the early church reverting to childish behavior because they couldn't cope with the uncertainty of freedom.

The Letter to the Hebrews is a classical example of Jesus devotees being lazy and refusing to grow up:

> By now some of you ought to be teachers, but you still need someone to teach you the basic principles of abba's teaching all over again. You need milk not solid food. Anyone who lives on milk is still a baby and is not expected to be familiar with the teaching about righteousness. Solid food is for the mature, who by constant use have trained themselves to distinguish good from evil (Hebrews 5:12-14).
>
> You have the potential to know right from wrong. To make the right choices that *abba* wants you to make. That's the message of the story of Adam and Eve. I, Satan, don't have to have the last word on the matter. You don't have to keep on being sinners. You can be wise and good. But you have to work at it. Train yourselves for it. But it's hard living without your favorite myths to guide you, even familiar Christian ones. It's hard living without heroes to look up to and victims to look down to. It's hard work living without me to blame for your failures. It's hard work coping with *abba*-direct. It's never easy being wise! The Old Testament Book of Job describes it in these words (words that were familiar to Jesus): Listen to me you wise men of learning. The ear tests words as the tongue tastes food. Let us find out for ourselves what is right; let us discover together what is good (Job 34:2-4).

One of the purposes of the Book of Job is to address not only kings for their failures in handling wisdom but also the wise men who claim to know so much about God and his ways. Get real, dear friends. If they can't be trusted, can you? In a few verses in chapter twelve, Job confronts the religious establishment of his day, by reminding it that true wisdom belongs only to a mysterious and transcendent reality beyond the sacred order of things, the reality that he calls Wisdom, the reality that Jesus calls *abba*. With sarcasm at times ('what great insights you have displayed'), Job goes on to demystify, as Jesus would do later, much of the traditional knowledge of his day. He treats as common knowledge a great deal of what the wise men claim to know, with wisdom even being found among the aged, 'for long life brings understanding'. No ageism here! Job also admits that to understand the secrets of nature (the source of a river, the movement of the stars) is quite an achievement but 'these are but the outer fringes of God's work' (Job 26:14).

Job finally points out that there is a deeper knowledge beyond the natural things which everyone can observe; the kind of knowledge before which individuals remain speechless and in awe; the knowledge that no one individual or tradition, however holy or special, can contain or manipulate. Consequently, counselors and priests are stripped of their office, judges are mocked, trusted elders and advisers are silenced, while kings and princes are treated with contempt and even deprived of the gift of reason. Even the supreme powers of creation, says Job, can say little or nothing on the matter, when asked to divulge where true wisdom lies:

> The Deep says, 'It's not in me',
> The Sea says, 'Neither is it with me'.
> Destruction and Death declare that ,
> 'Only a rumor of it has reached our ears'.
> (Job 28:14, 22)

Job was a pioneer in a movement that was looking for new ways of thinking about what it means to be human, as well as new ways of thinking about the reality that people referred to as God. Job was pioneering a new kind of knowledge and wisdom that reached its climax with Jesus; a wisdom that was encapsulated not in the myth of the superhero but in the story of ordinary individuals becoming sovereign: the sovereignty that Jesus believed could only be granted by *abba*; a sovereignty based on the type of divine humility that I find repugnant.

Spiritual Maturity or Death

The person who edited the first five books of the Bible, long after monarchy had disappeared in Israel, was eager to remind his readers that since the beginning of time, *Homo sapiens* were meant to be the crown of creation: *Homo sapiens*, the noblest of creatures, a living example of divine rule on earth – each person sovereign in his or her right, exercising power as responsible caretakers of planet earth. Psalm 8:3-6 is a wonderful example of an ancient author giving human beings ideas above their station in life. He addresses the Creator of the whole universe with these words:

> When I contemplate the heavens as the work of your fingers, the moon and the stars, which you put in their place. What is so special about human beings that you care for them? You made them a little lower than the angels and crowned then with glory and honor. You made them rulers over the works of your hands. You put everything under their feet.

Rulers over the whole of creation? I don't think so. You can't even rule your own hearts not to mention fulfilling your responsibility in maintaining the harmony that lies at the heart of the universe! Some of you can't even let go of what the Letter to the Hebrews (6:1-2) refers to as 'the elementary religious teachings' of the apostles. These are the type of believers who are always going on and on about having changed their lifestyle for *abba*'s sake; the ones who, stuck on the basics of their faith, think that teachings about the resurrection and judgment are the be all and end all of what it means to follow Jesus; devotees who know all about the meaning of baptism, and what it means to be a member of the church, but not much else; Christians who, trapped in the circle of tradition, are happy to recite the same old creed Sunday after Sunday, year after year, *ad nauseam, ad nauseam*. Amen; Christians who feel safe in the arms of dogma and doctrine, at home in the womb that has become the tomb called Mother Church.

The church, like many other institutions, is part of an increasingly fetal world, expert by now at keeping individuals in a permanent state of dependence. But it's the right kind of institution for a world in crisis; a world where people can proudly become spiritually-stunted creatures, clustering together in a collective monstrous womb which never gives birth but is always devouring. I am the devouring. My ability to persuade humans to commit spiritual suicide, is my specialty. I know that many would rather undergo spiritual death than face the truth about themselves. They hide behind rules and customs, happy to be fenced in by iron walls of prohibitions and dogmas. Protected from the truth, their souls clean and unblemished by the earth! Can you blame the heavenly judge for declaring 'Take them away and cast them into eternal darkness?'

Many see no need to move onto the risky, yet mature, stage of *abba*-direct and the practical enlightenment that it brings: the step that would take them beyond the basics, and even Christianity itself, since '*abba* is spirit and his worshippers must worship him in spirit and in truth' (John 4:24). Jesus teaches that

> When you pray go into your inner-self, close the door and pray to abba who is invisible. Then abba who sees what is done in secret will reward you (Matthew 6:6).

This is the '*abba*-stolic' faith, pure and simple. The mystery of *abba* is what is most hidden and inexpressible in the human heart: the spirit that helps individuals understand all that is necessary for their wellbeing; the truth that guides everyone into the intimacy of their innermost being, no matter what one's religion, or none. The '*abba*-moment' is when you move beyond the immature 'daddy' or 'mummy' utterances of a child and embrace the divine name that can only be understood in the depth of the heart.

The name known only to you. The name forever concealed in its own mystery. The name that can never become a religious idol.

This is the knowledge that brings freedom from the seductive power of all myths, religious ones included. The love that alone can free the world from every aspect of the satanic principle.

The Gospel of Wrath

So where does the God of Wrath fit into all this? The biggest disappointment in my life is the fact that in the realm of the Sacred I don't have a monopoly on violence. I have to share it with God's Wrath. That's why the shortest of all the Christian Creeds has never been a threat to me, because very few actually believe it. It's the one in John's first letter (1 John 4:16) that states categorically that 'abba is love'. But the popular Christian God is a mixture of a limited kind of love with plenty of wrath thrown in, just like all human beings. I've mentioned him often enough in my book. It's the kind of God who thrives on fear, because his is a religion based on fear. *Abba*'s is a way of life free of fear. One New Testament writer expressed it in these words:

> There is no fear in love. Perfect love drives out fear, because fear is to do with punishment. The person who fears is not perfected in love (1 John 4:18).

"abba"

I also feed on fear, fully aware of the fact that many of you find it difficult to turn your backs on the God of Wrath. Even Paul couldn't do it, and he broke free of most sacred things for the sake of Jesus. Along with other New Testament authors, he too

was a man of his times. A walking paradox, he could honor the spirit of Jesus in the same breath as he was sanctioning sacred wrath!

> Do not repay anyone evil for evil. As far as it is possible live at peace with everyone. Do not take revenge but leave room for God's Wrath, for it is written, 'I will do the avenging', says the Lord (Romans 12:17-19).

See what I mean? Christianity grew, not because people were excited about forgiveness and reconciliation but because they were afraid of the Wrath of God and the 'fires of hell'. God does move in the most mysterious ways! Mind you, so do I! An early fifth century theologian and bishop called Augustine developed a brand of Christianity where God even loves punishing babies. This isn't ancient satanic theology but a piece of twenty-first century Christian teaching that is still popular. A supposedly loving God is more than ready to send babies into eternal hell-fire if they are not baptized into the Christian religion.

Everyone has blind spots. Wrath was Paul's, a big blot on his spiritual landscape. You see, God's wrath is always handy to fall back on when things don't go your way, especially when you're not prepared to give me the credit. I've used rulers in every age to serve my principles, and Paul sings their praises as he struggles to make sense of *abba*'s love and his fear of God at the same time. Along with many others, Paul also betrayed Jesus in this respect, by promoting a theology that was the total opposite of what he had died for. And we're not just talking of the 'war on terror' here but 'God's War on Terror'. This is the key text in Paul's Letter to the Romans (13:1-5), with my comments in brackets, which I can't resist including!

> Everyone must submit to the ruling authorities because they have been set-up by God. He who rebels against the status quo (as Jesus did), is rebelling against God's Will. Those who do so will bring judgment on themselves (as Jesus did). For rulers are no threat for those who do right, but for those who do wrong. Do you want to be free from fear of the one in authority? (See what I mean about the all-pervading presence of fear). Then do what those in authority tell you and you will have nothing to worry about. For he is God's servant to do you good. (It just gets better!) But if you do wrong, be afraid (Be very afraid), for he doesn't carry the sword for nothing. (Thank God that violence always wins through in the end). He is God's servant, an Agent of Wrath to bring punishment on the sinner. It is therefore imperative that you submit to the authorities (Romans 13).

Unlucky for some! Unlucky for millions since the dawn of Christianity!

This is definitely one of my favorite passages in all of the world's holy books. Absolute faith in divine love was always going to be an impossibility. This is why there's nothing wrong with Jesus being a person's love token, as long as you have a reservoir of wrath to fall back on. And it's one hell of a fucking reservoir – God's sacred slaughterhouse: a spectacle of epic proportions full of sacred savagery and ruthlessness; an orgy of hatred, vindictiveness, blind destruction and fury. Love it!

Traditional Christianity is really an up-market version of your ancestors' need to please 'Big Daddy': a composite of all the imaginary beings that emerged over the millennia and that grew to represent their brightest hopes and darkest fears, but with one big difference. In Christianity, scapegoating remains the key, but this time round God supplies the victim – his only son. This God is so All-Mighty, and his holiness so perfect, that in human terms he must be thought of as the ultimate consuming fire, burning away all human sin and wickedness. Since this holiness can never be compromised, it is imperative that he executes (good word that!) judgment against all sinners. This is, after all, the 'righteous anger' of him who is perfect love. You must admit that 'righteous anger' doesn't sound as bad as wrath. And theologians assure me that it's the kind of anger that has nothing to do with vengeance. That kind of behavior is reserved for nasty and cruel pagan gods. Strange that I seem to recall many references to vengeance and punishment in both the Christian and Jewish holy books. Here are just a few. In Deuteronomy we read;

> If I should live for ever, I shall lift my sword to heaven and bring judgment on my enemies, taking vengeance on them who hate me. My arrows will be drunk with their blood and my sword will eat their flesh". (Deuteronomy 32:40—42)

Do you enjoy singing sacred songs or psalms? What about this one?

> May they always sing God's praises while holding a sharpened sword in their hands. To inflict vengeance on the nations, divine punishment on all people of the earth. To take their leaders prisoners, tying them up with chains of iron, in order to carry out the sentence passed against them. All this is done to bring glory and honor to God's saints (Psalm 149:6-9).

The final editor of Luke's gospel even put words into Jesus' mouth at least thirty years after his resurrection. Words that Jesus would never have said.

> The time of punishment has come to fulfill what has already been written. It will be horrific in those days for pregnant women and nursing mothers. There will be great distress in the land and wrath against this people (21:22).

By the time Paul was writing his second letter to the Church in Thessalonica in 51AD, Jesus' followers were still getting more and more anxious because of his non-appearance. So they revert to their old myths to make sense of things. Since abba's love was powerless against the 'Wicked One', at least God's tried and tested wrath could be relied upon to punish his enemies.

> *God is just. He will pay back trouble to those who trouble you. This will happen when the Lord Jesus is revealed from heaven in blazing fire with his powerful angels. He will punish those who do not obey the gospel of Our Lord Jesus. They will be punished with everlasting destruction and shut out from the presence of the Lord and from the majesty of his power* (2 Thessalonians 1:6-9).

It may be diabolical, dear friends, but God's wrath is pure and just. Sinners deserve to be at the receiving end of it. Or God's son, as the case may be, in the more refined brutal theology of the Christian kind – a Christianity forever trapped in mediaeval myth and its code of honor. God has to judge, exclude and destroy everything that resists and violates his commandments. The good news is that he decides to destroy his son this time round and spare humanity. Jesus was the substitute who had to suffer in place of *Homo sapiens*. Jesus was the price that had to be paid in return for God forgiving human sins. God was well satisfied once the payment was made.

'All you need is love'

Jesus would have found this theology not just weird but obscene, an insult to *abba*'s love. Jesus was no substitute. He invited his followers to share and participate with him in establishing the new peace agreement that would help bring about a new humanity. Jesus did face and confront all the wrath in the world but it wasn't the wrath of some imaginary 'God' but all human wrath, anger and revenge since the dawn of history.

I shall let you into a secret.
I was there.
On Golgotha.
As close as I could get.
I witnessed a mystery
that I will resist until hell freezes over.
Jesus was like a sponge absorbing every vile human act ever committed.
A love so powerful that it could transmute every evil act into its opposite.
It takes a courageous kind of love to look as deep as he did into the perversity that is the human heart.

Abba is free to love and to love absolutely. *Abba* loves without having any ulterior motive – unconditionally, expecting nothing in return. Human love always has strings attached to it, but *abba* is love itself. So much so, that there is no evil at all in *abba,* except in as much as *abba* embraces evil and transforms it by love. *Homo sapiens* are not this kind of love. It never has been. But Jesus believes that everyone can learn to be loving by being loved by *abba.* That's the theory! Jesus didn't do theory. Jesus practiced what he preached. No need to debate it. Just get on with it. *Abba*'s love was the be all and end all for Jesus. He loved everyone absolutely because of *abba*'s absolute love. In fact, Jesus believed that you only live to the extent that you can love, and that you love to the extent that you can forgive, and allow yourselves to be forgiven.

I never thought that being honest meant sharing this crap with you. I love, but not for your sake. I love for my own sake. I love you out of egotism. I love to glorify myself and to extend my power. Jesus was absolutely free of all ego because he wanted to be totally there for humans, and their adoption of *abba*'s New Peace Agreement. I'm a realist. I've been around long enough to know that, while it may have worked for Jesus, it'll never work for you.

I love the fact that one of the most perverse ideas in the whole of Christian theology is the belief that *abba* took a back seat and abandoned Jesus to his fate; allowed him to suffer and die a godforsaken death; dropped him in some 'deep shit', as you would say. *Abba* and Jesus were one in love, a love so intense that Jesus was *abba* in human form. Total presence. Nothing held back, not even an iota of love.

Abba is an 'all or nothing' kind of love. No healthy 'thirty-something' human being wants to die young. I remember the moment when it was crunch time for Jesus:

> My soul is overcome with sorrow to the point of death. Abba, everything is possible for you. Take this cup (of suffering) from me. Yet not what I want l but what you want l (Mark 14:34, 36).

Abba didn't abandon Jesus, as Ecclesiastical Christianity maintains, any more than Jesus abandoned *abba*. Jesus did, however, abandon the Sacred Order of things. He took a path outside the comfort zone of myth, religion, culture and nationalism. He continued to struggle with the reality of true sovereignty right to the bitter end. I heard him recite three psalms (Psalms 21, 22, 23) that embodied the challenge facing him.

> O Lord, the king is happy because of your power. He takes great pleasure in the victories you give. You welcomed him with rich blessings and placed a crown of pure gold on his head. You have conferred on him luxuries beyond measure. The king trusts in the Lord. Because of the unfailing love of The Most High One he will remain firm. (Psalm 21:from1, 3, 5, 7).

Jesus may have been at-one with the love that was *abba* but he was shaken to the root of his being because of it. Was it all a mistake? Maybe he was mad after all to throw his lot in with *abba*? He continued with the psalms, and as he recited the words for the last time, he wondered whether the wrath of the God of old would 'swallow' him up and 'his fire consume' him. Or maybe he should have accepted that he was the New Melchizedek after all, fully prepared to destroy his enemies and 'wipe out their descendants from the face of the earth' (21:9-10). No such luck! Jesus was prepared to make a stand for all the innocents who have suffered throughout human history. I am the sum of all your innocent victims crying out for revenge. Jesus was determined to show that the cycle of violence, especially sacred violence, could be broken.

Jesus reached psalm 22 and the words 'My God, my God, why have you forsaken me?' (vss1). So many theories have been built on these words. Let me put the record straight, as I have done throughout my book. Truth and falsehood continued to confront him in the space of a few verses. Jesus wasn't referring to *abba*. He was acknowledging the death of the 'God-of-old' and his impotence in ordering the universe:

> Our fathers put their trust in you. They trusted you and you freed them. They cried to you and were saved. They trusted in you and were not disappointed (22:4-5).

In spite of their trust, God's people had not been delivered. Disappointment was their worldly lot. Enemies regularly triumphed over them. As to the reality of Jesus' own predicament? The 'suffering servant' is finally humiliated, when people gloat over his imprisonment by evil men, his hands and feet pierced, his body tortured to starvation (22:16-17).

'Deliver my life from the sword'? (22:20) Not likely! Jesus had done the very opposite when he willingly delivered himself to the power of the sword. 'I will proclaim your name to my brothers' (20:22), but his brothers had rejected both him and *abba*. Jesus suffered the pain and humiliation of the Cross, for the sake of all living warring brothers and sisters, as well as 'a people yet unborn' (vss31) and believed to the bitter End, that 'the poor will eat and be satisfied' (vss26) with *abba*'s heavenly bread. Didn't I say he was mad? There was to be no 'green pastures' for Jesus or even a 'green hill far away', although he still hoped that he would dwell in *abba*'s kingdom forever. His anointing was as a mere son of man, and his cup did overflow but only with pain and humiliation. Meanwhile, he could still declare that 'even though I walk through the valley of the shadow of death, I will fear no evil, for you are with me' (23:4). Jesus feared no one, because of *abba*'s love. He would serve his fellow human beings, no matter the cost. What's more, shocking though it may sound to Christian ears, Jesus wasn't a sacrifice. He was the humble one who wanted to do away with human scapegoating in all its forms. John's gospel got this one right about Jesus' life:

I give my life willingly (John 10:15).

There was nothing accidental about Jesus death. It was a freewill act, a voluntary gift for abba's peace-agreement and humanity's future survival. Jesus didn't submit to a cruel fate.

Innocent? Yes. A victim? No. Cruel? Yes.

Bloody cruel! Jesus accepted that he had to suffer for love's sake, and 'be rejected and killed' (Mark 8:31). He stood in solidarity with all victims, oppressed and oppressor alike, since both are ultimately victims of the Sacred Order.

Many of Jesus' followers, as well as his early interpreters, realized that there was something unique in Jesus' life and death, but no one was able to grasp its full implication straight away – except me, of course. It's not easy grasping profound theological truths. It's even more difficult to break out of a mythical way of thinking. Millions of Christians to this day cannot break out of the 'sacrificial mentality'. This is why they continue to believe that the Eucharist or Holy Communion is a celebration of Jesus' sacrifice. Roman Christians even call it the Sacrifice of the Mass! The author of the Letter to the Hebrews is a classic example. Like all of you, he gets some things right and others wrong. He is right in saying that Jesus' death on the cross was a 'once and for all act'. He even agrees with the teaching of the Jewish prophets that, as far as *abba* is concerned, sacrifices aren't necessary any more (Hebrews 10:5). But he goes on immediately to contradict himself by describing Jesus as a sacrifice, albeit the best and the final one. He falls into the trap of religious one-upmanship. Jesus' sacrifice is better than pagan and Jewish ones, because he is the new Christian hero as High Priest. Jesus is forever the Supreme High Priest in the famous and prestigious Order of Melchizedek (7:17) – the very role that Jesus had rejected at the start of his ministry! What's ironic is that the author knows that Jesus didn't exercise a priestly role on earth, so he promotes him to the best priestly job in heaven!

Some Home Truths

1

Since Jesus came to break,
and not perpetuate
the age-old Cycle of Violence
in all its guises,
some painful truths for devout Christians,
who appear unwilling or unable
to take on board,
what Jesus thought of his religion:

Jesus was no High Priest.
Jesus was no Sacrifice.
Jesus was no Victim.

The Crucified Jesus
is not the absolute sacrifice,
but the absolute end of all sacrifice.

2

I'm not complaining,
but the Jesus who came
'to make all things new',
is not
'The Christ'
who now fronts
one of the most
dogmatic institutions
on earth

3

A Trinity of Betrayals

Jesus
never intended to sanction
a new and highly divisive
sacred system.

Jesus
never intended to sanction
the power
of religious rulers
ever again.
Jesus
never intended
to sanction
a new religion
of competing
and rival sects.

Jesus? Never!

4

I'm delighted
that
the means
of salvation
offered
by Jesus,
has become
a mechanism of religious domination:
an oppressive monarchic machine,

with a
monstrous pseudo Jesus
monitoring behavior.

The Heresy That Is Freedom

Freedom

There is no standing still
in the life of the spirit
because with abba
you grow
or diminish.

Followers of Jesus teach,
that it's only on the basis of freedom
that something can really be said to exist

That only in freedom
can anyone come to realize something creative
and therefore something new.

Freedom is a spiritual act that
entails stepping beyond the boundaries of everything
that has become fixed.

You don't get more fixed than religions
with their
buildings, books and boundaries.

Curses

Curses on those who teach
that in freedom and fellowship one is beyond obedience and

law

Curses on those who teach
that human freedom can only grow
as individuals encounter others different from one's self

Curses on those who teach
that only in freedom
can there be a truly joyful celebration of common-union.

The Curse of Freedom

The more aware you are
of the world around you,
the more open you become
to everything that isn't you.
It's the kind of openness
that just keeps on growing,
if you don't hold it in check.
The openness
that's always reaching out
to make connections with others.
It's the freedom to
encounter and engage
with strangers who live
outside your space.
Outsiders.
Aliens.

It's not normal.
It's not natural.
It makes you
vulnerable.
Anxious.

Fearful.
Unsure of yourself.
It puts your identity at risk,
your very being.

It would be irresponsible of me,
not to point out the pitfalls
of freedom and openness.
All this can be avoided
when unfreedom is embraced
and put into practice.

Be warned, dear friends.
Jesus is all about spaciousness.
His spirit is freedom.

Freedom is expansiveness and communication.
Unfreedom is the principle of survival,
which closes itself off
from everything
that isn't you.
Closed-off in a small world.

A secure world
of petty-sovereignties
at peace with itself.
A world where you know exactly
where you stand.

A world
governed by
labels
and the limits
of clearly marked boundaries.

A world
where you are free
not to be free.

That familiar world
where you have a right
to boldly defend
the limited space
to which you have retreated.

Obsessed with your identity
and independence.
And pleased as hell
with your precious purity.

Submerged
in your
safe
sacred
space,
slowly
being swallowed
by a
self-centered
salvation.

Stupendous!

Trapped

The truth can be so intoxicating
in a perverse sort of way.
Entertaining even.
Front row seats in my Kingdom of Fear.

Watching millions of lost souls
who think that they are free
is highly satisfying.

Unaware of the fact that
the viciousness of fear
pits your life against itself

The more you defend yourself,
the more you frustrate yourself

.

The more secure the more frustration.
The more frustration the more security
The more security the more isolation
The more isolation the more deadly your fear
and the more you try to hide the emptiness
that gnaws at our vitals

What are you afraid of?
What is there to defend against?
Life. Your own life. Freedom. Openness.
I have the most secure defense against life.
I am the one and only secure defense against life.
I am Death!

Living on the defensive is actually dying on the defensive.
Waking up late in life to discover that you have never really lived at all.
And all of it fuelled by the fear of freedom.
A fixated life,
though I prefer to call it 'anchoring' in the storm
that is life.

God

Welcome to a world
where you can take comfort
in your God.

The god
who allows you to hide away,
secure in teaching
that is
unshakeable,
objective and
absolutely true

A god who has been
well and truly
encapsulated in a
religious system

A god
enslaved
by dogma

A dogma god
Mad god

A manageable god

By your side
like a dog.

A trapped god
My kind of god

God.

Anarchy

To really exist
is
to love
and
to love
is
to step outside the world of things and objects

To really exist
is
to go beyond one's immediate self
and its desires
and thus
to regain
spontaneity and freedom

To really exist
one must
love unconditionally

To really exist
you must be free

Religious leaders can't stand for that

It would be a real 'free for all'

Anarchy!
Bloody Anarchy!
Fucking Bloody Anarchy!

Splendid Isolation

Mine is a splendid isolation
where I can never again be
questioned
or
crushed
by
another

Mine
is a world where
if I must talk of love
then let it be a love
directed exclusively inward

Mine
is a love
that loves only itself
and
its own survival
A love
so closed in upon itself
that it has become
totally alienated
from all others

The kind of love
that knows
that the only thing
that matters
is me
and my kingdom
of petty leaders.

Small gods
isolated
in their self-important
little universes.

Inferior bastards!

Tomorrow's Bread Today

'You can't teach an old dog new tricks', goes the saying. You can actually, if today's dog whisperers are to be believed. What about seasoned Christians? It can't be easy letting go of cherished beliefs that have sustained you as individuals for decades, and the church for centuries. Maybe now you can appreciate how challenging and painful it was for the people who heard Jesus' message for the first time. Hearing his words was offensive enough. Seeing Jesus in action was even more disturbing, especially the heart of his prophetic campaign, which meant sharing table-fellowship with sinners, mixing with the scum of the earth. Mind you, I regularly mix with them!

Jesus knew all about the tradition that looked forward to the Great Banquet at the Endtime, when people will come from east and west and north and south to take their places at the feast of the Kingdom of God. Special guests will include Abraham, Isaac, Jacob and the prophets. But as far as Jesus is concerned, that meal is already underway and the special seats are reserved for the 'oddballs'. Outsiders. Aliens. It is an act of solidarity with all those who don't fit into people's religious expectations. It is also a sign, a celebration of the heavenly bread, the spiritual blessings that *abba* offers freely to everyone. These gifts include togetherness (which I can also offer, though I call it orgies) and other practical and down to earth skills like forgiveness, compassion and tolerance. I abhor them!

'Food glorious food!' Of course Jesus wants the poor to be fed and resources to be shared in a just way, but his ministry was, and still is, an advertisement for *abba*'s new kind of sovereignty that would usher in a new kind of humanity, and not a third world aid program. The first test that I gave him had set the scene.

> After fasting for forty days and forty nights, Jesus was hungry. I came to him and said, 'If you are the Son of God, tell these stones to become bread.' Jesus answered, 'It is written: Human beings don't live on bread alone, but on every word that comes from God's mouth. (Matthew 3:2-3).

Abba's Bakery produces spiritual rolls, and they get distributed freely and in abundance. But nobody wants *abba*-bread. What do you expect when you're always thinking about your stomachs – and other physical needs as well? Remember the Sunday school story called 'The Feeding of the Five Thousand'? It had nothing to do with Jesus satisfying people's needs; it was a sort of miraculous picnic to win people over. Jesus didn't 'do' myths, any more than he did grand miracles and spectacles to catch people's attention. 'Why is this generation obsessed with miraculous signs? I tell you the truth, no sign will be given to it' (Mark 8:12). I wish he had opted for miracles when I tested him. It would have been one hell of a bungee jump from the highest point of the temple. A crowd puller of a story was needed. That's why the true message of the Five Thousand event was twisted to suit the more dramatic and immediate needs of the early church. Miracles always pack them in. I'll tell you what really happened. A crowd had been with Jesus all day long. They were tired and hungry. The disciples, having clearly missed the spiritual significance of the gathering, tell Jesus to send them away to buy something to eat. Jesus tries to get them to think about what's going on in an *abba* way, and challenges them with the words 'You give them something to eat'. In effect, 'Let's see what you come up with. Earthly bread or heavenly bread?' Jesus invites those with food to share a piece with ones who had nothing, in anticipation of what will soon take place when *abba*'s kingdom arrives. There may have been little food available in physical terms, but a spiritual feast is on the horizon. Remember how they had been told to pray to *abba*, 'You give us today the Bread of Tomorrow!' (Matthew 6:11). The Endtime banquet was underway. The Five Thousand shared a foretaste of Heavenly Bread in anticipation.

> Taking the bread, Jesus looked up to heaven, blessed and gave thanks. Then broke the bread and gave it to the people (Mark 6:41-42).

What's more, the foretaste of *abba*'s sovereignty is available for everyone, unconditionally, unlike the ritual that the church later developed with its hierarchical regulations. A heretical Jewish celebration of Endtime unity and togetherness has become an Ecclesiastical Christian cultic act, celebrating division and rivalry. The church has by now a near business monopoly as exclusive distributors of *abba*'s heavenly bread. What do you expect? Middlemen always adulterate the food which they supply. Christianity has turned Jesus' Endtime celebration into a ceremony for those who have qualified as one of the chosen, and transformed *abba*'s bread not only into a badge of membership but also into a way of controlling the faithful – yet another example of dogmatic attempts to trap, domesticate and tame Jesus.

Pagans had meals where they shared 'holy communion' with their deities, as well as memorial dinners that linked them with their ancestors. Jesus' meal was all about the future and not the past, about *abba*'s plans for the future welfare of the human race. What came to be known as the Last Supper is actually the First Supper, Jesus' inaugural celebration of *abba*'s new way of doing things. The 'breaking of bread' equates the broken and rejected Jesus with human brokenness. This entails everyone acknowledging their weaknesses as well as their strengths, their failures as well as their successes, their darkest fears as well as their brightest hopes.

In and through a simple act of sharing, *abba*'s new peace agreement can start to take effect. Forgiveness can become a way of life, scapegoating a thing of the past, as people learn to stand in solidarity with each other, no matter what their backgrounds. Violence is abandoned forever as the answer to the world's problems. What idealistic rubbish!

Painful though it was for him, Jesus also rejected the Passover, the supreme Jewish religious, national and cultural ritual. If Jesus had wanted to link his work with the Passover, he would have arranged the First Supper to be held on the festival evening. But he didn't. He held it a day before, on Thursday night, April 6. The lambs to be eaten on the Friday evening, when Passover was held, were killed on the Friday afternoon when Jesus was dying on the Cross. This is why Christians wrongly equated Jesus as the true Lamb of God. If Jesus must be equated with an animal then he made his choice quite clear – Jesus is a donkey. But lambs have a better pedigree: an ideal image of submission and innocence with which to control the faithful. Jesus' message was unequivocal. No more innocent suffering, be it human or animal. No more capitulation to that passivity which is the very reversal of *abba*'s freedom and responsibility. As Paul says later on, you had better work out your salvation in 'fear and trembling' (Philippians 2:12). Since Israel also has a key role to play in *abba*'s salvation, Jesus' First Supper has more of a universal flavor to it than that envisaged by the Passover meal. The Exodus account is straightforward enough, and helps put Jesus' actions into context.

> God said to Moses; 'Each man is to take a lamb for his family. Wait until the chosen time , when all the people of Israel must slaughter them at twilight. Then take some of the blood and put it on the sides and tops of the doorframes of the houses

> where they eat the lambs. Eat the meat roasted over the fire, along with bitter herbs and bread made without yeast. You must eat it as if in a hurry, for it is the Lord's Passover. On the same night I will pass through Egypt and strike down every firstborn, both men and animals, and I will bring judgment on all the gods of Egypt. The blood will be a sign for you on the houses where you are; and when I see the blood, I will pass over you. No destructive plague will touch you when I strike Egypt.' (Exodus12: from 3-13)

Jesus had a different agenda. While the twelve disciples represent a restored Israel, it was a nation renewed for a purpose, namely to bring the pagan nations under *abba*'s sovereignty as well. Jesus, ever the idealist, had said on one occasion, that 'I have other sheep that are not of this sheep pen. I must bring them also. They too will listen to my voice, and there shall be one flock and one shepherd' (John 10:16). Jesus couldn't let go of the hope that human beings could live together as one loving family.

The First Supper was the penultimate subversive act of the infamous Jewish Heretic, Jesus of Galilee. While Melchizedek had shared bread and wine with Abraham (Genesis 14:18), Jesus had shared *abba*'s heavenly food with anyone and everyone since the start of his ministry. It was his invitation to *abba*'s Endtime party. As his mission reached its climax, Jesus, in absolute humility, having rejected New Melchizedek's power and prestige, shared bread and wine with a bunch of twelve ordinary men – a motley crew, if ever there was one! It was meant to represent a new Jewish way of bringing about a world of peace and harmony. Isaiah III had looked forward to the day when everyone would 'maintain justice and do what is right, for God's salvation is near at hand'. (Isaiah 56:1)

In order that he didn't passover and ignore the shedding of human blood anymore, Jesus turned his back on the most sacred and special Jewish festival. To establish true justice, he had to bring an end to all victimization, violence and vengeance, by offering himself as a sign that there is another way of doing things. No matter how much he loved his people, remembering Israel's past slavery was no longer a priority; his commitment was to humanity in the present and its fate in the future. By rejecting every aspect of earthly power in favor of abba's sovereignty, Jesus believed that all nations can be part of a more profound liberation – freedom from Satan and all heavenly and earthly powers!

The First Supper is about reconciliation: new kind of at-oneness between *abba* and *Homo sapiens,* as well as between every human being. Notice the sequence in the story of feeding the five thousand, when Jesus handles the token food that symbolizes *abba*'s heavenly bread. 'Taking the bread, Jesus looked up to heaven, blessed and gave thanks, then he broke the bread and gave it to the people' (Mark 6:41-41). He did the same on the night before he was crucified, but this time the bread took on a deeper significance. Jesus' body would be battered and bruised for the sake of the New Peace Agreement. For him, it was the only way to usher in *abba*'s sovereignty. But there was an even deeper significance to the bread this time. 'Jesus took bread, gave thanks, and gave it to them, saying "Take and eat for this is my body."' There is no mention of Jesus 'looking up to heaven', because *abba* is present in a unique way when the 'bread is broken' this time. Remember, that it's all about '*abba*-direct'. Jesus is prepared to die for the sake of *abba*'s total presence in the world. Jesus is talking for *abba* when he says

> This is my body. Take it and eat it.
> This is my Cup of the new Peace Agreement. Drink it.

Just as Jesus is able to be totally present for *abba*'s sovereignty, ridding the world of all rivalry and hostility, individuals can, in a similar way, die to my satanic power-systems and thus become focal points for the New Peace Agreement. If you've got the guts, and can stomach the truth, you are the Peace Agreement!

Abba's sovereignty can be shared immediately with those who want to taste the riches of heavenly bread and drink the lifeblood of the new humanity. If you dare take the leap of faith, and embrace the truth that Gospel of the Fallen Angel is the answer to the world's problems, then there's no need for priesthoods and regulations.

Buy a loaf and a bottle of wine.
Share the bread and the wine.
Be the bread and the wine.
I dare you.

You don't have to think about it.
You don't need to get trained in it.
You don't have to wait to become it.
You just get on and do it.

I bet you never thought that a loaf of bread and a bottle of wine could be so subversive? More subversive than you could ever imagine! That's why the church has never been fully honest with you as to the true meaning of Jesus' words, 'Do it in memory of me' (Luke 22:19). A better translation is, 'Do it in renewal of me.' *Abba*'s love, continually renewed in the world.

Ecclesiastical Christians are like pagans in this respect. When they remember a past event, they do so by recalling it inside their head. They tap into a storehouse of memories, and repeat it in a symbolic way. The two thousand year-old myth of a dead and rising god is regularly re-enacted as priests endeavor to conjure up Christ's mysterious presence in a pseudo-magical way. It's a private, inner-affair, between you and Christ. When followers of Jesus 'break the bread', they too make present Jesus' saving and liberating death. They actually 'recharge' themselves by sharing, once again, a common union with *abba*'s energies of love and forgiveness. But while some Christians keep on traveling back to the past, the future is actually present now when followers of Jesus 'break bread'. Instead of sharing a token meal, a pale imitation of the original, followers of Jesus actually sit at table as peacemakers in *abba*'s Endtime Banquet. And this is no exclusive members club. *Abba*'s freshly baked bread is available for everyone. It's a communal event that all are challenged to partake of.

This re-enactment is not an act! It's real human theatre. Just as modern soldiers talk about the theatre of war, followers of Jesus celebrate the theatre of the new peace agreement. You stand with Jesus in solidarity with your ancestors, Cain and Abel. As Jews participate in the Exodus from Egypt, Jesus' Endtime celebration means that you are actually present at the first murder when Cain killed his brother Abel. You are challenged to remember that both are kinfolk, members of your human family. The first murder is present in the Cup of the new Peace Agreement. In a mysterious way, Jesus' blood is also Abel's blood. Abel's wounded body is your broken body. Cain's guilt and remorse is also your guilt and remorse. Every broken body, every drop of spilt blood in human history, past and future, is present in your digestive system and deep within your body's DNA. If Jesus and Paul are to be believed, you are also the new Adam and Eve: outward and visible signs of the new breed of *Homo sapiens*.

For Jesus' sake, stop being religious and get on instead with the work of incarnating and grounding *abba*'s spirit in the world, and thus bring to an end all hostility and rivalry. I dare you!

Up, Up and Away

I'm sure that many of you are curious by now as to my honesty about the real Jesus. 'What's the method in his madness?' I can hear some of you ask. There's no method. By getting to know the historic Jesus, you can make up your own minds as to whether his plans for *Homo sapiens* are ridiculously out of touch or not. I also hope that you now appreciate that I'm not as bad as many have made me out to be. My satanic principles have served you well over the centuries. And if I had to pick one word that makes me supremely confident that most human beings will never follow Jesus, it's the word 'exalted'. Jesus said that his followers are to be 'the salt of the earth' (Matthew 5:13). Not the main course or even the starter, but the salt that keeps the whole meal tasty. But Christians want to be the whole meal. Ecclesiastical Christianity wants to be the Banquet itself. And why? When it comes down to it, Christians are only human. It's natural for them to want to get on in the world; to get to the top, to climb to the top of the ladder, to 'be exalted'. People love getting exalted. Human culture is motivated by it. The economy of nation-states is driven by it. You don't set out to be second best. You set out to be rich and to be powerful, to assert yourself on the world stage.

I'll be watching developments closely in Asia over the coming decades, in particular among the trinity of Japan, China and India. Or should it be India, China and Japan? It will be interesting to see how issues of race, nationality and identity develop in that part of the world, especially with China's current feelings of racial superiority. She occupies today the position that Japan found herself in seventy years ago: insecure, chauvinist and aggressive. The run-up to the 2008 Olympic Games proved that she will not be lectured to by the West. She stands on the threshold of world domination, but her rise as a new world super-power threatens Japan, whose economic revival in turn threatens China. India's emergence as an economic and political super-power is a threat to both. A potentially dangerous Asian power struggle is on the horizon. President Bush Jr, when he was head of the most exalted, and therefore most powerful, nation on earth, had the wisdom and imagination to align the USA with India, the largest democracy in the world.

In a world or rivalry you always have to take sides. But you'd expect such wisdom from the most exalted person on planet earth! After all, God personally chose him to be president, just as he personally saved him from the demon liquor. I'm glad that Bush's stunning pre-emptive attack on Iraq, and the catastrophic war that followed, was nothing to do with me. While Bush's God was going about his business, I was waiting in the wings, picking up the pieces, as I've always done. My load became much lighter when the early church convinced itself that Christ had come to establish the imperial and glorious authority of God on earth.

But Jesus negates every Western image of the Christ of Glory, though the church refuses to accept that truth. Ecclesiastical Christianity must have its exalted Lord, because it's part and parcel of the sacred world of patriarchy. What is probably the very first Hymn to Jesus in the New Testament captures the essence of what true humility is all about, as well as its opposite. It's the only perfect type of humility that I've ever encountered. As the New Melchizedek, Jesus could have had it all, but he rejected it for the sake of *Homo sapiens*. The author of the hymn challenges his readers to adopt the same humble attitude in their lives:

> Though his form was divine, Jesus had no desire to play at being God. Rather he emptied himself of all divinity and took instead the form of the most humble of human beings, a lowly servant. He then walked the path of perfect humility, that led to his death on the cross (Philippians 2:6-11).

But in the second part, the author reveals his slavery, not to the spirit of abba and Jesus, but to the spirit of patriarchy and its love of exaltation. The message is of Jesus 'being exalted' and everyone in heaven and on earth bowing before him as Supreme Lord. All of it done, mind you, for abba's fame and glory. That's not the abba that I know!

The Christian fixation with, and bondage to, 'being exalted' is a serious spiritual illness. As a sufferer myself, I have no desire to be cured of it. Jesus has no interest in satisfying anyone's lust for power, including the church, since he unmasked all fantasies of omnipotence on the cross. Christians imitating 'the way of the world' is a joy to behold, but sad if you are a follower of Jesus. The New Testament even closes with the image of Christian worship imitating the adulation once accorded to the Roman emperors. In the Book of Revelation (4:12), 'You are the worthy One, our Lord and God', sings the heavenly choir to God and the Lamb, thus imitating the acclamation used to greet the Roman emperor during his triumphal entrance. The emperor Domitian even insisted that he always be addressed by the title 'our Lord and God'.

Language is a potent enslaving power, religious language in particular.

Paul knew that the power of Jesus' resurrection was related to *abba*'s eternal love, but even he failed to find a new language to describe what Jesus was all about. It isn't that patriarchy has failed to come up with a new language. Patriarchy doesn't want to, because new language means letting go of outdated, and by now utterly meaningless, ways of behaving and of ordering the life of the church. Paul transforms the 'son of man' into his very opposite, namely the 'man of heaven'. He ends up equating resurrection not just with exaltation but also with elevation. It was alien to Paul's thought patterns to think in terms of incarnation, and to follow the Risen Jesus into the mystery of what it means to really be en-fleshed. For *abba,* the deeper you can bring Jesus into the flesh the better, since the only true divinity is a sensuous, living being: a creature of flesh and blood. For Paul, it's the very opposite! Resurrection is a movement upwards, just as spiritual power has always to be equated with the sovereign power of kings. I'm not complaining, since this is my kind of theology. I love the fact that Jesus has been promoted to the status of a monarch and cosmic lord, instead of becoming even more deeply the Jesus of passion, the humble one, *abba*'s final word and spirit, one hundred per cent present in the world.

It's ironic that I've come to know the son of man better than any of you. *Ecce homo,* as Pilate said of Jesus. 'Behold the Man!' Yes, look at him; really look at him, all of you, if you dare! Face the fact that the absolute sovereignty of *abba* is to be found in the absolute humility of Jesus.

For Jesus there is only one name under the sun before which people should bow, and that is the almost unutterable name of '*abba*'. Jesus doesn't want to be exalted to the heavenly throne but the church has placed him there – on a throne that's become big enough to include the church also. When I hear the Hymn to Jesus being read, I always hear Christianity exalting itself and the humble 'son of man' pushed aside. I hear leaders yearning for that moment when their fellow human beings bow to them in obedience. I hear the Church basking in the glory of its exclusive and all-conquering Son of God, and the power that he has given them.

I leave the last word in this chapter to one of the great Jewish-Christian prophets of the modern era, the German anti-philosopher and atheist Friedrich Nietzsche (d.1900). His warning to Western culture about the dangers of exaltation are ignored at your peril. I quote from his gospel entitled *Thus Spoke Zarathustra.*

> Christians! If you have ears to hear, then you too must listen.
>
> You are treading your path of greatness: now it must call up all your courage that there is no longer a path behind you! And when all footholds disappear, you must know how to climb upon your own head: how would you climb upward otherwise? You, however, O Zarathustra, have wanted to behold the ground of things and their background: so you must climb above yourself, up and beyond, until you have

even your stars under you!

'O Zarathustra,' he said mockingly, syllable by syllable, 'you stone of wisdom! You have thrown yourself high, but every stone that is thrown must fall!

'O Zarathustra, you stone of wisdom, you projectile, you star-destroyer! You have thrown yourself thus high, but every stone that is thrown, must fall!

'Condemned by yourself and to your own stone throwing: O Zarathustra, far indeed have you thrown your stone, but it will fall back upon you!'

(F. Nietzsche, *Thus Spoke Zarathustra,* from Part 3)

Yes, dear friends, it will fall back upon you!

Chapter Six

The Only Stairway to Heaven

"Scribe: What message am I to preach? What is the 'good news' that the faithful need to hear? As a child I heard my grandparents speak of the plague that devastated Europe. A catastrophe that haunts the Church to this day. Every village was affected. Every family suffered, be they rich or poor, witnessing the tortuous deaths of their loved ones. Afterward? People did as they pleased. They believed that Holy Church had failed them, that the Mass had proved an ineffective shield against diseases.

Bishop: And what do you believe?

Scribe: I believe in a message of 'good news' for our people now.

Bishop: (furious) What message preacher? I'll tell you what message. The virtue of holy obedience. That's the 'good news'. The Church did not fail them, neither was it God's fault. The lesson of history is a simple one. The faithful must be more obedient. Obedient to the words of Holy Bible. Obedient to the rules of Holy Church. Obedient to their superiors."

'Deo Gratia' by Geraint ap Iorwerth

A play set in 1406 A.D. Wales

The Way of Humility

Jesus handpicked twelve messengers in readiness for *abba*'s New Age. This had nothing to do with setting up an earthly institution, least of all what is known today as 'the church'. The twelve were to represent the New Israel and its different kind of sovereignty in the world. Jesus called them 'the little ones' or 'the humble and lowly ones'. It's in this context that you must understand that Jesus wasn't undermining John the Baptist's pre-eminence (as the early church did) when he said, on one occasion, that the 'least in the new Kingdom was greater than John' (Matthew 11:11). Jesus was talking about humility, the true mark of the new emerging sovereignty. He was highlighting the fact that, in worldly terms, the most insignificant in *abba*'s new creation would find themselves greater than John, and he was 'The Greatest'.

Humility has always been one of the greatest challenges for the leadership qualities that Jesus had in mind. But humility has never been part of my way of operating in the world. It just doesn't work. People need, and like, strong leadership built on a hierarchy that clearly spells out where everybody stands. Orders that come from 'on high' always have more of an impact. I've never had any trouble with leaders who follow my principles, rulers who know how to exercise authority by 'lording' it over their subjects. And enjoying it in the process. You should see the queue when I'm holding job interviews. I never get any trouble filling vacant posts worldwide. But I never see many applying for jobs that advertise, 'If you want to be the first then you must be the very last, the servant and slave of all' (Luke 22; 26), as Jesus would have it. How pathetic! Try telling that to your kids before they go off to a careers evening at school. 'Get real Mum and Dad!'

Mary Magdala was a close companion of Jesus and an integral part of his mission team. He confided in her and she in him. Because of the incredible love between Jesus and her, I could never really get close to Mary. Theirs was a truly intimate relationship. Mary was to become pre-eminent among Jesus' followers, men and women included. When talking about the women around Jesus, the gospels always mention her first, with 'Mary Magdala and the other Mary' being the standard formula. She helped finance Jesus' mission and, along with a close circle of women, traveled with him and his disciples. She was also a close friend of Mary and Jesus' sister. She stayed loyal to Jesus, standing by him with the other women at the foot of the cross. And it was she who went to the grave on that first Easter morning to attend to Jesus' body. Some of the gospels found this so unbelievable, that they couldn't bring themselves to record the truth, preferring instead to write, that 'the women went to the tomb' (see Mark 16). But the truth is that 'when Jesus rose early on the first day of the week, he appeared first to Mary Magdala' (John 21; 1).

As a patriarchal religion, I'm sure that early Christianity would have airbrushed Mary Magdala from its history, if it wasn't for her fame and popularity. How embarrassing to have a woman as Jesus' right hand man. It was even more embarrassing to have a woman as the first messenger to deliver the news about Jesus' resurrection to her fellow disciples. But facts are facts. Mary clearly had an incredible vision by the graveside, though no one will ever be able to tie it down in scientific terms. That's what I like about religion. There's never definite proof to put before your eyes.

Come to think of it, that's what I like about Jesus. Nothing in his life was free from ambiguity. No truth about him is self-evident. This means that the church will always consist of people who are always arguing and quarrelling about what he really said: arguments that help sow the seeds of bitter ecclesiastical disputes and theological battles – seeds that eventually lead to wars. I don't know who said it, but I wish it had been me – 'God gave us spirituality but the devil invented religion'. There's no doubt that Jesus certainly didn't. Much to my disgust, it was never on his agenda to set up another religion. And yet, I shouldn't complain. His so-called followers have done me proud over the centuries. By arrogantly claiming that their hybrid creation called 'Christianity' is the best, most superior, of all religions, they have guaranteed that I'm going to be kept busy for centuries to come, as other religions also jump on the 'ours-is-the-only-true-religion' bandwagon.

"Mary Magdala"

'Deliver us from nonsense'

One of the joys of having an extended vacation is that I get to watch a lot of TV. I never thought there could be so many documentaries on so many subjects with so many experts. In a religious documentary on the family of Jesus in 2006, one such expert was Fr Dean Bechard of the Pontifical Biblical Institute in Rome. He started the program, shown on the UK Channel 4, by saying that as a professional historian he had been trained to be as critical as possible when looking at the evidence. But he then went on say that as a Christian he always begins his research on the assumption that the tradition of his church is always trustworthy. 'Reality check, brother!' From my experience, I would never equate academic integrity with the history of the Church of Rome. My curiosity was immediately awakened. He then proceeded to gently mock those Christians who, because of their naivety and curiosity, generate 'fanciful, speculative and imaginary stories' about the family of Jesus. He did admit, however, that most of the history of the first Jewish Christians, of which St James the brother of Jesus was the leading figure, is lost. Our expert, Fr Bechard, failed to mention, however, that we may know only a little about St James, but what we know is historically accurate. He also failed to mention that we only have limited knowledge of what happened to St Peter after Jesus' death. Fr Bechard chose to ignore that point. I couldn't.

I've since seen numerous documentaries where Roman historians and theologians go on to mock the ideas behind Dan Brown's global phenomenon known as *The Da Vinci Code.* When I first read it I thought that Brown must have had special tuition and training by Roman clerics in the art of manufacturing a false history. What did Jesus say?

> Judge not and you will not be judged. In fact, if you do so, you will be judged in the same way that you judge others. Your behavior will be measured by the same standard that you use for others. Why do you look at the speck of sawdust in your brother's eye and pay no attention to the plank in your own eye? You hypocrite. First take the plank out of your own eye, and then you will see clearly to remove the speck from your brother's eye (Matthew 7:1-5).

The whole idea that St Peter had anything to do with Rome is more than just 'fanciful, speculative and imaginary'. It is a downright lie. As the Prince of Lies, I had to get involved. Any hope of resting my investigative skills for a while would have to be sacrificed for the sake of the truth. Now I never thought I'd hear myself saying that!

To crown it all, the May 2006 edition of the publication called *Inside Vatican* carried a quote, in an article entitled 'Faith and Reason', that said that 'Faith has the power to deliver us from nonsense'. And Cardinal Ratzinger, as the current Pope was called in 2005, said in a homily, 'Let us be children no longer'. But Rome isn't practicing what it preaches. Its faith is built on nonsense. I've already pointed out the historical and biblical truth that Jesus appointed no successor. He also had no plans for setting up an earthly institution of any kind, least of all a church. To this you can now add the historical truth that St Peter was never in Rome. 'So how come,' you ask, 'that the Church of Rome to this day maintains that St Peter was Christ's vicar on earth? Why do they continue to believe such silly nonsense?' I've told you already. It's your mythic imagination. It has too firm a grip on you. You need not only a superhero, but also, if possible, a famous pedigree that gives added fame and prestige – and power. Always the power! And if you haven't got a legitimate history, then you invent one. The Church of Rome set about creating its own myth. And then went on to manufacture its own saint.

"Peter kissing his wife"

Batman in Gotham City is joined by St Peter in Rome City.

What the Church of Rome did to Peter is totally alien to the spirit of his Master. It is a betrayal of *abba*'s sovereignty, which, as I have already explained, is grounded in the most humble of lifestyles. I've also made it clear that Jesus made use of only one title to refer to himself, the 'son of man' or 'one of you lot'. I doubt that he would have adopted a title that could be misused by those who craved a superhero, at least not while he was still alive. He would also be horrified at the thought of Peter as his religious No. 1, but it's no surprise to me. When Rome became an

important Christian center, its early theologians had to compete with pagan imperial theology, which stated that the Emperor was not only the Son of God, but also Lord and Savior. With the title 'Lord' already in use as the Jewish name for God, hey presto, Jesus also had to become 'the Son of God'. Consequently, his earthly lieutenant, Peter, had to move up in the world.

Jesus' whole life was characterized by a total lack of interest in anything to do with human pride, pomp and ceremony. He had no interest in writing a new myth or in spawning a new breed of superheroes. He also says that 'My kingdom is not of this world. My sovereignty is from another place' (John 16:36). Jesus even entered Jerusalem for the last time as a holy fool riding on a donkey – Jesus, the original religious clown. In fact, his humility started to irritate me towards the end of his life. I thought at first that it was just a ploy. Sacred spin. A strategy to draw people's attention. But he couldn't be anything else. He was humility incarnated.

So why did Rome boost Peter instead of one of the other disciples? James, the brother of Jesus, would have been the ideal choice to fabricate a history about. But he was based in Jerusalem and history is clear about what happened to him. Paul did go to Rome but since he wasn't one of the original twelve, he wasn't good enough. He didn't have the pedigree. Though Mary Magdala was known to have been close to Jesus, she was a woman, so she was definitely out of the picture. So it had to be Peter. He had to be God's *supremo* on earth. But Peter was no such thing. Could I prove it? I decided to put my investigative skills to the test once more, and the result was a fascinating trail of deception and lies at the highest level.

'Promise to tell the truth, the whole truth...'

Let's look at Peter's life in a bit more detail. Peter was a fisherman, a working man, passionate and, by all accounts, impetuous. He ran the family fishing business with his brother Andrew, working on the Sea of Galilee. Like his fellow disciples, Peter was slow at grasping what Jesus was all about. My followers and I have no problem in that respect. Ironic really! The New Testament openly admits that demoniacs knew who Jesus was from the start. Not a bad claim to fame in theological circles. Maybe you all need to acknowledge the demonic element in you, if you want to know the truth about Jesus and *abba.*

Peter was a married man, though we don't know his wife's name. He wasn't a celibate priest but a family man, and on one occasion we know that Jesus healed Peter's mother-in-law. So, to put it another way, Peter had a wife and enjoyed a carnal relationship with her. They made love. In modern language, they 'had sex' – and unprotected sex at that! Peter's wife accompanied him on some of his missionary travels after Jesus' death.

Peter was a prisoner in Jerusalem. There is even a small church on the west coast of Britain, in Southern Snowdonia, Wales, dedicated to this event. It's called St Peter ad Vincula, which is Normanized Latin for 'St Peter in Chains'. It is the only one of its kind in Wales. You can find the story of this historic event in Acts of the Apostles, chapter twelve. England has a dozen or so such dedications, one of them being the parish church of the Tower of London, a famous tourist haunt of mine with its long history of torture, beheadings and imprisonments. These churches don't claim to do anything other than commemorate the event, as does the church in Jerusalem, which was dedicated to the memory of St Mark and is now under the care of the Syrian Oriental Orthodox Church. A church in Rome is also dedicated to the same event, St Pietro in Vincoli, but with one difference. It claims that Peter was also imprisoned in Rome and has on display the original chains! Lies! More damned lies, though I applaud them!

So let's summarize what we know so far:

Peter wasn't Jesus' spiritual heir. If anyone has the right to that title it's his brother, James. Jesus didn't even appoint him to carry on with his work, but James took the job on after his experience of the risen Jesus. Like Paul, James wasn't even a disciple of Jesus, 'one of the twelve' as history has it. There was a hierarchy at work here, but it has nothing to do with later church hierarchy. It was Jesus' family hierarchy. When James was later martyred, his brother Simon took over the leadership of the Jerusalem Assembly.

James, and not Peter, was the first leader of the first formal gathering of Jesus' followers in the world. James was the patriarch, the overseer:

When Peter escaped from prison he sent a message to James.

> When Paul arrived in Jerusalem four years after his conversion, it was James who made him welcome.
>
> When Paul returned to Jerusalem fourteen years later, it was James, once more, who welcomed him.
>
> It was James who presided over the Council of Jerusalem in XXAD, when the heated debate took place between Jewish and Gentile followers of Jesus.

There's no denying that Peter was one of the twelve disciples and a close companion of Jesus. He became a traveling preacher after Jesus' death, supporting himself financially with profits from the family fishing business. He never charged for his services as an apostle. He wasn't a rich man, at least in material terms, and once admitted publicly to a beggar, 'I have no silver and gold' (Acts 3:6). He never claimed any seniority or primacy for himself, neither did the early church give him any. Peter was given a role by the Jerusalem Council as an evangelist to fellow Jews. So let's cut to the chase. I shall demonstrate that Peter was never in Rome. Consequently, Peter was not the first 'bishop of Rome'. Peter wasn't even among the first leaders to establish Jesus assemblies there. The logic is simple and straightforward. Since Peter had no connection with Rome, any claims made by the Pope have no scriptural or historical authority at all.

Built, as it is, on a lie, namely the Papal tradition that Peter lived in Rome for twenty-five years as its bishop, the whole Roman edifice comes tumbling down. He didn't.

Equally false is the belief that Peter was eventually martyred in Rome in 67AD. He wasn't. Neither was Peter buried under the High Altar of the church in Rome that bears his name.

Let's take a closer look at the evidence, especially in the writings of Paul.

While Peter would never have referred to Jesus as the 'son of God' (it was alien to his religious and cultural mentality as a Jew), the early church did adopt the title. Jesus was 'the Messiah, the Son of God'. It quickly became one of the first 'Confessions of Faith' for new believers. In fact, all who decide to follow Jesus recite it, and because of their faith, they too become rocks or building blocks on which the church is built. Many firm rocks of faith all coming together as 'living stones' to be 'a spiritual house acceptable to God' (1 Peter 2:5). Peter was one of those rocks, albeit an important one, Jesus the chief cornerstone. All true followers of Jesus are 'rockys', and not just the first disciples. If Roman propaganda is to be believed, the other eleven disciples chosen by Jesus weren't all that special after all, since they had no faith. Peter was the only proper man of faith among them. But Rome takes the argument even further, twisting the words of the New Testament to suit its own ends:

> You are Rocky and on this rocklike faith I will build my church, and the Gates of Hell will not overcome you (Matthew 16:18).

'Charming', if you follow Rome's interpretation! Since Peter is the only real Rocky, the Gates of Hell will never overcome him, but the other disciples haven't got a chance! But there's more startling news:

> To you Peter is given the keys to the Kingdom of Heaven, with power to bind or free evil spirits t both on earth and in heaven (Matthew 16:19).

In other words, to Peter alone was given 'the key' or the power to forgive sins or not to forgive sins, as the case may be. Once again, all the other disciples are ignored. We are asked to believe that Jesus chooses twelve men to be his special representatives, but only one of the twelve is actually treated as a special representative. What utter nonsense! What the Church of Rome has done to Peter is a classic, textbook example of devious religious opportunism and the ingenious doctoring of a religious text that to this day continues to fool millions of people. But not me! Since Rome wants to be in charge of all Christians, a fantastic lie has been concocted. Forget *The Da Vinci Code*. The Roman Code is even more incredible! Here are its core beliefs for an eternity of human history: the promise of leadership is made to Peter alone, who becomes Christ's supreme and permanent infallible authority, who passes the promise on to his so-called successors, one celibate man at a time, all of whom happen to be bishops of Rome.

But everyone who makes the confession of faith that 'Jesus is Lord' is a 'rocky'. Share the good news about Jesus with others, and you too become a pope, a patriarch, or a bishop. Every follower of Jesus is given the power to forgive human sins, the release from Satan's control. Every believer has the destiny of the world in his or her hands, because love and forgiveness is the way into *abba*'s kingdom. But Jesus' good news has never involved the refusal to forgive sins. That was the church's decision: a wise strategy to punish people and withhold the forgiveness of sins from them. They are meant to be left forever in chains. My chains! Good news indeed!

'...and nothing but the truth'

What I find strange is that none of the contemporary records have anything to say about Peter's presence in Rome. St Jerome, writing at the end of the fourth century, does supply us with a few dates, but his fabrication serves only to expose the lie even more. According to him, Peter is supposed to have arrived in Rome in the second year of Emperor Claudius' reign, and martyred in the last year of Nero's reign. So we're talking about a quarter of a century between 42 to 67AD. The Church of Rome initially saw this as being divinely ordered, and so it was decided that no pope would exceed twenty-five years in office. Rules are rules, after all. But Pope Pius IX would have none of it.

His reign lasted thirty-two years. Mind you, when you have the last word on any matter, you can change the rules as well as invent them!

Paul wrote many letters, or epistles as they are called, to some of the early churches. He wrote one to the large church in Rome in 59AD, which he sent via a woman called Phoebe. By that time, had he been there, Peter would have been bishop of Rome for seventeen years, although there was no such office or post in any church at that time! The existence of the Roman church, or congregations to be more accurate, was already well known in the Christian world. It was set up without any help from the original twelve disciples. Founder members included Andronicus and Junias, whom Paul referred to as apostles. It was a Greek speaking church comprising mostly of Gentile Christians, though there was also a small Jewish Christian presence. Paul had a habit of greeting local leaders in his letters, so let's look at the congregational leaders in Rome. It's quite a roll call!

> Epaenetus, Mary, Amplias, Urbane, Stachys, Apelles, Perses, Rufus, Asyncritus, Phlegon, Hermes, Patrobas, Hermas, Philologus, Julia, Neurus and his sister, Olympas, Herodion, the grandson of Herod I, two families referred to as the Tryphaena and Tryphosa, the Household of Narcissus as well as the Household of Aristobulus, who was brother to King Herod Agrippa (Romans 16).

Now unless he had changed his name, there is no mention of Peter, which isn't surprising because he wasn't there! Paul even makes a point of talking about 'all those in Rome, beloved of God and called to be saints' (Romans 1:7). How odd that Paul doesn't salute their bishop. How discourteous of him, especially since Paul and Peter knew each other, even if they weren't big buddies. And anyway, if Peter was the leader of the Roman congregations,

Paul wouldn't have written to 'his' church in the first place. It's an irrefutable fact that Paul had made it crystal clear from the start of his ministry that he would never interfere with the authority of other leaders. So it isn't just a case of Peter's absence from Rome. Roman Christians had no one overall leader exercising authority them in 59AD.

One of the congregations was well known to Paul. It was a house-group that met in the home of wife and husband, known as Priscilla and Aquila. These were Jewish Christians whom Paul knew well and with whom he stayed when he reached Rome in 62AD. They had been expelled from Rome in 49AD and accompanied Paul on a missionary journey to Syria and Ephesus, returning eventually to Rome to consolidate the Christian mission that they had played a key part in establishing. This dynamic husband and wife team were later responsible for the conversion of the wise man called Apollos, who was to become as famous an apostle as Paul with his mission work among the Gentiles.

I suggest that Priscilla and Aquila should be honored, if not as the founders (because that we will never know), but as being among the chief patrons of the original Christian congregation in Rome. It would be very fitting because Peter, after all, was also a married man. Peter was a Jewish Christian but he couldn't have been in Rome in 49AD, his seventh year as bishop, because that's the year when Emperor Claudius had expelled Jews of all persuasions from Rome. Let's look at some more facts.

Paul arrived in Rome in the autumn of 62AD, on board a ship called Castor and Pollox. When news of Paul's arrival reached the locals, groups of Christians went to meet him on the Appian Way, some traveling up to forty miles to be there. Under the escort of a centurion, Paul was allowed to live for two years in his own rented accommodation. If Peter had been in Rome, surely much would have been made of the meeting of these two famous apostles. What's even stranger is the fact that one of the first things that Paul, a learned Pharisee, did was to get in touch with members of the traditional Jewish community and invite them to debate with him. These Roman Jews knew nothing about Paul or Jesus, because they didn't mix with Gentile Christians. This is very odd, because if Peter (chosen by the apostles in Jerusalem to evangelize among his fellow Jews) had been bishop of Rome for twenty years, some of the locals Jews would have met with him and would have some knowledge of the Christian message.

Paul went on to write a number of letters between 62-62AD while under house arrest. In none of them does he mention such a famous fellow-worker and apostle as Peter. Why? Because Peter wasn't there. So where was he? Peter wasn't executed in 67AD. The Acts of the Apostles is clear on the matter. It tells us that he had 'departed and gone to another place'. When Jews were sent into exile to Babylon centuries before, it was such a traumatic event that Jewish tradition ended up never saying or writing the name 'Babylon'. It became taboo. Instead it talked about going 'to another place', as in the Book of Ezekiel (12:3):

> Therefore, son of man, pack your bags for exile and leave your home and 'go to another place'.

Babylon was a large city in the first century AD, with a significant Jewish population. It was located near Al-Hillah, in present day Iraq. In the first letter that bears his name, Peter acknowledges the fact that, being illiterate, he dictated it to Silvanus. He signs it with the words, 'The Elect who is in Babylon, sends you her greetings, as does my son Mark. Greet one another with a kiss of love. Peace to all of you who are in Christ' (1 Peter 5:13-14).

By 150AD, the church was led by Bishop Abdias, whose writings confirm that Peter had established the church. And what about Paul? In all probability, he left Rome on a mission to Spain, where he was to die of old age, buried in an unmarked grave in one of the Roman towns of Spain.

Spanish Christians eventually caught the Roman disease. They couldn't have Peter as their religious mascot so they claimed James, one of the original twelve, as their patron saint. He was transformed into a Christian warrior-saint to fight their Muslim enemies. To support this lie, they invented a ridiculous story that James' body had miraculously floated ashore in Spain in a marble coffin in the eighth century. To this day, it rests under the High Altar of the grand cathedral of Santiago de Compostella in Galicia. This Christian fraud lured hundreds of thousands of pilgrims from all over Spain to see the coffin in the Middle Ages. Forged documents resulted in every parish in Spain being taxed to support the cathedral of St James until the nineteenth century. In spite of the blatant fraud becoming public knowledge, pious Spanish Christians still flock to Compostella for blessings by touching the casket of someone who clearly isn't St James. Sad!

Britain wasn't much better. In 1220, the pious abbots of Glastonbury, in the west of England, even forged The Charter of St Patrick to support the lie that the famous Patrick of Ireland had been to Glastonbury. He never visited the place. I thought that it was the responsibility of the Holy Spirit to guide Christians into the truth, instead of filling them with a load of silly, superstitious nonsense. The magnificent mediaeval Cathedral of Chartres in France was built with money contributed by pilgrims, again flocking in their hundreds of thousands to see and worship Jesus' foreskin. There's only one possible response to that – Bollocks!

Roman Forgeries and Fakes

But nothing can compete with the Roman forgeries. In the middle of the third century AD, Roman clergy began to use Peter's alleged connection with their city as an excuse to justify the primacy of the Church of Rome. It's ironic that the fallible and all-too-human, married Peter should become the prototype of the celibate and infallible papacy. The first bishop of Rome to claim supremacy over other bishops was Stephen I. Cyprian. The bishop of Carthage in N. Africa had the wisdom and courage to reject his claim, and to this day every other major sect in Christendom has done the same. By the eleventh century, the East and West churches, known respectively as Orthodox and Roman Christianity, had separated. They remain alienated from each other.

Frustrated that there was no historical evidence to support its claim that the bishop of Rome had a sacred right to exercise authority over all Christians, the Papacy set about forging it in the ninth century. The Dan Brown of his day was Benedictus Levita of Mentz and he initiated a massive forgery for his Archbishop, called Antocarius. Nicholas 1 was the first Pope to make use of the forged *Decretals,* as they are known. The forgeries arrived in Rome during June 864 and it was timely that on Christmas Day of the same year Nicholas made it known that they had always been in the Vatican archives. Christians had long pretended that Jesus had been born on December 25, so a precedent had already been set for a festival of lies.

All of Nicholas' successors sanctioned this blatant fraud, and in 1559, when Jesuit scholars set about proving that the Forged Decretals were genuine, they were so thorough in their research that all they succeeded in doing was confirming that they were forgeries in the first place! Unlike Dan Brown's Christian fiction, the papacy's forgeries weren't just an ingenious work of fiction but the result of senior Christian leaders setting out to deliberately deceive the faithful. And what about the claim that Peter's remains are buried under the High Altar at St Peter's? In 1939, Pope Pius XII ordered an excavation hoping to prove their authenticity. He announced to the whole world, with great pomp and ceremony on December 23, that Peter's bones had been found in the vault under the solid marble altar. Once again it was a pack of lies. What he failed to mention – and it doesn't get better than this – was the fact that the bones found belonged to a woman.

And where is Peter? Jesus' followers had no interest in relics of any kind. While Peter's real remains rest in an unmarked grave somewhere in Iraq, the WMD's in Rome continue to benefit financially from his memory. WMDs in Rome? Wielders of Mass Deception!

The odd case of Padre Pio is a good modern example of the fact that frauds will eventually be exposed. He was born in a small town near Naples in 1887. When he joined the Capuchin Order, he took the name Padre Pio, which means 'the pious one'. When he was twenty-three years old, the wounds of Jesus' crucifixion, or the stigmata as it is called, started to appear on his body. A cult soon grew up around him, which threatened Roman Catholic authority because of its popularity among the masses. Padre Pio could not only foresee the future but also be in two places at once, like Peter and James, only they were dead at the time! The 'odor of sanctity' that followed him around came in fact from his favorite eau de cologne! Padre Pio was eventually banned from celebrating Mass by church authorities. Then, a strange twist of fate: A young Polish Christian went on a pilgrimage to have his sins forgiven by Padre Pio. He became Pope John Paul II and he made Padre Pio a saint! Well, if you've got the authority, why not promote your favorite saint to heavenly stardom!

Padre Pio was made a saint in June 2002, when half a million gathered in St Peter's Square in Rome. Seven million pilgrims a year now visit Padre Pio's tomb in a church near the friary where he lived. That many people can't all be wrong. Can they? In 2008, just under a million pilgrims pre-booked to make sure that they could see his exhumed body. He is such a dead superhero (sorry, I mean 'saint') that the Christian faithful are convinced that he has a better chance of delivering miracles than prayers to the Virgin Mary and even Christ himself! And what about Mammon? Padre Pio has done more to transform the economy of rural southern Italy than sixty or so Italian governments. Padre

Pio's tomb was opened initially in 2008 to see the signs of the stigmata that made him famous. Only one problem – No stigmata! Neither his hands nor his feet showed any sign of the wounds expected of a saint who the church says bled, as Jesus did on the cross, on and off for more than fifty years. His critics had been proved right. Padre Pio was a fake, a self-harmer, who regularly used carbolic acid to create the wounds in the first place.

'Your Highness'

In 1520, when the rebel Roman Catholic monk Martin Luther brought about the religious division of Europe into Roman and Protestant camps, he had an ideal opportunity to reassert Jesus' teaching of '*abba*-direct'. With no bishops and priests to interfere any longer between heaven and earth, I thought for a moment that Jesus' teaching would at long last begin to make a real impact on European spirituality. I needn't have worried. Simple faith in *abba* is just that: too simple. Humans need something more real and tangible. Luther became the new pope, the true spokesman of the City of God. Along with seventy trusted interpreters of God's Word, Luther also became the Guardian the Bible. The Bible became the idol of the new Protestant faith. Luther and his colleagues, the professors, had the final say in all discussions of religious and national interest. This was a big difference from the early Church, when it was the emperors who had the task of defining Christian doctrine, but the link between church and state was just the same. In the fourth century, key points of theology were incorporated into the imperial legal system, so that Christian orthodoxy could be protected by both secular and church law. From then on, heretics were also condemned by the state. The emperors' motivation wasn't theological but political. Christians bickering amongst themselves was a threat to imperial unity. Religious unity has always had an important part to play in furthering political cohesion and stability.

The Protestant state became the guardian of Luther's new religion and he became a loyal citizen of the State. Out went the bishops and priests who had governed every aspect of an individual's life. In came the civil authority to take care of both security and salvation. The Roman Catholic sovereignty that had replaced *abba*'s sovereignty was replaced in turn by secular princes, who, to all intent and purposes, became the new priests. They were the High Magistrates, armed with God's authority to do their bit in carrying out God's righteous reform. This was their way of showing their Christian faith in the most practical of ways. In addition to looking after civil order, they became responsible for looking after marriages, trade and property dealings. Large and small, rich and poor, be their titles ordinary or grand, these secular princes were equals in the responsibility they exercised towards their subjects.

Abba's sovereignty took on a different slant. Every Protestant Christian was taught that by honoring the secular authority they were honoring themselves. Whatever their religious leanings, humans will always need strong leadership, be it tribal or national. Someone had to be found in Protestant lands to replace the security and splendor of Rome's very visible authority. It was imperative that a new figurehead be found to worship. So important was the Christian role of the high magistrate that he was always addressed as 'Your Highness'. I once heard a prayer to God's new right hand man, which contained these words, 'Let him stand high. Let him speak out clearly what the law is. Let him be strong enough to protect our property and our family against emperors and popes'. New messiahs followed, fed by a reservoir of blind obedience and trust. It's no wonder that Hitler's Nazi regime would receive much more religious devotion than was ever directed towards the pope, bishops or clergy.

As the power of the State grew in Protestant lands, the decline of Rome's political power resulted in a bloody power struggle in Italy. The new secular powers that took over behaved just as badly as the religious authorities. Power is power! Who it is that wields that power has never bothered me. With the loss of the religious veneer to hide behind, rulers no longer had to pretend that they were anything but tyrants. The worship of naked power means that talk of *abba* and his heavenly kingdom becomes a personal affair, the church a peripheral bit of theatre except when it is needed to sanction the use of that arbitrary power.

One man's justice is another's tyranny. It always comes down to power, no matter what century you live in. You can enjoy the escapism of your epic poetry as much as you like, but only raw power keeps you safe. Over seven hundred years ago, Dante, one of the world's greatest philosopher-poets, yearned for the time when the Emperors had been the true judges of Christianity. The pope and the cardinals had long left Rome for France and settled in Avignon. Here they came under the influence of the French Court. This was against Dante's Christian principles. The Papacy should never be subject to any sovereign other than the Emperor himself. The French princes were, after all, servants of the Emperor. And while both Emperor and Pope may have been equal in authority, the Pope was superior in honor. But in submitting to a lesser power, the papacy had forfeited that honor and was guilty, in Dante's opinion, of renouncing the Christian religion. Pope Clement V died suddenly in 1314 and the apostate cardinals continued to disobey God's will. Dante had no alternative but to turn to the emperor as God's new legal vicar. Ultimate authority would rest from now on in imperial power, to which trust and obedience was due. In fact, humanity is most like God when it is united, and it is nearest unity when it is subject to one prince.

The Prince of the World.

Military power alone guarantees that peace and unity. It exists in order that every person may reach his or her own liberty and power. That sounds good in principle but Dante realized that, in reality, men, even Christian men, still had to be compelled and controlled to behave in the right way. They had to be commanded to be virtuous. The Emperor may be the guardian of heavenly law, and his army may represent God, but it's still the power and majesty of his sword that triumphs in the end against the powers of evil. I've always been attracted to religions where God can always be relied upon to provide timely intervention and success on the battlefield; religions where people can live their individual moral lives from day to day because of the security that the emperor's army provides. 'But Jesus said to him, "Put your sword back in its place", for all who live by the sword will die by the sword.' (Matthew 26:52).

Confusing? There has never been a universal morality that is binding on all. Well, there has been, but you soon found ways to rationalize your ways around it. 'And God said "You shall not kill"' (Exodus 20:13). But you have always replied, 'We will', and I'm glad that you did. Life isn't all black and white. What is legitimate today may have been illegitimate years ago. This is why states have a right, indeed, the sole authority, to decide and determine the right and legitimate use of violence to promote, protect and preserve its way of life. Wise leaders know that ethics, the traditional systems of 'rights and wrongs' only apply to individuals in their petty day-to-day lives. In religious language, you could say that the State is God.

As the twenty-first century unfolds, many believe that military power is the new morality. Maybe it has always been so. War is not an illness of a state but a healthy strategy. Enthusiasm for violent and brutish political transformation at other people's expense has never been higher. From now on, the democratic West can begin to choose the sort of war it wants to wage. It can decide how to shape future peace by making wars to lay the foundation for peace. Small wars will prevent bigger ones. Small wars and its use of force (please note, 'force' not 'violence') will be used more and more to promote Western values throughout the world. This is the thinking that guides the American military historian, Philip Bobbitt, as he describes the contemporary situation in one of the best books that I've read during my satanical. It's called *The Shield of Achilles: War, Peace and the Course of History*. I think of it as a modern Bible. Mind you, I was bound to be attracted to a writer who claims that war is 'a creative act of civilized man'. He dedicates his book to God's grace and the loving kindness of his friends. How sweet! I wonder which God he's talking about?

Bobbitt views everybody's nationalism as leading inevitably to war and ethnic cleansing (as in the Balkans) but American nationalism as principled and sincere: the same America that regularly supports tyrants who treat with contempt the principles of freedom and justice which many Americans hold in such high esteem. Bobbitt isn't as narrow-minded as his law abiding fellow citizens, since he allows America the right to break its own rules when it comes to neutralizing threats from envious states or malevolent 'non-state actors', as he calls them. I call them terrorists! Never forget, dear friends, that a nation's moral obligation to comply with the rule of international law is voluntary – a matter of choice, or tactic. This is why targeted assassinations by nation states are a virtue because it avoids many more being killed. Your leaders have a moral duty to adopt such methods. Great leaders are even above the common principles of morality, be they religious or secular leaders. I should also add, a great people also.

Bobbitt is adamant. Without the security that violence brings, the State ceases to exist. This is why it is imperative that laws are regularly invented to legitimize the ever-changing needs of the State.

This is why one man's legitimacy is another's act of terror. I feel for you who live in the world's leading democracies. I admire your high ideals, but it's the evil and immoral behavior of others that prevent you from living them. 'Kill or be killed' is still a good principle to follow, or as politicians call it 'pre-emptive strikes'. Get rid of the bastards that threaten your way of life as quickly as you can, in order that you can carry on living your moral lives. I love it when religiously sanctioned barbarity teams up with humane rationality. And why? Because I'm a realist. If Jesus was alive today, my realism would force him to abandon his idealism and face the necessity of power and violence. Realists know that all collective behavior is necessarily conflictual and Jesus' way an illusion. Human sinfulness cannot be overcome in the real world. It can only be tempered and contained. Realists have enough experience of human history to know the necessity of having to make conscious choices of evil for the sake of the common good.

'Holy Father Church'

It's often those who take the moral high-ground that cause untold human suffering. Slaves to a twisted sense of morality, Christian leaders are in the forefront in this respect. Some countries have a higher abortion rate than others because the Vatican prevents doctors from prescribing contraceptives. Celibate priests must realize that teenagers will have sex whatever grownups and the church say. In the real world, the poor world, women who have no ready access to contraceptives will do everything in their power to terminate unwanted pregnancies. When the Pope, on behalf of 'Holy Mother Church', behaves in a wholly irrational manner and has the arrogance to tell his bishops that they must stand up for 'traditional family values', I wonder which family he's talking about. I assume a family with celibate uncles and no mothers! I've often wondered why it isn't called 'Holy Father Church' since its patriarchs know sweet F.A. about motherhood!

It's strange that a male celibate religious movement calls itself 'pro-life' while, at the same time, condemning women to untold suffering and death simply because they are not allowed to take responsibility for planning their own families. George Bush, a Protestant Christian, is no better. By using his presidential powers to block aid for charities that promote safe abortions, during his term in the Oval Office he was directly responsible for replacing contraceptives with the hygiene and skill of 'back-street' abortions. This is proof that supposedly intelligent people, proud of the God-given gift of reason, are more often than not seriously wrong with the decisions they take. Instead of acting in a rational manner, they end up being totally irrational because their reasoning is based on false theological and moral presuppositions. Nothing illustrates this better than the current debate on embryo research, where Roman Catholic bishops and politicians believe themselves to be experts in the field. For them, the newly fertilized egg, which is a mass of growing cells no bigger than a pinhead, has the same right to life as an adult. But more than sixty-five per cent of fertilized eggs are lost naturally. If each of these eggs is really a person, an eternal soul, as Roman Catholics teach, then we have a pretty absurd situation. Heaven is mainly populated by trillions and trillions of 'pin-heads', only a very small percentage of which 'might' have ended up with the 'potential' of becoming human one day.

And Jesus said, 'Leave them, for they are blind guides. Should a blind man lead a blind man, both will fall into a hole' (Matthew 15:14).

Magical Mystery Tours

Since dogma is God, I wasn't surprised in 2006 when a doctrinal hardliner became Pope. The age-old ritual of the Roman Church is, for Benedict, on the same level as revealed doctrine. That's why for him there is no room for innovation or creative freedom as far as worship or liturgy is concerned. In fact, religion and innovation are totally incompatible in his opinion. He is the church's humble servant, who will do everything in his power to uphold and faithfully transmit Roman tradition. The same applies to his views on contemporary society. To him, the enemy that must be overcome is not only the modern world but also the modern church or, as he calls it, 'the church of the heathen'. Trapped in the degraded embrace of a corrupt society, this is the church of those who call themselves Christians but are in fact pagans. But the Pope is unaware of the contradiction that lies at the center of his worldwide Christian empire. His is a sacred organization that wants to reform individuals by promoting its own counter-values, but they are the same values, namely ambition, competition and avarice! Similarly, young people in particular are criticized for being obsessed with sex, but so is the Roman church. It's always going on about it! Rome also professes to respect unconditionally the rights of individuals and yet maintains, contrary to what Jesus taught, that without its own particular Christian brand, the individual has no power to oppose and defeat Satan. Benedict is the ideal leader not only to take the whole church back to the bedrock of traditional values, but also to point out the deficiencies of other Christian groups and religions. And all this under the camouflage of inter-church and inter-religious dialogue and bridge-building. But you don't have to build bridges when you are the Pontiff, God's only bridge on earth.

Pope Benedict XVI is adamant that the Roman Church will never betray what it knows to be the truth. By speaking out honestly, he wants participants in any dialogue to be as clear about their own identity as he is. That sounds sensible, until he proceeds to tell others who they really are! In a consumer society, where people are attracted to strong brands that protect their identity, the Pope made it clear on taking office that his priority was to make sure that 'staff and services bearing the label "Catholic" are what they say they are'. Benedict has no intention of allowing talk of ecumenism and multi-culturalism to blur the differences between the various competing labels!

Benedict doesn't pull any punches either. He tells it as it is. In the summer of 2007, the Vatican came out with all guns blazing, stressing the fact that there were major defects among the non-Roman churches. In fact, they are not proper churches at all but 'mere ecclesiastical communities' or congregations. In addition, Protestant ministers are effectively phonies, with no right to administer Holy Communion. And what about Orthodox and Anglicans? They are defective but not as defective as the Protestants. And why are these congregations defective? Because they don't recognize the primacy of the Pope and the Roman Church as the 'One True Church of Christ'. There may be elements of the truth in other Christian denominations but only the Roman denomination or sect, as I prefer to call it, is 'fully Christian', according to the heretical gospel that Rome champions. Benedict made it clear during his first sermon as Pope that he would work tirelessly to rebuild the full and visible unity of all Christ's followers. It is his ambition, nay his 'impelling duty'. That sounds like a wonderful commitment to ecumenism or a 'one-world' vision of Christians working together for greater unity. But don't be fooled. Since Rome is the One True Church, the desired unity is for everyone to become Roman Christians. Benedict's goal is to make sure that his church grows in power to eventually gain tight control over all churches in the west.

Did you know that there is a department in the Roman Church called the Congregation for the Doctrine of the Faith? It used to be called the Inquisition. It is hell bent on safeguarding Roman Catholic doctrine from error, ambiguities, harmful interpretations, serious confusion and misunderstandings. After coming clean on the 'The Peter Deception', I suggest that the pope puts his own house in order first, before, for example, attacking scientists on contemporary issues. Just before Christmas 2007, Benedict XVI launched a surprise attack on climate-change prophets of doom, warning them that any solutions to global warming must be based on firm evidence and not dubious ideology. Come again? He wants the international community to base its policies on firm scientific evidence and not be dictated to by the fundamentalist dogma of the environmentalist movement. I suggest that the pope first acknowledges that three major Roman beliefs are a work of religious fantasy.

The first is known as The Immaculate Conception. In 1854, Pope Pius IX declared that Mary was conceived in her mother's womb without any stain of human corruption. This meant that she was immune to human sin of any kind. She was conceived in the normal way, with her father's sperm joining with her mother's egg as a result of sexual intercourse. But the instant they became the new life that grew to be an embryo, and eventually Mary, she became a unique species.

The human sperm and egg were not worthy in themselves, but had to be doctored in a mysterious way by the Holy Spirit. Mary became perfect and sinless but not as perfect and sinless as her son, Jesus; otherwise, there would have been no need for a perfect male savior to have been born in the first place! Mary would then have been the Great Redeemer. So what of Paul's teaching that 'all have sinned and fallen short of God's glory'? (Romans 3:23). Mary is the exception in the whole of human history. Not so much 'alone of all her sex' – just alone. Not quite on the same level of perfection as her son and yet unique when compared to every other human being who has ever lived. Do I detect an ultra-unique-superhero status here?

Next comes the teaching called Papal Infallibility. It states that infallibility belongs in a unique way to the pope as head of the bishops. He alone of every human being on earth is protected exclusively by the Holy Spirit from even the slightest possibility of error when making declarations about matters of faith and morality. Well, someone has to do it when you think that there are about thirty thousand denominations on the planet all claiming to know 'the truth of the Bible'. With so many rival bishops eager to assert and hang onto their own authority in spiritual matters, it's good to know that one man is prepared to take on the responsibility. Having one supreme shepherd and teacher of all the faithful does make sense after all. Rome claims that the seeds of 'infallibility' are in the Bible but they are pretty strange seeds. The truth is that papal infallibility was invented in 1870 at the first Vatican Council in Rome. John tells us that Jesus said to Peter before his death 'feed my sheep' (John 21:17), which Roman theology informs us is synonymous with 'the pope is infallible'. Do you want another 'seed'? Luke tells us that Jesus said to Peter, 'I have prayed for you that your faith may not fail' (Luke 22:32), which Rome assures us is synonymous with 'I will make sure that every pope in the future will be infallible as far as my teaching is concerned'.

Devout Roman Catholics assure me that the mere fact that the Roman Church teaches that something is definitely true is a guarantee that it is true. Rome has spoken! The case is closed. Dissension is not allowed.

Thirdly, there is the Roman teaching known as Mary's Assumption. The pope used his infallibility in 1950 to declare that when Mary died, she didn't ascend into heaven, since that would have put her on par with Jesus, but rather was 'assumed' or 'taken-up' body and soul. Proof? Since her grave was never found, it is assumed that, since she was such a unique person, she must have ended up in heaven. Similarly, Rome tells us that other Biblical figures also went to heaven but they were not unique like Mary, since they were mere humans. And anyway, when I checked the relevant verses in the Bible, those concerned were still alive when they were taken up. But Mary had died!

> As Elijah and Elisha were walking and talking together, suddenly a chariot of fire and horses appeared between the two of them, and Elijah went up to heaven in a whirlwind. When Elisha saw this he cried out, 'My father! My father! The chariots and horseman of Israel.' And Elisha never saw him again. (2 Kings 2:11-12).

I've often wondered why the Pope didn't go the whole way and book the chariots of fire for Mary's assumption with Elijah at the reins. Now that would have had an authentic Biblical ring to it. Rome further supports its fiction about a dead Mary's journey to heaven, by quoting some verses from Matthew's gospel about what happened the moment Jesus died on the cross. Supposedly,

> the earth shook and the rocks split. Tombs broke open and the dead bodies of many holy people were raised to life. After Jesus' resurrection they went into Jerusalem and appeared to many people' (Matthew 27:51-53). Scary!

But these verses are pure fantasy and are based on the belief of some of Jesus' early followers, who believe that the moment Jesus died he was immediately resurrected. Being resurrected, Jesus kick started the general resurrection of the righteous who were dead and buried. So to be fair, it isn't just Roman Christians who come up with weird ideas. Mind you, nowhere do the verses speak of one of them going off straight up to heaven after visiting Jerusalem. And even if they did, it would mean that there was nothing unique in Mary's 'assumption' after all.

To avoid any confusion, let me summarize Roman teaching on this matter. The likes of Elijah simply 'went up to heaven' in a chariot of fire, while still alive. Jesus however, 'ascended' to heaven after his death and resurrection, while Mary, after she died, was 'assumed' up to heaven. Clear now?

'One Church, One Faith, One Lord'

In March 2008, Islamic scholars met with Vatican officials to see if they could come up with ways of improving Muslim-Christian relationships for the sake of world peace. With over a billion members each, Muslim and Roman Catholics form a significant part of the global population of 6.5 billion. In 2006, Muslims comprised 19.2% of the world's population (1.25 billion) and

Roman Catholics 17.4% (1.13 billion). The total Christian population currently stands at about 2.2 billion souls. The discussions centered on a document entitled 'A Common Word Between Us and You' and challenges Christian leaders to unite with the Islamic world on the shared essentials of the two faiths. I've no doubt that the Vatican made it quite clear at the start where it stands in relation to other religions. Here is an exclusive summary of the Roman perspective.

The Roman Church's Christ is the sole and universal mediator of salvation for all humanity, i.e. for every person on the planet and therefore for all religions. He offers everything necessary for a person's spiritual health and there is nothing in other religions that can complete what Christ has already achieved for humanity.

It must be firmly believed that the Roman Church is the unique signpost to, and instrument of, salvation for all people. Pope Benedict XVI has not an iota of doubt that his brand of Christianity has to be accepted as the God-given true religion.

The small seeds of truth and goodness that exist in other religions are only a limited participation in truths already contained in Jesus, but such seeds come originally from Jesus' mediation work and no one else. In the same way, the Spirit that works for the salvation of Christians and non-Christians alike, is the Holy Spirit of Jesus.

This Holy Spirit can work in other religions for the salvation of non-Roman Christians by preparing them for the full and perfect salvation on offer in the Church of Rome. But these other religions are obviously not ways of salvation because they don't have Jesus.

It's even wrong to think of other religions as complementing the salvation on offer by Rome, because they contain too many 'omissions, insufficiencies and errors' regarding fundamental truths about God, humanity and the world. Similarly, non-biblical holy books and religious texts must not be thought of as complementing the Bible. I disagree. I know *abba* as well as anyone does. I don't think *abba* would be daft enough to build only one 'stairway to heaven'. Strange then that the Hindu Scriptures should also know of '*abba*-direct'. In their holy book, known as the Upanishads, the mystery that is the divine is described in these few words:

> not easily perceived,
> deep within the abyss,
> the original secret place. (Katha Upanishad 2, 12)

Written sometime between the fifth and second centuries B.C., the Bhagavad Gita is one of the best loved Hindu gospels. Known also as the 'Song of God', it is in the form of a dialogue between Krishna, an incarnation of God, and his disciple, Arjuna. These words appear in the gospels' final chapter. Krishna says to Arjuna:

> The Divine One dwells in the heart of all living things, as he dwells in yours. O Victorious Man, go to him for your salvation. Receive from his Grace the Supreme Peace, which is your home in Eternity. I have given you words of wisdom more secret than all the hidden mysteries of the world. Contemplate my Divine Word in the deepest silence of your soul. They are my words of salvation. Give me your mind, and your heart, and your sacrifice, and your adoration, for I love you. You have my word of promise: in truth you will come to me for you are dear to me (18:61-65).

Arjuna replies,

> I am deluded no longer. My doubts have gone and my faith is firm. Now I know that it is through Divine Grace that I call to mind the Light within me. Now I can truly say 'Thy will be done'. (vss 73)

But for Roman Christians, one religious book alone prepares the way for Jesus, and that is the Jewish Scriptures, or the Old Testament, as Christians call it. But Jesus' religious heritage is of no value in itself. It's only valuable as a preparation to the Christ event. As his closest adversary, I can assure you that Jesus would be saddened by such an idea, though I love its narrow and exclusive Christian viewpoint. While I would never presume to put words into his mouth, if I were Jesus' twenty-first century press officer, I would counter such Christian elitism by reminding all people, irrespective of their religious persuasion or none, of the simple and yet profound words of The Beatitudes. I think of them as Jesus' equivalent of the Ten Commandments:

> Happy are the poor in spirit: abba's kingdom belongs to them.
> Happy are those who are in mourning: they will be comforted.
> Happy are those who push themselves to the limit for the sake of abba's way of doing things; they will be satisfied.
> Happy are the merciful; they will be shown mercy.
> Happy are the pure in spirit; they will see abba.
> Happy are the peacemakers: they will be called abba's sons and daughters.
> Happy are you when you get persecuted for doing things abba's way: abba's kingdom belongs to you also.
> Happy are you when people insult you, saying all kind of evil things about you because of me. Be really Happy, because great is your reward in heaven. They treated the prophets who came before you in the same way
> (Matthew 5:1-10).

I wonder what kind of Sermon on the Mount Jesus would deliver today in the context of religious tolerance, multi-faith dialogue and co-operation? I think it would be a woolly-minded and liberal one. In case any of you are tempted to get involved in genuine inter-religious work, here is my version:

Should you be foolish enough to enter into dialogue with members of other faiths, decide at the outset that you are going to be stubborn and bloody-minded. That is your sacred right.

Behave like a pack of hungry lions, and enjoy going in to kill-off beliefs different from your own. Be spiritually smug since you know that your religion is the right one. The only one!

Should you be stupid enough to stay in dialogue, don't remove the theological beam from your eye. It is an attractive theological accessory.

Blessed are you when you feel self-sufficient in the company of other religious devotees.

Blessed are you when you do not give-up your precious religious convictions.

Blessed are all religious authorities for preventing change and genuine reconciliation between faith-communities.

Blessed are you for doing all in your power to defend the vested interests of your religion.

Woe to you liberal theologians for believing that there are many different paths to the Truth.

Woe to you, religious people, when you forget that you have a monopoly on the Holy Spirit.

Woe to you should you decide to follow abba's way of love and compassion.

As long as the Sacred Order exists, God and Satan will always belong together. Many of you would be lost without it. That's why it will continue, no matter what Jesus says. You know where you stand within that Sacred Order – always safe and secure. It alone is your true salvation, and not Jesus. I'm proud to be part of that security, and thus integral to your salvation.

I've really enjoyed writing *Gospel of the Fallen Angel*. The demonic detective has played his part in revealing the true Jesus to you. You've also discovered in the process, the secret to the tragedy that is *Homo sapiens*. By reading my gospel, I've also given you an in-depth look at the virus called the Satanic Principle and its antidote, Jesus! I hope that you can now appreciate my predicament. You made me! I'm your creation, a creature of your cunning, invested with the power of destruction, which I never had originally. In order to survive, I have to spread myself around as many humans as possible. Kill me off and I'd have nowhere to live. I'd soon be dead. But to be a successful super-virus, you have to learn to tread carefully, as I've done for millennia. Kill me off and you'll have nowhere to live! You'd soon be dead, all of you!

And there was war in heaven.
Michael and his angels fighting against the dragon,
And the dragon and his angelic army fought back.
But he wasn't strong enough,
and he lost his place in heaven.
And the great dragon was hurled down,
that ancient serpent called Satan,
who leads the whole world astray.
He was hurled to the earth,
and his angels with him.

Therefore you heavens, rejoice, s
and you who dwell in them!
But woe to the earth and the sea,
Because Satan has come down to you!
He is seething with fury, because he knows that his time is short.
(from Revelation 12:7-12)

Time is short? Don't you believe it! I may have been banished from the Holy Council, but who can doubt, as you survey planet earth, that MINE is 'the kingdom, the power and the glory, for ever and ever'?

Ah well, back to my current paperback...

He was aware of a power, a force that felt truly demonic, colder, more hostile, more sinister than anything he had ever experienced before. His scalp prickled with fear and he shivered, his shirt clammy on his back. He was cold, bitterly cold. He took a few tentative steps forward. The Cave of Demons. The place where the final confrontation had been fought. Where, according to the legends, God had defeated and banished Satan. And where the demons waited, biding their time for the fallen Master's return. Good could win again. The secret was in the Bible; it was there, quietly and unobtrusively, but plain for all to see... I really thought then it was just a question of good versus evil. 'But there's no longer good versus evil in this world,' Rorke continued, 'Good versus evil has become bad versus evil. You try to change, but in the end it's you who gets changed, Molloy. Power corrupts, and absolute power corrupts absolutely. Great men are almost always bad men.

Conor stared at him. 'That's your excuse, is it, Rorke? Is that how you justify murdering my father and mother?'

Rorke shrugged. 'It's all a matter of perspective. For you what I have done is evil, for me I look upon it as necessary for a greater good. Everything depends on how you look at it, Molloy. You look at me and see a monster; I look in the mirror and I see a gentleman.' He smiled. 'But I'm sorry we couldn't do business together. Really I am. You and I are the same beneath the skin.' Glancing out of the window again and back at the mountains, he remembered a line from a poem he had read years before. It was from Shelley, he thought. Yes, Shelley... 'Sometimes, The Devil is a gentleman.'

He smiled.

(Peter James, *The Alchemist*, from pp 658-660 and 669)

Acknowledgements

Many books have challenged me over the last few years, but in particular the works of the Biblical scholar Margaret Barker and the literary critic René Girard. Without the nourishment of their ground-breaking books, I think that both my intellect and emotions would have died of starvation.

Albert Schweitzer's *The Quest of the Historical Jesus* reignited my own quest to look again at Jesus of Galilee. Read his books on Paul as well as Jesus. It was Abraham J Heschel's *The Prophets,* in the early 80s, that first alerted me to the fact that Jesus was a real historic Jew and not a Christian.

The journalist Robert Fisk regularly provides wisdom and hope in a world that is becoming increasingly brutal by the day.

And why did I decide to let Satan tell Jesus' story? For the praise of my Master Jesus and not blame. I wanted to let Satan speak in order to bring him to the point where he ends up refuting himself.

My next book will be the second in the trilogy, entitled '*The Gospel of Sophia* - subtitled *From Trinity to Quaternity*', it follows my spiritual journey from the narrow confines of the traditional trinity to the more wholesome life of the quaternity, where the Divine Feminine is sovereign.

Geraint ap Iorwerth
Southern Snowdonia, Wales, and The Gironde, France
Summer 2010

References

Many thanks to the following for granting me permission to quote from their works

Peter James for permission to quote from The Alchemist, Orion 1999

Tess Gerritsen for permission to quote from Body Double, Bantam 2010

Robert Fisk for permission to quote from 'In the Colosseum, thoughts turn to death', The Independent 15.09.2007

The White Lioness by Henning Mankell, published by Harvill. Reprinted by permission of The Random House Group Ltd

SPCK for permission to quote from The Great Angel by Margaret Barker 1992

SCM Press for permission to quote from The Quest of the Historical Jesus by Albert Schweitzer 2000

Thanks to Continuum International Publishing Group for permission to quote from Things Hidden Since The Foundation Of The World by Rene Girard 2003. Athlone Press sold the US rights to Leland Stanford Junior University.

Orion Publishing Group for permission to quote from The Closers by Michael Connelly 2009.

The Closers by Michael Connelly. Copyright 2005 by Hieronymus,Inc. By permission of Little, Brown and Company.

Abacus, imprint of Little, Brown Book Group for permission to quote from The Gospel of Judas by Simon Mawer 2005

Penguin Group (UK) for permission to quote from the following:

Complete Dead Sea Scrolls In English by Geza Vermes (Allen Lane, The Penguin Press, 1997) Copyright G Vermes, 1962, 1965, 1968, 1975, 1995, 1997.

Crime and Punishment by Fyodor Dostoyevsky, translated with

BOOKS

O is a symbol of the world, of oneness and unity. In different cultures it also means the "eye," symbolizing knowledge and insight. We aim to publish books that are accessible, constructive and that challenge accepted opinion, both that of academia and the "moral majority."

Our books are available in all good English language bookstores worldwide. If you don't see the book on the shelves ask the bookstore to order it for you, quoting the ISBN number and title. Alternatively you can order online (all major online retail sites carry our titles) or contact the distributor in the relevant country, listed on the copyright page.

See our website **www.o-books.net** for a full list of over 500 titles, growing by 100 a year.

And tune in to myspiritradio.com for our book review radio show, hosted by June-Elleni Laine, where you can listen to the authors discussing their books.

MySpiritRadio